SOCIAL HOUSING, WELLBEING AND WELFARE

James Gregory

First published in Great Britain in 2022 by

Policy Press, an imprint of
Bristol University Press
University of Bristol
1–9 Old Park Hill
Bristol
BS2 8BB
UK
t: +44 (0)117 374 6645
e: bup-info@bristol.ac.uk

Details of international sales and distribution partners are available at
policy.bristoluniversitypress.co.uk

© Bristol University Press 2022

British Library Cataloguing in Publication Data
A catalogue record for this book is available from the British Library

ISBN 978-1-4473-4791-0 hardcover
ISBN 978-1-4473-4850-4 paperback
ISBN 978-1-4473-4854-2 ePub
ISBN 978-1-4473-4858-0 ePdf

Cover design: Clifford Hayes
Front cover image: tom-iurchenko iStock
Bristol University Press and Policy Press use environmentally responsible
print partners.
Printed and bound in Great Britain by CMP, Poole

For Andrea

Contents

List of figures, tables, and boxes

Figures

Tables

Boxes

Acknowledgements

Two people are owed a special thanks. The first is Alan Murie, who first encouraged me to write this book and continued to offer guidance, and correction, throughout. The second is Lin Tian. Lin conducted the empirical modelling of Chapter 6. Alan and Lin have both played a key role in the developing the arguments I present in this book, offering new insight and, at times, patiently steering me away from error. Any remaining errors are my own. Stefan Angel and Danny McGowan have also helped me to develop my understanding of the data I present in Chapter 6. Richard and Carole Fries, Lee Gregory and Tom Hampson all gave valuable advice on the overall structure and argument of the book.

In Chapter 5 I present the results of two projects conducted with colleagues. They all played an important role. So thank you to: Laura Ballantyne, Natalie Brown, Susanne Espenlaub, Giulia Giunti, Andy Lymer, Lin Tian. Finally, I would like to thank Andrew Fisher, whose generous support of CHASM has made this research possible.

1

Introduction: housing, wellbeing, and welfare

This book is about the relationship between social housing and wellbeing in the UK today. Over the past 40 years there has been a strong political and cultural bias against social housing. The assumption is that those who are able to buy their own home will naturally prefer to be owners. By becoming owners they will take an important step towards greater wellbeing, emotionally, psychologically and financially. But for those who cannot own their home, social housing is often seen as a tenure of last resort, suitable only for the most vulnerable in society. So even if a social home is the best available option, social tenants would and should prefer to own, if they have the means to do so. By the same token, it is assumed that private renters are in a kind of limbo between ownership and social housing, waiting and planning for the opportunity to own.

My aim in this book is, in part, to challenge these assumptions. The dominance of ownership as the cultural norm rests on a wide range of beliefs and values, some of which we can challenge with empirical fact, or by carefully unpicking the assumptions on which they are based. In this spirit I confront, head on, what is perhaps the most powerful assertion that is made about social housing: that it has a negative impact on a tenant's behaviour and worldview, sapping their will and creating a state of passive dependency on the welfare state. The contrast – sometimes tacit but often explicit – is with the positive effect that ownership is thought to have on a person's sense of independence and agency, creating the virtuous and responsible citizen. From this it is a short and easy step to the further claim that owners, unlike social renters, are not a burden on the welfare state. Not only is ownership the natural aspiration; it is also the *right* aspiration.

Viewed from this perspective, it is clear that the task of this book is more complicated than a process of empirical refutation. To defend the value of social housing we need to do more than challenge the dependency argument on empirical grounds. Prior to this we need a clearer view of the *purpose* of social housing, and of what we want or expect it to achieve. We may view social housing as a means of reducing poverty, providing homes that would be beyond the reach of lower-income households. Beyond this we may also see social housing as a way of creating stable and socially mixed neighbourhoods. Other views of purpose will naturally take us in a different direction, as becomes evident when we consider the view that social housing should only be a temporary stopping point for those in acute need.

My argument is that a turn to the concept of 'wellbeing' allows a clearer understanding of the role we want social housing to play in the UK today. How we understand and measure wellbeing is therefore a central theme in this book. For the present, however, I rely instead on the familiar shorthand of 'happiness'. Instead of just asking whether or not social tenants are more or less likely than owners to be physically healthy, educated and employed, I advocate for the inclusion of a number of happiness questions. Are social tenants less likely than owners or private renters to be happy or satisfied with life? Are they more likely to be depressed or anxious? If so, is this just because social renters are more likely to experience these emotions even before they become social tenants? These questions are, I believe, every bit as important as metrics of poverty or life chances.

But I want to stress from the start that I am not suggesting that wellbeing is a *better* metric of the value of social housing. It should instead be used alongside other modes or criteria of assessment, including poverty and life chances. Of equal importance is a recognition of the limitations of subjective wellbeing as a metric of social value. The measures I employ do not ask if people are 'really' happy or satisfied with life. The data I present is simply the reported state of mind of a survey respondent at the time of the survey.

Few people would say that this does justice to our considered views of wellbeing. For this we would need to enter into more 'objective' accounts of wellbeing – of what it is to truly flourish as a human being. These judgements will often conflict, and the meaning of wellbeing will be vigorously disputed, reflecting the richness and complexity of human experiences. It would be absurd to attempt to capture all of this and expect an easy consensus, or to think the task of completeness can be achieved through survey questions or responses. So I argue for the value of a pluralistic approach to the meaning and measurement of wellbeing, drawing on ideology, tradition and rhetoric as well as presenting statistical data.

This pluralism is particularly important in the context of the social housing debate, so much of which is driven by underlying normative beliefs in the nature of agency, desert and independence, all of which carry with them tacit ideals of individual virtue and correct behaviour. From here it is a short step to objective ideals of wellbeing. In Box 1 I present a brief sketch of the three main perspectives on wellbeing that, in differing forms and with different inflections, animate the debates in this book.

In Chapter 2 I elaborate on the plural meanings presented in Box 1.1. Nevertheless, the starting point for my argument is some straightforward and uncontroversial descriptive facts.

Box 1.1: Three views of wellbeing

Subjective or hedonic wellbeing

A commonly used definition of subjective wellbeing defines it as 'a person's cognitive and affective evaluations of his or her life' (Diener et al, 2002, p 63). In practical terms this is often assessed by asking individuals how far they agree or disagree with variants of the following statement: 'Overall, how happy did you feel yesterday?' The counterparts to this are questions that ask people about anxiety and depression. Hedonic wellbeing therefore overlaps with some aspects of mental health care and assessment.

Satisfaction with life

A standard question in wellbeing surveys is: 'Overall, how satisfied are you with your life nowadays?' Sometimes referred to as 'evaluative' wellbeing, this question invites greater reflection than hedonic questions. But it is still a *subjective* account: it is taken for granted that when a respondent says she is satisfied with life she really *is* satisfied. We also assume that she is right to be satisfied – it is her subjective judgement that carries the greatest weight.

Objective or eudaimonic wellbeing

The Aristotelian concept of eudaimonia captures notions of human flourishing, based on an ideal of what it is to fulfil our human essence. For adherents of this kind of approach, wellbeing is not simply a subjective feeling or experiential state; there are objective criteria that must be met if we are to say that someone has achieved a true state of wellbeing. This type of account is closely related to concepts of individual virtue.

Social housing in the UK today

Until the late 1980s the majority of all subsidised housing in the United Kingdom (UK) was owned and allocated by local authorities. This 'council' housing was a key part of the UK's housing system, at one point housing around a third of all people in the UK. In the public imagination this association remains strong – we often still think of all subsidised housing as 'council housing'. But with the rise of housing associations, policy makers and practitioners increasingly referred to 'social housing' as a description of both council and housing association housing.

A full treatment of the place of social housing in the UK today would raise many more issues than I am able to address in this book. Not least of these is that, since the 1998 devolution settlement, there is no unified system across the UK, and social and economic context vary significantly, even within the devolved nations. I come back to these issues in Part III. They are briefly summarised here.

Housing need and supply

In England in 1997 house prices were on average around 3.6 times annual gross full-time earnings, yet in 2016 workers could typically expect to spend around 7.91 times their annual earnings on purchasing a home ONS, 2016). Moreover, across all housing types (socially or privately rented as well as owner-occupied) 2.2 million working households with below-average incomes spent a third or more of disposable income on housing.

In Scotland the average house price increased by 61 per cent between 2004 and 2014, from £118,932 to £191,072 (Shelter Scotland, 2018). Shelter Scotland also reports that a growing proportion of its caseload comes from people in the private rental sector who are struggling with rental or living costs – 46 per cent of all its cases when only 14 per cent of all Scottish households live in the private rental sector (Shelter Scotland, 2017). There are also 137,000 households on the waiting list for a social home, in a population of 5.25 million. There are similar patterns in Wales. The average cost of buying a home was three times annual gross earnings in 1997, rising to nearly six times earnings in 2017. As in other parts of the UK, there is also a growing problem of rising rents and low incomes, which has an impact on tenants in the social as well as the private rental sector (Archer et al, 2018). There are now just over 60,000 households on a waiting list for a social home, in a population of 3.17 million.

Turning to Northern Ireland we see another aspect of the housing crisis. In contrast to a pattern of rising house prices elsewhere, prices in Northern Ireland are 41 per cent below what they were in 2007 (Wallace et al, 2018a). This has left many owners living in homes that are worth less than the price they were bought for ('negative equity'), while they are still struggling to afford their monthly mortgage payments. It is perhaps to be expected that this has received somewhat less attention than the negative equity crisis of the late 1990s, which was largely an English crisis.

It is therefore unsurprising that we regularly see media reports of a housing crisis. The headlines, however, tell more than one story. Typical examples include the following: 'The sacrifices you make to get on the housing ladder' (BBC News 2018); 'Millions of millennials will never own homes so it's time to make renting work better' (Moore, 2018); 'Edinburgh housing crisis as rent prices soar' (*Edinburgh Evening News*, 2018); 'More than 1m families waiting for social housing in England' (*The Guardian*, 2018).

Table 1.1: Percentage of working-age adults in low-income groups by housing tenure, UK, 2017–2018

Income thresholds – Below median

Tenure	Before housing costs			After housing costs			All working-age adults
	50%	60%	70%	50%	60%	70%	
Owners	7	11	15	7	11	14	24.4
Owned outright	12	16	21	10	13	18	8.3
Buying with mortgage	5	8	12	6	9	12	16.1
Social rented sector tenants	18	31	45	32	45	57	6.0
All rented privately	11	17	25	24	31	42	8.8

Source: Table 5.8db. DWP (2019) Households below average income: 1994/95 to 2017/18. DWP, [online], Available from: https://www.gov.uk/government/statistics/households-below-average-income-199495-to-201718

In Table 1.1 we can see that housing costs have a direct impact on income poverty in the UK. This applies not just to social tenants, but also to private renters, for whom the gap between before and after housing cost poverty (taking this as 60 per cent of median household income) is ten percentage points, just below a 12 percentage point gap for social tenants. These figures are shown in Table 1.1, which shows the percentage of working households in the UK experiencing poverty before and after housing costs.

The UK's housing crisis is thus wide-reaching, affecting people from all income groups and walks of life, and extending across all types of housing provision – a social problem and a political challenge that holds the promise of potential consensus, yet one that eludes a deeper consensus on how to address it.

Housing tenure and the tenure 'split'

Housing tenure refers to the legal status of a person's right to occupy their home. That status will typically be either ownership or the contractual obligations between landlord and tenant, social or private. For 'home' the more correct technical language is a 'dwelling' – simply a building used for residential purposes. There are a number of dwelling 'types'; for example, flat, house, or terraced house. A social home can be any of these dwelling types, but the tenure remains the same, and the dwelling type of an owner-occupier does not tell us anything about their tenure status.

When we look at the proportion of different forms of housing provision we can see that the 'tenure split' has changed significantly in the past 40 years.

Figure 1.1: Tenure distribution, the UK, since 1951

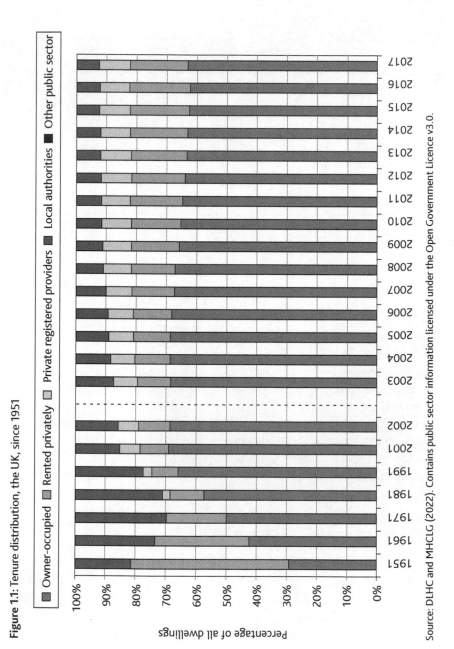

Source: DLHC and MHCLG (2022). Contains public sector information licensed under the Open Government Licence v3.0.

Figure 1.2: Tenure distribution in the UK, 2009/10 to 2019/20

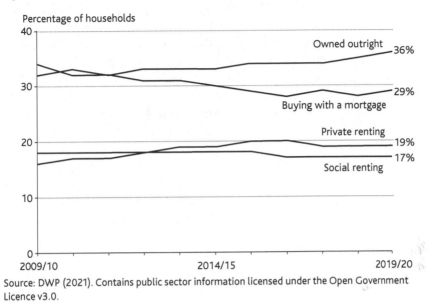

Source: DWP (2021). Contains public sector information licensed under the Open Government Licence v3.0.

In the last year shown in Figure 1.1 there were approximately 4.8 million social homes in the UK. This represents nearly 17.5 per cent of all homes or 'dwellings' (see Figure 1.1), compared with just over 19 per cent of privately rented homes, and just over 63 per cent of owner-occupied homes. The tenure split has not always looked like this. Back in 1979 over 33 per cent of all dwellings were social homes, the vast majority of which were the 'council housing' of the local authorities. At this point owner-occupation stood at about 55 per cent and the private rental sector a mere 11.5 per cent of all homes in the UK. However, we can also see a dramatic rise in the proportion of privately rented homes over the past 20 years.

Figure 1.2 nicely illustrates two more recent trends over the past decade. The first is the point at which the proportion of owners with a mortgage declines relative to outright owners in the early 2010s. The second is the point at which the proportion of private rental housing becomes larger than the proportion of social housing. Both of these trends are set to continue and have significant implications for the future role of social housing in the UK.

The rise of the small landlord

One of the recurrent themes addressed in this book is the insecurity of financial pressures faced by many, though not all, private renters today. In some respects the resurgence of private renting presents us with a historically familiar case for a strong social housing sector, with the government offering a viable (and widely accessible) alternative to a private market associated with poor conditions and a lack of quality supply at an affordable price.

There are, however, two significant differences. The first difference is that, in contrast to the steady growth of local authority housing from the inter-war period until the early 1980s, the impact of the state in the housing market is largely driven by direct support for renters, via the Housing Benefit (Local Housing Allowance, or LHA) now wrapped into the Universal Credit system. For the past two decades this has helped sustain a private rental market that has in many areas seen dramatic increases in rental prices. The only significant market intervention we have seen is the introduction of housing benefit caps in 2013, which was sometimes defended as a means of suppressing continuous price increases, though in practice rents have risen while the real hit has been on the ability of tenants to pay while maintaining a reasonable standard of living.

I later argue that we should not dismiss the housing benefit system as inherently flawed in principle. Nevertheless, without the systemic constraints of a more balanced approach to housing support – including far greater capital investment in new housing supply – it has undoubtedly helped create and sustain a dysfunctional housing market. Unwinding this negative dynamic therefore presents us with a significantly different set of challenges than those presented even in the comparatively recent past of the 1960s and 70s.

The second difference lies in the characteristics of today's private landlord. The difference is not primarily one of scale. Small landlords, perhaps with only one property, predominate both periods. Rather the difference lies in the institutional context and the process of property acquisition. The liberalisation of mortgage markets pre-dates the rise of the private rental sector and ultimately allowed a new form of mortgage – the Buy to Let (BtL) mortgage – introduced in 1996. This product allowed individuals with relatively little capital (though enough for a deposit) to invest in housing stock in a period of low interest rates and, from 2003 onwards, rapidly rising rents. Until 2021 individual investors were also supported by generous tax relief on mortgage interest payments. Not all investment has relied on debt. One estimate is that about half of all investment purchases in the UK last year were cash buys (Hamptons, 2021). But the BtL mortgage market has been significant and has helped shape the changing housing market, bringing some unfamiliar challenges for social policy.

Another characteristic of property acquisition has been the resale of former local authority properties, originally sold under the Right to Buy scheme (discussed in more detail later in the chapter). It has been estimated that as many as 40 per cent of former local authority homes have been sold to private landlords (Inside Housing, 2017). In many cases the private tenants in these homes are reliant on housing benefit to access expensive housing that was, originally, built as a more affordable alternative to the private market.

In some ways, this ironic – some would say perverse – outcome presents us with a crystallisation of some most pressing issues of principle that we must face if we want to shift the way in which social housing in the UK is understood, socially and politically, and distributed. We can, rightly, regard the use of former social homes as rental investments as a distortion of the political justification of the Right to Buy as a route to wider owner-occupation. Yet the story of former council homes in the new private rental sector is still one of *ownership* and, specifically, one that is embedded in narratives of a property-owning democracy.

I discuss these narratives later in this chapter, and then at a number of critical points throughout this book. But we need to bear one, crucial, point in mind when first approaching the structure of the private rental sector today. Under the normative prescriptions of the Thatcherite property-owning democracy, if the former tenant continues up the property ladder (putting social and physical distance between their 'dependent' past) and goes on to use her former home as a rental investment, then so much the better. This entrepreneurial spirit would, if anything, be seen as a vindication of the policy rather than an unintended consequence. This does not necessarily imply that it was a *foreseen* consequence – but serendipity has never been ruled out of court in the politics and ideology of the modern welfare state.

Diversity in and across tenure: who owns what?

There is a temptation in these debates to set up a simple contrast between the housing circumstances of owners and renters, as if we can compare one homogenous housing sector with another.

The simplest expression of this contrast is one in which owners invariably live in better quality housing, with stronger rights and greater security than renters. This is often true. Owners will certainly have stronger legal rights than private renters, particularly in England and Wales, which lag behind Scotland when it comes to reform of the private rental sector, in which the default rental contract is for only six months, after which the tenant can be evicted with only two months' notice.

However, in a direct comparison with social housing, owner-occupiers are not necessarily more secure than social renters, either financially or in their contractual right to occupy and control their home. One obvious distinction is between the circumstances of mortgaged versus outright owners. As seen in Figure 1.2, there has been a steady increase in outright owners compared with mortgaged owners. This is largely driven by two factors: mortgage maturation among owners who bought earlier in their lifecycle and, compared with this generation of owners, the greater financial challenge of accessing sufficient mortgage debt to buy a home in today's housing market.

It has been long known that owners are a diverse group with different needs and different financial circumstances (Forrest et al, 1990). In 2003 it was found that 'half the poor' were owner-occupiers, split fairly evenly between mortgaged and outright owners (Burrows, 2003), indicating that this was not just a case of asset-rich but cash-poor pensioner poverty. Although there have been fluctuations in poverty among owners, the overall rate has been consistent over the past 20 years.

The percentage rate of owner-occupied poverty needs to be viewed with some caution. In total numbers, there are more social tenants in poverty than owner-occupiers. All things considered, owning your home without a mortgage greatly reduces housing costs and therefore the risk of poverty. Nevertheless, in considering all things we must include the quality of the home and the ability to maintain a decent standard (see the section on quality and amenity) and, crucially, the fact that the proportion of mortgaged to outright owners is steadily declining (see Figure 1.2).

With this trend there is also a change in the profile of mortgaged owners (see Wallace et al, 2018b). Compared with the early 1990s, there are fewer manual workers and fewer self-employed people buying their home, and a greater predominance of owners in a managerial or professional occupation. This may suggest greater financial stability and resilience. But the level of debt now required to enter the housing market will still stretch many households financially, and the margin between stability and financial stress can be finely balanced. In this context, calls for a stronger safety net for owners are as important as ever (see Stephens et al, 2008; Wallace et al, 2018a).

How far we can and should integrate this into a more universal and tenure-neutral social housing system is an issue considered in Part III of this book. There I seek to draw out the shared 'social' elements of housing support in the UK.

Security of tenure

The diversity of housing circumstances within different tenures reflects the structure of legal rights as well as the differing financial circumstances of owners.

Later I discuss the rights of ownership in some detail. But there are some clear cases in which owners may have less security than social renters. The most obvious example is the legal status of mortgaged owners, where the lender retains rights of ownership that can be exercised in the case of mortgage default. Other restrictions of ownership rights include the use of restrictive covenants – for example, where the owner may not be able to make certain changes to the property, or where there is a price cap that limits the profit an owner can take if and when they sell the home.

There is also an important distinction between freehold and leasehold owners in England and Wales. Whereas a freeholder owns the land on which their home is built, a leaseholder does not, and therefore must pay rent to a landlord (the freeholder). For the year 2019–20 there were roughly 4.6 million leasehold homes in England, just over half of which were occupied by the leaseholder (Wilson and Barton, 2021b). Of these leaseholds, the great majority are flats.

A similar system – with the telling title of 'Feuhold' – existed in Scotland but was effectively abolished in 2000, as one of the earliest post-devolution divergences from Westminster. This little-noticed reform could prove to be very significant in retrospect, viewed from the perspective of the 'fleece-hold' crisis facing a growing number of owners in the major cities of England.

Historically the duration of an English leasehold would typically be around 100 years, but tenant-owners have had the right to extend or buy the lease since 1993, and the more recent norm on new leaseholds is up to 999 years. Rent on the land will still be payable, but can be almost negligible (a 'peppercorn' rate) and would rarely exceed £50 a year. This paradoxical position is less counter-intuitive when we consider the practicalities of building and managing a block of flats. Joint freeholds of flats are not uncommon, but they require an effective system of resident management, and a separation between the leaseholder occupant and an external manager-landlord is potentially beneficial for the resident.

Yet over the past decade it has become increasingly clear that the terms of freehold and leaseholder contract can be inequitable, sometimes to the point of exploitation. Leaseholds on new properties have been as short as 80 years (even with the right to extend the lease this is a significant disadvantage) and ground rent (which does not include any charges for services) can start at hundreds of pounds a year, with steep rises built into the contract. There is now concerted action – and legislation backing it – to check these abuses.

Quality and amenity

Finally, we must acknowledge the diversity of housing conditions within the three main tenures. In stark comparison with the other tenures, social housing is in fact the clear winner when it comes to the quality, comfort and design of the home. In light of the 2017 Grenfell tragedy,[1] any discussion of the relative merits of social housing requires some care. But it is important to preserve the truth that social housing in the UK is a high-quality product, better than a lot of owner-occupied housing – as we see all too clearly with the ongoing cladding crisis – and certainly a superior form of housing to much of the private rental sector.

This assessment is consistently borne out by national housing condition surveys, conducted annually by all of the devolved nations. In England the most recent survey finds that 12 per cent of all social homes do not meet the 'decent homes' standard, compared with 16 per cent of owner-occupied homes and 23 per cent of private rental homes. In Scotland, Wales and Northern Ireland, there is a similar picture.

Yet social housing continues to be portrayed, and perceived, as an inferior choice. Of course, not all social housing is up to scratch. The period of high-rise building of the 1960s played some role in damaging the reputation of local authority housing (Dunleavy, 1981), but it is also true that the desire to build more social homes led to a trade-off between cost and quality in the rush to volume of the 1950s and '60s (Malpass, 2005). Just as we have seen in the case of owner-occupation, there are pitfalls in treating social housing as one homogeneous tenure, to be compared with and ranked against other forms of housing provision.

Yet we will not get far without some generalisation – and there are two generalisations that are hard to dispute. The first is that there is a disconnect between the actual quality and amenity of social housing today and public perceptions of its value, even among those who live in social homes.

Despite the high quality of social housing, a 2018 opinion poll in Scotland found that only 13 per cent of people thought that it would offer a good home (*Scottish Housing News*, 2018). In the same year the British Social Attitudes Survey found that when asked to state their ideal tenure, 86 per cent of respondents expressed a preference for owner-occupation, roughly the same proportion nearly a decade earlier (Ministry of Housing, Communities and Local Government [MHCLG], 2011). There is also a pattern of lower housing satisfaction among social renters compared with both owners and private renters. In the most recent data from England we can see that over 90 per cent of owners are satisfied with their accommodation, compared with over 80 per cent of private renters, and around 75 per cent of social renters (DLHC and MHCLG, 2021a).

The second generalisation is that social housing continues to be framed as a policy problem rather than as part of a solution to market failure and unmet need. The British Social Attitudes Survey, conducted in 2018, really brings this point home with the inclusion of one simple question: 'In general, how comfortable or uncomfortable would you feel about living next to this [social] type of housing?' (MHCLG, 2019).

Overall, it is reported that more people (41 per cent) are comfortable with this than are not (24 per cent), with answers varying, in part, by respondents' age, income and personal housing situation. Owners are more likely than private renters to feel uncomfortable living next door to social housing, and Londoners are, overall, more comfortable in this position than the sample from England as a whole (MHCLG, 2019). Perhaps unsurprisingly, survey research has also shown a consistently greater opposition to new housing development among owner-occupiers (MHCLG, 2019).

There are a number of interesting nuances in these responses, offering some insight into the attitudes – and relative social position – of people who wish to maintain literal spatial distance between themselves and social tenants. We learn, for example, that people who think that social housing allocations are generally fair are less averse to living next to social tenants, compared with those who regard the system as unfair.

But the most striking thought is that the question needs to be asked at all. To understand why the question arises, we need a deeper understanding of social housing and neighbourhood.

Neighbourhood *or* housing?

So far I have highlighted some of the pitfalls of overgeneralisation in contemporary housing debate. However, one generalisation that is based firmly in the empirical facts accepted across the field of housing research is the central importance of neighbourhood for individual wellbeing. The data presented in Chapters 5 and 6 fits a broader body of evidence showing satisfaction with area and neighbourhood is strongly correlated with higher subjective wellbeing (Kearns, 2000; Araya et al, 2006; Bond, 2012; Badland, 2017). This is likely to have a disproportionately negative effect on social tenants for the simple reason that, compared with owners and private renters, more social renters report dissatisfaction with the area they live in.

The 2019–20 English Housing Survey shows that nearly 90 per cent of all owners are satisfied with the area they live in, compared with nearly 84 per cent of private renters, falling to 78.6 per cent of all social renters (MHCLG, 2020a) This pattern has remained broadly stable over the past decade, though we can see a gap opening between local authority and housing association tenants in 2019/20, with a higher proportion of local authority tenants being dissatisfied with the area they live in.

This of course raises further questions about neighbourhood quality and, specifically, the aspects of neighbourhood that may account for the lower levels of area satisfaction among social tenants. The data presented in Part II does not directly answer this question.

But there are some useful insights in recent research conducted by Wallace et al (2018b). Drawing on the British Household Panel Survey (BHPS), Wallace and colleagues find that mortgaged owners in poverty are more likely to live in the lowest-value properties in their local authority area than other mortgaged owners. They also show that owners at risk of poverty tend to live in the same deprived local areas as financially stretched social or private renters.

This is not quite the full picture. There is also some divergence, with private as well as social renters more likely, overall, than low-income owners to live in a degraded physical environment (Wallace et al, 2018b). This presents an important challenge. We need to better understand the extent of and contributory factors leading to this kind of physical degradation, and we need effective policy responses to deal with it. Some of these issues are addressed in Chapters 7 and 8.

But the broader message is, once again, that the experiences of owners and renters are frequently very similar. Poorer areas are, overall, just as likely to be neighbourhoods of owners, not just renters And if we exclude the status of owner versus renter, we see that owners are a diverse and stratified group, sometimes at or near the bottom of the socioeconomic pecking order (Forrest et al, 1990; Burrows, 2003; Wallace et al, 2018b).

There are in fact some scenarios in which owners are significantly worse off than renters. We have seen this in some post-industrial areas in England, where overall economic stagnation created pockets of decline so severe that there were some cases of neighbourhood abandonment. The Housing Market Renewal Initiative (HMRI) bought and demolished vacant (and in some cases abandoned) houses in nine areas in the Midlands and North East, seeking to correct an oversupply of housing that had left some neighbourhoods with an excess of empty and sometimes derelict properties (Leather and Nevin, 2013). The same phenomenon of depopulation also depressed the value of owner-occupiers' homes, restricting their ability to sell and move on (Leather and Nevin, 2013). From the start the scheme was met with hostility in the mainstream media, a typical headline from a *Guardian* newspaper comment piece being 'Housing madness' (Carter, 2007).

It was against this background that the then highly influential think-tank, Policy Exchange, openly called for the abandonment of such areas as a lost cause, social and economic, that does not justify the resources required by regeneration policy (Leunig and Swaffield, 2007). The fact that this call was publicly slapped down by the Conservative Party leader, David Cameron, does not itself present the whole picture. As Chapter 3 demonstrates, testing the water of public opinion is one of the roles of political think-tanks; a different public reaction could have prompted (or allowed) a very different response from Cameron. In any eventuality, the HMRI was promptly scrapped when Cameron became Prime Minister in 2010.

As we can see from the case of post-industrial decline, some of the factors shaping neighbourhoods must be viewed from the perspective of economic geography. Other factors, however, are more micro, recurring at different times and in different locations, sometimes regardless of wider economic and regional influences. Historically, class, race and income have all played a role in local housing markets and the creation of local neighbourhoods, sometimes with results that do not conform to our expectations of the relatively advantaged owner-occupier.

The precedent for this insight is set by Rex and Moore's classic 1967 study of housing and race in Birmingham, where there was a systemic racial bias against Commonwealth immigrants in the council's allocation process (see Rex et al, 1967). With similar race-based exclusions in the private rental sector, many immigrant households found ways into homeownership instead, typically at the lower end of the market and often by pooling resources from extended family. For many of these households, the offer of a social home would have been a good option. But the history of council housing is not always one of democratic class solidarity and social justice, no matter how misty-eyed some recent expressions of the 'true' purpose of social housing have been (see Chapter 4).

These two types of problem – regional economic decline and more localised institutional and market forces within regions and cities – represent different but potentially overlapping challenges. The regional challenge presents a scale and complexity that is largely beyond the scope of this book. But it serves as a warning that there is no single housing market or 'crisis' in the UK. It follows that there can be no single policy response, though the principles I advocate are intended to apply across different regions and housing markets. Regional cases are symbolically important too, in the sense that they are mobilised in political argument to express – and sometimes test – broader political ambitions. Whatever transpires of the current 'levelling up' agenda, the good it does (if any) will depend not just on very significant economic investment, but also on genuinely regional plans that go beyond a politically easy North–South map of the UK.

Ideology and institutions: social housing in a property-owning democracy

In my discussion of housing stratification I have sought to emphasise the material reality experienced by social tenants. As we have seen, there are significant similarities of experience across tenures: lower-income owners may be closer to social tenants than they are to higher-income owners. Yet the negative perception of social housing remains. How are we to address this?

One response to this would be to reiterate that popular perceptions and political depictions of social housing do not fit the facts. At the very least, as we shall see, the social problems attributed to social housing – and associated with those who live in it – are grossly exaggerated. Yet such beliefs are so deeply entrenched in our political and policy discourse that facts alone are not enough to shift the debate.

An understanding of the ways in which these beliefs are created and sustained must therefore go beyond the particular beliefs to explore the social conditions in which they take hold. These conditions can be complex and subtle, unspoken and perhaps unknowable in full. But there are also much more tangible aspects that we can seize and subject to empirical scrutiny. There are two aspects in particular that have played an important role in the housing debate.

The first is the ideological backdrop of 'property-owning democracy'. This became part of a mainstream political discourse in 1946 when Anthony Eden, then Deputy Leader of the Conservative Party, told the Conservative Party Annual Conference that "ownership of property is not a crime or a sin, but a reward, a right and a responsibility that must be shared as equitably as possible amongst all our citizens" (cited in Jackson, 2005, p 419.). The highpoint, however, is the sale of council houses through the Right to Buy initiative in the 1980s, which became the defining expression of Prime Minister Margaret Thatcher's own brand of property-owning democracy. Over the 35 years following the Housing Act 1980 approximately 2.7 million homes were sold below market value to council tenants – but, notably, not housing association tenants – across the UK (Murie, 2016, p 66). The value of these discounts has varied over time and (after 1986) by whether the purchase was of a flat or a house. One estimate puts the total cost of these discounts over the first 30 years of the Right to Buy at somewhere between £150 billion and £200 billion (Hills, 2013, p 187).

There are a number of good historical accounts of the property-owning democracy that underpinned the Right to Buy (Gamble, 1994; Jackson, 2005; Francis, 2012; Sutcliffe-Braithwaite, 2012). For my part, the key point to stress is the *responsibility* that Eden yokes to the right and reward of ownership (Gregory, 2016). As we shall see in Chapters 3 and 5, this is the essential normative thread running through the ideological push towards ownership in the UK today. It represents a view of the world in which social housing is seen not just as an inferior tenure, but also a source of moral failure, allowing and encouraging the vice of welfare dependency. In this worldview we should *want* to maintain a clear social distance between ourselves and social tenants.

The second issue to play an important role in the housing debate is the effect of identifiable policy drivers. In the context of the ideology of property-owning democracy, it is the Right to Buy (brought in by the Housing Act 1980) that had the clearest impact. From 1980 to 2015, 2.8 million social homes were sold, bringing in capital receipts of £58 billion (Murie, 2016).

We can see the effect of the Right to Buy in the steadily declining proportion of council housing in Figure 1.1. Even with the rise of housing association provision, there is a steady and profound overall decline in social housing, halving as a proportion of all housing over 40 years. Although we cannot say that the Right to Buy is solely responsible for this decline, its impact has nevertheless been highly significant, and is reflected in the changing pattern of housing tenure in the UK.

Perhaps the most important of these effects is that the Right to Buy created a new political context that the Conservative Party was then able to exploit. This is usually presented as a story of electoral bribes, based on the calculation that the promise of a highly subsidised property would garner the votes of the affluent working class (Gamble, 1994; Jones and Murie, 2008). There is little reason to doubt this account. But the sale of council homes also allowed the creation of a new social archetype – the image of the undeserving and feckless social tenant (Jacobs et al, 2003). When a third of the population lived in social housing, this attack on moral integrity would be hard to sustain intellectually, as well as being electorally hazardous. But with greater targeting – and with much of the most desirable social housing bought by the more affluent – it became easier to create the discourses of dependency we confront today.

There was also an important spatial dimension. In the early stages of the Right to Buy take-up was predominantly in rural areas and small towns, with households typically buying good-quality houses, with gardens, in low-density neighbourhoods (Murie, 2016). As council homes were not being replaced at the same rate as they were sold (due largely to restrictions on how local authorities could use the capital receipts from sales), the housing stock shrank. A further step along this path occurred once take-up within cities increased: many of the more desirable homes were sold, leaving new entrants a pool of housing that was increasingly concentrated in high-density estates of the type that are now caricatured as 'sink estates'.

Although the fate of council estates after the Right to Buy was not necessarily one of unavoidable decline, the broad pattern fed into a process of residualisation and social separation. Murie draws this out in the following passage:

> As more affluent tenants bought and became owners, so the profile of public housing narrowed further. But at a neighbourhood level the pattern was not the same. Estates that emerged with higher levels of public and social renting mixed with significant private renting developed an increasingly narrow social base associated with social deprivation, and the contrast with some other estates increased. ... Rather than the Right to Buy reducing concentrations of deprivation or introducing more social mix, it has introduced a new process generating polarisation and segregation. (Murie, 2016, p 112)

People, places and spaces – from cost rent to 'fair rents' and housing benefit

There have also been more subtle policy drivers at work. These include much broader changes that have had both direct and indirect effects on housing provision in the UK, such as the deregulation of financial markets, and the introduction of institutional mechanisms through which social housing is allocated. For the most part, this book steers clear of the technicalities of housing finance. However, there is an important distinction to be drawn between financial mechanisms that subsidise the construction of social homes, versus a broader strategy that offers less (or no) construction subsidy, but instead provides individuals with a form of income support that subsidises their personal housing costs (see Box 1.2).

There are three dimensions of subject subsidy, as it has developed in the UK, that have a bearing on the analysis and argument of this book. The first is the very fact that subject subsidy still falls under the remit of Westminster. Unlike *housing* policy, subject subsidy for housing costs does not fall under the remit of devolved policy. The LHA is set centrally as a percentage of local housing markets, and at a level that has created significant hardship for private renters in many areas across the UK. Social renters tend to fare to better as there is a limit to the chargeable rent (set by the devolved governments), though some social renters have been hit by the 'bedroom tax', which deducts housing benefit for social renters deemed to be under-occupying – that is, having more bedrooms than they need. This is also driven from Westminster and circumvents devolved housing policy, though devolved governments may seek to mitigate the impact through discretionary payments to households.

The bedroom tax and its impact have been discussed extensively. My concern is with a second dimension of subject subsidy: the spatial impact of centrally imposed restrictions on housing benefit. To an extent this is also an issue for the bedroom tax. The stated logic of this, aside from the familiar language of fairness to the tax-paying, non-social tenant, was that it would encourage social tenants to move to a smaller property and thus allow local authorities to alleviate overcrowding for larger households. The reality is that the steady diminution of social housing stock, and a failure to build smaller social homes, has left very little scope for 'over-occupying' households to move, even if they wanted to.

Yet there is a potentially huge spatial effect on private renters in market hotspots across the UK, most dramatically in London. Research from Crisis (2019) suggests that as little as 8 per cent of private rental market in the UK would be covered by the LHA in 2018/19. This creates the prospect of increased spatial sorting of private renters by income. With rising rental prices there are also greater costs for land acquisition and the development of new social housing. These effects will be felt more slowly than the immediate impact of LHA caps on household poverty and material quality of life. But they will also be far harder to unwind, and will likely set in train the same kind of social and economics dynamics that are associated with the Right to

Buy. There may well be tenure diversity, but markers of social and economic status will be attached to localised geographies.

The third and final dimension of subject subsidy I wish to stress is more general and concerns the way in which social housing development is funded. In this section I touch, in a very cursory way, on some complex issues in the history of housing finance (for greater detail see Malpass, 2005).

Even with generous capital (object) subsidy, projected rental revenue has always been used to raise and then service the debt finance needed for new development. However, the extent to which debt and therefore rental income is needed depends on the generosity of capital subsidy. Faced with the challenge of building housing that is affordable for lower-income households, one solution is to increase building subsidy, which in turn lowers rents. The rental level was set accordingly and with reference to 'cost rent', that is, rents was set at, and no higher, than needed to finance construction and maintenance. Historically, and until the early 1980s, even though the extent of capital subsidy varied, cost rent was the standard financial model.

Yet it was also the subject of increasingly divisive ideological debate. What appears to be a technical issue of housing finance was also contested in terms of fairness. There are, again, a number of dimensions to this, and two that are important here. The first is that the cost-rent model sets rents without consideration of current and future market rents. In this respect it is not sub-market. It is outside of the sphere of the market altogether. By contrast, social rents today are set and debated with reference to the private market: 'affordable rent' is set at 80 per cent of market value, and social rent (in England) at around 60 per cent.

This insulation from the market protected tenants from the rising costs of private housing provision in the 1970s (Malpass, 2005) and therefore fed into a pre-existing debate about 'fair rents' for council tenants, based more on what they *could* pay, rather than on minimum rental levels needed to build the home they live in. This legislation explicitly intended to reduce financial assistance as income household income rises. The further objective, as argued by Merrett, was to push higher-income tenants out of social housing and into owner-occupation (Merrett, 1979, pp 188–189). A fair rents policy for council tenants was introduced in 1972 but only lasted three years before being repealed. It nevertheless hastened the residualisation of social housing, accelerating a trend for more affluent renters to become owners (Malpass, 2005; Murie, 2016).

The standard of 'fairness' resonates today. This strand of thinking re-emerged in the 2010s with the proposed policy of 'pay to stay', in which better-off social tenants would either have to pay a higher rent, or move out of social housing. The earlier contention, in the debate of the 1960s and '70s, was that many council tenants had an unfair advantage over those who had to either buy their home or pay market rates for private rental. But, from the perspective of today's housing discourse, there is an important twist. Council tenants were portrayed as a privileged group who did not *need* such support (Jacobs et al, 2003). The assertion at this point was not that social housing encouraged welfare dependency and a reluctance to work, but that it was inefficient (as well as unfair) for subsidy to be 'wasted' in this way. Only later, once there were fewer 'privileged' tenants, and once the longer-term impact of needs–based allocations took hold, did it become viable to portray the remaining tenants as feckless and workshy.

Both the pay to stay and fair rents were policy failures. But they were both politically powerful and should be viewed as expressions of a broader approach to social housing. Yet, as argued in Chapter 7, we may still recognise the desirability of a more flexible approach to social rents, without presenting it as a choice between tenures, and without introducing divisive social hierarchies either between tenures or within social housing.

Box 1.2: Follow the money: households or bricks?

Cost rent. The expansion of council housing from 1918 to 1957 was driven by a cost-rent model. This refers to a funding model in which the rent that tenants paid was directly related to the cost of building the property, and social rents were unrelated to market rents. As the cost of building was subsidised by capital grants from central government, councils were able to set rents below the going market rate. The greater the capital subsidy, the lower the rent councils were able to charge.

Object subsidy and subject subsidy. In housing finance, the capital grant used in the cost-rent model is referred to as 'object subsidy'. The 'object' refers to the dwelling – the bricks and mortar of the home. 'Subject subsidy' is the direct financial help an individual or household is given to pay for their housing costs. The most familiar of these is the housing benefit system or, more recently, the LHA. Subject subsidy has been available to both social and private tenants since 1972, when a rebate system was extended to the private rental sector.

Hybrid and cross-subsidy. Over the past three decades there has been a steady decline in capital (object) subsidy for the development of new social housing. Social landlords have therefore turned to more mixed funding models. The most common approach is for local authorities to require private developers to build some social homes as a condition of planning consent – so-called 'Section 106' agreements.

Residualisation: where 'effect becomes cause'

I now turn to the second explanatory perspective employed in my exploration of social housing and social distance.

This process is widely known as the 'residualisation' of social housing. This describes a process in which social housing has come to be distributed on the basis of greatest need while, at the same time, the available stock of social housing decreases, so that a limited supply is distributed only to those in greatest need. The processes are far more complex – and contested – than my crude snapshots suggest (see Forrest and Murie, 1983; Murie, 1997). The conclusion, however, is not altered by this complexity: we have moved from a point in which social housing was a valued social good, to one where it is easily portrayed as an inferior good, and as a negative marker of social status.

In this way social housing becomes something that is only 'for' the poor and most marginalised in society, easily resented and regarded as undeserving. This has important consequences for the *meaning* of social housing: negative characterisations of social tenants also tell us something about what social housing 'is', of the value placed on it as a social good. By this I mean that, if we were to ask an advocate of the dependency argument to tell us what social housing is, one of the likely answers would proceed along the lines of who it is 'for'. Underlying this will be a normative belief about who it *should* be for. But it is also an empirical claim, a description of the actual distribution of social housing and 'who' (which type of person) receives it, and this becomes enmeshed in the meaning of social housing.

My argument here is not new. The role of institutions in these processes has been extensively discussed in political science and in the sociology of welfare states. From this literature I borrow two concepts that have been usefully employed as analytical tools in the study of social housing and the welfare state (see Lowe, 2011, chapter 1). The first is path dependence, which has been most closely associated in political science with the work of Paul Pierson (1993) and describes how policy decisions taken at one point in time will limit the range of policy options at a later point. The second, related, concept is that of feedback loops, which occur when, in Pierson's phrase, effect becomes cause.

There have also been influential accounts of the ways in which different types of welfare provision may affect wider social relations. The central message is that targeted welfare provision – available only for those in acute need – creates a sense of social distance. Bo Rothstein expresses this pithily: 'the very act of separating out the needy almost always stamps them as socially inferior, as "others" with other types of social characteristics and needs' (Rothstein, 1998, p 158). This logic applies beyond social housing and was developed, first, as a way of understanding attitudes to direct income support, with a focus on support for the unemployed or economically inactive (see Larsen, 2008). The contrast is with universal welfare provision, covering the whole population, when it is called for, as a social right and without an assessment of the claimant's social and economic status.

In this context, social distance is metaphorical: the experience of needing to rely on an inadequate means-tested cash transfer from the government is one that many people will not have experienced. For some people it may be hard to even imagine. The same goes for all the traps and pitfalls that come with poverty. There is a large social scientific literature on this form of metaphorical social distance. One strand within this literature addresses the psychological impact on the 'other' of this social distance. Another strand addresses the ways in which this social distance creates and sustains attitudes to welfare provision and economic redistribution. This research is often based on repeated surveys over many years, asking how (for example) respondents feel about the generosity of unemployment benefits, or whether or not they believe that generous support creates welfare dependency.

There are some significant insights in this literature, some of which help to drive forward the argument of this book. The issue of 'othering' social tenants fits the same pattern identified in this literature. As a targeted and means-tested good, it may be thought of in the same terms as (for example) unemployment assistance. Could we imagine what it is like to need social housing? Would we want to be the type of person who had to live next door to a social tenant, and what would that say about us? But there is a limit to the vertical analysis of social distance. It does not account for the ways in which actual, spatial distance may feed into negative discourses of social housing, and into broader attitudes to the welfare state.

This spatial dimension is especially important in the case of social housing. More than other welfare good, social housing in the UK is, or has been, tangibly, visibly identifiable. High-rise towers may have never been the norm, and huge 'mono-tenure' estates may now be a mix of different tenures. But social housing is still often easily identifiable, and even in cases of mistaken identity the social power of association is undiminished: the 'estate' is still physically there. Hastings and Dean (2003) best capture the essence of this. The following comes from a study of three regeneration projects, all of which were mixed tenure:

> tenure preferences alone do not explain negative attitudes. It is also the idea of living in social housing estates, especially larger estates consisting mainly of flats, which people have turned against. Indeed, estates per

se are increasingly viewed as problematic in the popular imagination and, indeed, emblematic of a whole range of social problems. (Hastings and Dean, 2003)

Taken together with a needs-based allocation system, this presents us with two, intersecting, dimensions of social distance.

Two dimensions of social distance: the special case of social housing

Here I present the two dimensions of social distance that are pertinent to this book and have special significance for social housing.

The social distance of experience and imagination. This is the *metaphorical* social distance felt by the person whose life experiences are disconnected from those who have needed targeted or means-tested welfare provision. The distance arises in the case of means-tested and conditional income support. It also arises through the needs-based allocation of social housing in the UK. The inability to place ourselves in such a position is a failure of empathy or imagination.

Spatial distance and social separation. This is the *literal, spatial* distance that exists where social housing is densely concentrated and disconnected from other types of housing and from surrounding neighbourhoods. The separation is such that: (a) there may be a strong visual association between social housing and a needy 'other'; and (b) the same spatial separation acts as a barrier to a greater degree of empathy and understanding of the lives and experiences of social tenants.

There are of course some important caveats to add to the analytical distinction I have drawn. The first is that it is not just social tenants who may be judged by where they live. This caveat goes beyond my emphasis on the changing tenure composition of estates. Spatial disconnection does not just run along tenure lines. It can occur more broadly, driven by socioeconomic status, with the lives and experiences of lower-income groups rarely, if ever, crossing paths.

The second caveat is that social housing is not the only sphere of welfare provision in which we find spatial distance and social separation. To some degree, we can see the same spatial–social distance in education, in the 'sink schools' of the 'sink estate'. We can see and judge children in a certain school, we can judge their parents, and we may think we can place where they live. Nevertheless, of Beveridge's famous 'five giants' of poverty – squalor, ignorance, want, idleness, and disease – it is only the first (housing) in which we see a systemic and sustained intersection of the two forms of social distance I have outlined.[2] The child in a stigmatised school is very likely to live in a household that relies on the type of assistance that creates a metaphorical social distance, and the school may well be associated with a social housing estate. But the school itself sits within a universal education system, provided to all as a right (and obligation) of citizenship.

With these two aspects of social distance in mind, I revisit, once more in this introductory chapter, the crucial question: 'How comfortable would you feel about living next door to social housing?'

The first form of social distance is metaphorical and hypothetical. Some answers to the survey question *may* be based on real experiences of living next to or near social tenants, but this is not what the question is really driving at. The more important questions are tacit. Do you expect a social tenant to be wholly unlike you? If we had no choice but to live next to social housing, what would this say about us, what would our social status be? Discomfort, I suggest, will reflect the social distance created by targeted welfare provision. Social housing is 'for' only a certain type of person, or 'other'.

The second form of social distance is spatial and literal. So we may ask two final questions. First, does this literal separation feed discomfort and anxiety – does it sustain the metaphorical social distance I have described? If it does, we may conclude that the structure and perception of social housing in the UK exerts a much broader influence on the ways in which we think about the welfare state as a whole. So the second question is one of strategy: how would people feel about living next door to social tenants if there were actually greater social mix and less spatial separation – would greater social proximity help more people to make the imaginative leap into the lives and circumstances of social tenants? In Part III of this book I argue that it would. But in order to make this argument we must address, head on, the beliefs and assumptions that underpin discourses of welfare and dependency.

Book structure and chapter outline

This book is structured in three parts, as follows.

Part I: Meaning and purpose: discourses of social housing

Opening the section on discourses of social housing, Chapter 2 is devoted to a detailed discussion of the recent rise of wellbeing in social science and policy debates. The aim is to draw out both the normative aspects of this debate and the key challenges we face if we are to use wellbeing as a guide to policy development. I advance the case for the value of subjective wellbeing as an important metric in the social housing debate, but one that carries risks if we place too much weight on it. I also argue that, at a deeper level, all policy debate is anchored in underlying beliefs about virtue and human flourishing. In the final section of this chapter, I introduce a visual model of the relationship between hedonic wellbeing and more 'objective' and virtue-based criteria of human flourishing. As I progress through my treatment of wellbeing in this book I refer back to this model. A key theme is the extent to which negative discourses of the value of social, together with virtue-based discourses of the value of ownership, may have an impact on the wellbeing and mental health of social housing tenants.

Chapter 3 brings the meaning of social housing into sharper focus. The central argument is that different types (tenures) of housing are viewed through the lens of *who* they house, rather than through technical or legal definition, and that as tenants have become poorer over time the meaning of social housing has changed too. This process is often described as the 'residualisation' of social housing. My argument is that the contemporary meaning and value of social housing today is closely tied to negative perceptions of social tenants that have evolved through residualisation; it is 'for' the 'undeserving' and 'dependent'.

Chapter 3 turns directly to contemporary discourses of social housing and dependency. The first task of the chapter is to clarify what we mean by 'discourses' and to provide a conceptual framework for the discussion that follows. My social constructivist argument is that our shared understandings and social practices create the 'goods' that we distribute in society, including the goods of social housing and owner-occupation, and, crucially, the goods of self-respect and esteem. This deepens the argument, made in Chapter 1, that we understand the different functions of the welfare state not just in terms of what they do, but of who they are for, with residual and targeted welfare provision tending towards social hierarchies of status and virtue. I explore these hierarchies through an in-depth examination of the apparent 'crisis' of social housing, central to the narrative of 'broken Britain' in the late 2000s, but also a recurring theme throughout the history of social housing. The narrative of a moral crisis of a 'broken' welfare state extends to all spheres of welfare provision. But it takes on particular resonance in the social housing debate, which is approached as the locus of dependency and 'worklessness', and is typically associated with an urban underclass, living in 'ghettos' or 'sink estates'.

These narratives of welfare dependency are found at different levels, from tabloid media to think-tank reports and political speeches. Examination of these sources shows that the social scientific evidence base – notably on social housing and life chances – is often misinterpreted, and sometimes distorted, to fit the broken Britain narrative. However, I also argue, in

Chapter 4, that it can be a mistake to take a myth-busting approach to such distortions, as they are part of a process in which 'social facts' are created, and that such facts are too powerful for direct rebuttal. I illustrate this argument with the idea of 'cultures of worklessness' and argue that apparently progressive counter-narratives can also be ideologically driven, with normative orientation sometimes driving, and distorting, the interpretation of empirical evidence.

Part II: Social housing, wellbeing, and experiences of the home

Comprising Chapters 5 and 6, Part II discusses the current evidence base on the relationship between social housing and wellbeing. I present my own empirical contribution in these two chapters. My first task in Chapter 5 is to introduce a further dimension to the relationship between social housing and wellbeing. This dimension is the way in which people experience their home and, in turn, the effect this may have on their wellbeing. 'Home' in this context is conceptually distinct from both dwelling and tenure, though perceptions of the social value and status of different housing tenures can play into our feelings about the home we live in. We can approach these issues through survey data and there have been a number of studies based on bespoke surveys designed for this purpose, many of which have combined survey data with in-depth interviews. These studies are generally relatively small-scale and regional rather than national. I discuss some of these in Chapter 5, before presenting the results of a recent study, conducted with colleagues from Universities of Birmingham and Manchester, of social tenants and owner-occupiers in South East England. I also present results from a similar study of social and private renters in the South West.

In Chapter 6 I move on to an analysis of large-scale longitudinal data, taken from the BHPS and its successor, Understanding Society. The primary analysis is the relationship between housing tenure and three measures of wellbeing: depression, happiness, and satisfaction with life. A secondary task is further analysis of the relationship between social housing and employment status, with additional analysis of the relationship between social housing and political engagement. The aim of this secondary analysis is to bring empirical scrutiny to the negative discourse of social housing, which can present social tenants as dependent on the welfare state and detached from the civic virtues of political and social engagement.

In this strand of analysis I follow a widely accepted view of subjective wellbeing, defined as 'a person's cognitive and affective evaluations of his or her life' (Diener et al, 2002, p 63). It is this kind of self-evaluation that we find in some medical screening questionnaires, specifically the General Health Questionnaire 12 (GHQ-12), that ask us to rate our current feelings of (for example) happiness, depression or anxiety. It is a great advantage for researchers that similar questions are also included in large-scale national surveys, and such surveys – in particular the BHPS and the later Understanding Society survey – underpin much of my empirical analysis in this book.

Taken alone, these data capture only fleeting moments of a person's sense of wellbeing. However, the same surveys also ask people a slightly different type of question, inviting a more reflective ('cognitive') evaluation of their wellbeing. In these questions respondents are typically asked to rate how satisfied with life they feel, giving us a more rounded picture of the person's sense of wellbeing. These data allow me to offer a fuller empirical treatment of the relationship between social housing and wellbeing.

My suggestion is that, in some circumstances, cognitive and evaluative judgements can move in different and opposing directions; in other words, we can be 'happy' but dissatisfied, or satisfied but a bit miserable. I believe this fits our shared intuitions about the human experience. Nevertheless, my position does not fit the common assumption that cognitive and affective wellbeing responses move in the same direction. Often they do. But it is where they do not that we can perhaps unravel some of the indirect effects that social housing could have on individual wellbeing, in particular the effect that housing can have on a person's perceived social status and sense of self.

Part III: Rethinking the 'social' in social housing; common needs, shared identities

Part III begins with a brief summary in Chapter 7 of the empirical conclusions we can draw from Part II. The immediate aim is to draw from this summary three broad, normative orientations that will help structure the discussion of the policy implications of the arguments and evidence built up in the preceding chapter. A key issue is the way we choose to balance different types of wellbeing, especially where the evidence suggests that they do not neatly fit together. If social housing has no impact on 'hedonic' wellbeing or mental health but does have an impact on satisfaction with life, this raises different challenges of policy and principle than we would face if, for example, the evidence pointed in the opposite direction.

A second thematic issue with significant practical implications is the relationship between empirical and social fact. The evidence presented in Chapter 6 is mixed, and suggests that there is a relationship between social housing and wellbeing, albeit one that has greater nuance than we might expect. Even where there is greater empirical certainty – for example, the absence of a causal relationship between social housing and worklessness – these are not necessarily the decisive facts. Politics and policy decisions are also driven by 'social facts', and at times these are more powerful than empirical fact. My case in point is the negative narratives of social housing and welfare dependency, mirrored by the belief in the superior value of owner-occupation. But the relationship between empirical and social fact is not the same across different spheres of the welfare state. I argue that the goods of one welfare 'sphere' take their meaning, in part, from other spheres, with a sphere being defined and understood in relation to what it is not; social housing is not, for example, the same type of social good as the universalist National Health Service (NHS).

In Parts I and II of this book I argue that the value of social housing has consistently been presented in terms of its binary opposite: the ideal of owner-occupation. I also argue that the interaction of the two forms of social distance I have sketched in this chapter should be at the centre of our thinking about housing, wellbeing and the welfare state. Spatial distance, I argue, entrenches a more metaphorical social distance or 'othering', shutting down the possibility of greater mutual understanding and compassion across society.

In Chapter 7 I propose a way out of this impasse, based on a more Bevanite and universal model of social housing that is integrated with both owner-occupied and private rental housing.[3] I pay close attention to contemporary political discourses and address a series of current policy dilemmas and value trade-offs. These include asking which is the more pressing 'right' – security in the home, or access to social housing for someone in greater need? Is there a right for social housing tenants to live in high-cost areas? And does the ideal of social mix trump the need for housing volume?

Chapter 7 goes on to outline my view of the future direction of social housing in the UK. The two principles driving this policy chapter are, first, that housing need is wider and more diverse in its form than it has been for most of the post-war period, and, second, that individual needs and preferences are far less fixed than they have been in the past. My aim is to suggest policy frameworks that take us back to a more universal system, based on a mixed economy and a transparent system of subsidy for all housing tenures. Housing associations can play a key role in creating this new offer, building for the open market as well as social rent. Often this practice has either been condemned as neoliberal or viewed at best as necessary means of cross-subsiding social housing. My argument is that it should in fact be viewed as a turn to a more genuinely inclusive model of housing provision.

PART I

Meaning and purpose: discourses of social housing

Wellbeing: meaning and measurement

In this chapter I propose a framework of measurement with which policy makers and social scientists can view the impact of social housing on those who live in it. In keeping with the analytical structure of the book, this framework needs to encompass owner-occupiers and private renters as well as social tenants. The emphasis within the framework is on subjective wellbeing. There are some important limitations in the use of subjective wellbeing, and I aim to present a balanced approach that acknowledges the importance of these limitations. My first task, however, is to set these limitations in the context of other social policy approaches to measuring impact.

Measuring 'impact': poverty, life chances and wellbeing

In the previous chapter I touched on some ways of thinking about the impact that different types of housing provision have on people's lives. I have also presented some basic facts about housing costs and income poverty. However, this is only one of a number of ways of thinking about the impact of housing on people's lives and, moreover, poverty itself is not an uncontested concept.

Poverty and housing

The poverty presented in Table 1.1 is relative income poverty. This is the most prominent and widely used measure of poverty and defines an individual as being in poverty if their household income is less than 60 per cent of national median household income. As such it is a relative measure: even if a household's income stays the same, if national household income drops, that individual household would be seen to rise out of poverty. It is widely accepted that this approach has significant limitations. For some commentators the very idea of relative poverty is ill-conceived. Relative poverty may be regarded by some as a measure of inequality rather than poverty as such. In 1989 the then Secretary of State for Social Security (John Moore) summed up this view: "what the relative definition of poverty amounts to in the end is that ... however rich a society it will drag the incubus of relative poverty with it up the income scale. The poverty lobby would in their definition find poverty in Paradise" (cited in Lansley and Mack, 2015, p 21).

The underlying objection is to the relativity of poverty. Lansley and Mack illustrate a common expression of this view of poverty in their discussion of reaction to the 2012 Poverty and Social Exclusion Survey, quoting a column in the *Daily Mirror*, asserting what poverty really is: 'It's about not having a roof over your head, living hand-to-mouth, wearing hand-me-down clothes, walking around in shoes full of holes' (cited in Lansley and Mack, 2015, p 35).

It does not take much to see that these claims are also relative, albeit in a way that can accept high levels of inequality. They are relative because the referenced standards are historical standards that change and evolve. Relativity in this sense refers to accepted standards of what constitutes a minimally decent life. This concept was most famously expressed by Adam Smith in the 1770s: 'A linen shirt, for example, is, strictly speaking, not a necessity of life. ... But in the present times, through the greater part of Europe, a creditable day-labourer would be ashamed to appear in public without a linen shirt' (Smith, 1776 [1981] chapter 1).

In contemporary social policy discourse this kind of relativity finds theoretical expression in the language of capabilities (a concept I visit later). But it has also been developed as an empirical reference point, underpinning attempts (primarily through survey work and focus groups) to identify a consensual list of the basic necessities of life (for a full discussion, see Lansley and Mack, 2015). Following several decades of design and development, some of the insights developed by these poverty researchers were incorporated in the Department for Work and Pensions' (DWP) survey on Households Below Average Income (HBAI) in 2002. The HBAI now includes in its list of necessities such items as the resources to pursue a hobby, to invite guests home once a week, and to be able to take an annual holiday

Significantly, the methodology is able to track changes in what are considered to be the necessities of life. For example, in earlier surveys being able to afford a joint of meat for a Sunday roast was considered a necessity – a crucial aspect of social life in the UK – but was considerably less important in later surveys. Nevertheless, many of the goods still considered to be necessities are clearly social goods: the ability to take a holiday or attend a wedding, for example, or to afford a home computer. These are the types of good dismissed for not meeting – or even coming near – the leaky shoes threshold.

One of the fundamental features of these consensual accounts is that they give us a means of thinking about what it is *like* to live in poverty, and to perhaps recognise the shame and stigma that can come with it (see Lister, 2003). To be free of such shame is one of the fundamental 'goods' we touched on when introducing our theoretical framework. As we shall see, this association of shame and stigma is not just a generalised characteristic of poverty (Beresford et al, 1999; Batty and Flint, 2013). It is also powerfully manifested in the more particular relationship between social housing and poverty. There are direct lines of connection here, for example, the fact that only low-income households will be eligible for social housing, or the historically strong (and now much-reduced) pathway through social housing into poor quality homes and material deprivation. Crucially, there are also indirect lines, following more symbolic connections between social housing and stigma.

Social housing and life chances

We have seen that there are direct relationships between social housing and poverty. The most obvious is the change in poverty rates once housing costs are taken into account. We have also seen that housing costs can push a large number of households that are in other tenures into income poverty. What we do not see is the same concern with the pathology of poverty outside the case of social housing, for example, among owner-occupiers. Over two decades ago it was shown that 50% of all people living in poverty were owner-occupiers, and that half of these owner-occupiers were of working age, excluding the easy explanation of the phenomenon as a case of pensioner poverty (Burrows, 2003). Yet it is only in the social housing debate that the default assumption is that poverty issues run deeper than the challenge of housing costs.

Using longitudinal datasets that track a panel of individuals over time, it is possible to predict the probable impact that childhood experiences could have on an individual later in life. This is represented as their 'life chances'. This framework has been particularly important in child development research policy (for example, Feinstein, 2003), first in the United States (US) and later in the UK, where it informed the development of Sure Start centres in the late 1990s. The use of life chances data in the context of social housing came later and is more limited in scope because there have been a limited number of studies. Despite this (as we shall see in Chapters 3 and 4) it has been highly influential and subject to competing interpretations in political and policy spheres of discourse.

For those born into social housing in 1946 there are no associations with later disadvantages in life, but for those born in 1979, social housing is strongly associated with a range of negative outcomes later in life compared with those born into other tenures. From 1979 onwards growing up in social housing makes it more likely that you will have, for instance, poorer health, lower levels of education, and higher levels of unemployment (Feinstein et al, 2008).

Correct interpretation of these results does not allow us to draw any clear causal conclusions, such as that living in social housing is the cause of later disadvantages. I discuss this in depth in Chapter 3, when I explore the transition of the life-chances data from the sociological to the political sphere of discourse. But my immediate point is that the dominance of life-chances measures has tended to take us towards an instrumentalist view of the value of social housing. The housing and life-chances debate has thus focused on the following types of outcome: mental and physical health; income and poverty; and education and employment.

There can be no doubt that such outcomes are intrinsically important. In practice, however, the public and policy discourse of life chances has become increasingly framed in terms of the outcomes that are of value to society rather than the individual's quality of life. The predominance of poor health among social tenants becomes a public cost and exclusion from the labour market becomes an economic and fiscal burden. We see this, in more general terms, in the aptly titled blueprint of the UK's turn to the conditionality of 'welfare to work'. 'Reducing dependency, increasing opportunity' (Freud, 2007) quickly became the *leitmotif* of welfare reform in the UK, pursued with particular vigour since the coalition government of 2010.

I am not claiming that this kind of instrumental calculation motivates the sociology of life-chances research, nor that life chances are not essential to the housing and welfare debate. However, I argue that, taken alone, the language of life chances is particularly susceptible to ideological manipulation, and that even without this risk it ignores an important social measurement: the extent to which a person's home helps to make them feel happy and satisfied with life.

Why wellbeing? A pluralist approach to value

Throughout this book I explore the ways in which the purpose and impact of social housing is debated in the UK today. I have stressed that this debate is driven by more than just hard statistical facts and metrics such as poverty and life chances. With the meaning of social housing so closely tied up with beliefs about who it is – and should be – for, measuring success in this context is not just a case of choosing a suitable metric. Similarly, the tests and metrics that we do employ are as much social constructs as are the concepts of housing tenure and the responsible citizen.

My view is that all of these approaches are valuable when taken as part of a wider approach to measuring impact. Moreover, the relative emphasis placed on utility, behaviour, and character helps to unveil underlying beliefs about the purpose and value of the value of the welfare state, as we shall see in Chapter 7, which compares social housing with other spheres of welfare provision.

But my immediate argument, in this chapter, is that we should view the normative or ideological perspective of policy proposals through the ways in which the different elements of impact, as presented in the previous chapter, are weighted and combined. This is in keeping with the kind of pluralist approach to distributive justice developed by both Michael Walzer (1983) and David Miller (1999). In some areas we may want to view policy through a life-chances framework. This makes intuitive sense in discussions of education and childcare support (for example), where the outcomes of interest are inherently development. In the case of disabilities rights a capabilities approach may come to the fore (see the section on capabilities and human flourishing), though life-chance frameworks will play a part too, as we want to keep track of emergent inequalities that may manifest later in a disabled person's life.

And, in the case of social housing, I suggest that the balance of empirical metrics – and the normative logic underlying it – is different again. There are two ways of viewing this. The first perspective is based on the tacit or overt assumption that social housing has some form of causal impact on the individual. This view is present in the dominant discourse of social housing and welfare dependency, discussed in the following chapter. From this perspective, a life-chances approach appears to offer a good fit for social housing; if social housing affects who we are and what we do, it makes sense to track its impact over time. As I seek to show, however, the underlying assumption is empirically false and, indeed, conceptually flawed. We should therefore view social housing from a second perspective – something akin to traditional utilitarian assessment.

Subjective wellbeing as neoliberalism, and neoliberalism as utilitarianism

This argument runs against a strong strand of anti-utilitarian sentiment. Much of this sentiment is well warranted. The language and logic of utilitarianism runs through a lot of recent policy that is based on ambiguous – and at times disingenuous – normative justification, with a similarly suspect approach to empirical evaluation. The exemplar of this brand of utilitarian discourse is found in the spheres of work and welfare, specifically in the utility-maximising model of the rational self, receptive to the welfare 'nudges' of 'libertarian paternalism' (see Chapter 3). These utilitarian discourses also make a great play of respect for the autonomy and free will of the individual, while simultaneously laying claim to a paternalist concern for the wellbeing of the workless, who will be happier (have greater utility) through work.

From this viewpoint it is easy to dismiss utilitarian logics of distribution. The turn to subjective wellbeing and happiness certainly *could* be a kind of ideological subterfuge of neoliberal ideology, just as the ostensibly paternalistic justification of welfare conditionality probably is. If this is the case, we would expect subjective wellbeing metrics to supplant, rather than complement, competing evaluative frameworks. Then the choice of subjective wellbeing as a metric would be an expression of belief about the underlying *purpose* of our distributive mechanisms, over and above a means of evaluating the impact of these mechanisms.[1]

There are good grounds for accepting this story. From a broadly Keynesian consensus among professional economists on the rules and standards of credible academic discourse, a new mainstream economics emerged, based on more 'classical' economic assumptions and models. Then under the label of rational and 'public choice' models of decision making, these assumptions migrate to broader public policy, leading to the pervasive marketisation of society and the construct of the consumer-citizen. Moreover, much of the intellectual groundwork behind New Labour's public services reform agenda in England emerged from the economics departments of leading universities, notably in the development of quasi-markets in the NHS and in the 'choice' agenda in state schooling. It is also from the same environment that the 'happiness' agenda emerged, bringing with it the metrics of subjective wellbeing that are the central theme of this chapter – with the merits and limitations that we have just discussed in the previous section. These, as I have indicated, should cause us to approach the use of subjective wellbeing with some circumspection, but not to reject it as a valuable part of a wider framework.

There are also good grounds for the stronger claim that neoliberalism employs subjective wellbeing as part of an ideological subterfuge. By shifting attention from the distribution of resources and the evaluation of impact in terms of material outcomes, the 'happiness' agenda could mask a systematic rolling back of the state and distract from growing inequalities of wealth, income, and life chances. This suspicion is well founded, especially when set in the context of the rather strained attempts to yoke benefits sanctions with a tough-love paternalism, ostensibly for the sake of the claimant's own wellbeing, while simultaneously denouncing the morally decayed class of benefit claimant who lives off the taxpayer as a 'lifestyle choice'.

Yet there is an important way in which utilitarian calculation can be *more* respectful of social tenants. Is the social tenant happy, or satisfied with life? Is there a greater risk of depression among social tenants than those living in other housing tenures? Crucially, in asking these questions, we are not *expecting* anything of social tenants. There are none of the demands that might arise from data on life chances, which naturally lends itself (regardless of the researchers' own intent) to behavioural metrics of evaluation. And we, as people concerned with social outcomes, have choice in these matters: we can choose when and where to use subjective wellbeing metrics. Doing so does not carry an excessive risk of our individual transmutation into unwitting neoliberal cyphers.

I return to these issues shortly. First, however, I turn to the more substantive line of criticism, that subjective wellbeing does not fit with our deeper notions of what it is that makes life worthwhile, that it does not connect to the values that we may really want to pursue in designing and evaluating social policy.

Subjective wellbeing

The fear that subjective wellbeing leads to an unacceptably attenuated view of human wellbeing is not a new concern.

It has been raised as an objection to utilitarianism since Bentham's earliest advocacy of it and continues to be a favourite staple of moral philosophy, which invites us to consider the attractions of classic utilitarianism from the perspective of devices such as Nozick's experience machine (Nozick, 1974). Such a machine would provide the sensation (the mental state) but not the reality of rich human experience: for example, love, success at work, great sporting achievement, and so on. The invitation of this thought experiment is to reject a framework of measurement that would allow such illusory pleasure to count. The experiment is extreme but provides a useful contrast with some accounts of objective wellbeing, where the objective account is based on a view of human flourishing that requires a standard of authenticity. I return to this point later in this chapter.

For my immediate purposes, though, a more salient example would be the problem of addiction. This scenario was introduced by Frankfurt (1971) in an influential philosophical discussion of freedom of the will. In this scenario, one addict may be struggling to break free, while the other, who comes under the unfortunate label of the 'wanton', is a 'willing' addict. The wanton does not seek to break free of her addiction and will at times (if she can communicate at all) report extremely positive experiences or mental states. Deliciously high on opium, reclining in her opulent country house library, we would have to say of this person that she is experiencing a very positive sense of subjective wellbeing.

So taken alone, as the overriding metric of social success and quality of life – individual and collective – this would indeed be a scarily narrow view of the human experience, and of the value of a life.

There will be times when the force of this concern breaks through and leads us to question the value of subjective 'wants'. The easiest examples are probably historical and viewed from the outside, with the benefit of detachment. Happy serfdom is likely to offend us, even if the happiness is sincere. Similar feelings are aroused when we see whole groups of people whose sense of the possible is constrained by social or historical circumstance. No matter how happy they are, we might still want to reshape social policy to encourage some younger people to look at university, or to explore different career options. If we knew for sure that the great majority of these groups were truly happy, would we be satisfied? At times we will not.

But there are, of course, risks attached to this kind of judgement. The clearest example is found in one of the central characters of this book: the happy social tenant. My conclusion is that this is a positive outcome. But, just as we might feel that social policy should not maintain limited career expectations, others may feel that social policy should not maintain happy social tenants. By this I do mean to imply the existence of a cadre of politicians and policy makers who want social tenants to be miserable. Their view is, rather, that social tenants should want 'better', and if their expectations of this 'better' have been thwarted or lost, then social policy should seek to change this. In this worldview, the social tenant as 'happy clam' is not a good outcome.

We might expect this influence to run through 'objective' accounts of wellbeing, taking the form of virtue-based arguments that may (for example) claim that happy social tenants are not really happy, or that they are unreliable judges of their own wellbeing. Perhaps they think that the good life is the one depicted by the recurrent comedy and tabloid theme of the contentedly idle benefit claimant, happy as a clam with a wide-screen TV. The caricature is grotesque in its blanket judgement. But there are more subtle manifestations of the argument. Most notable of these is the tough-love paternalism of active labour market policy in the UK, the 'work is good for you' trope of welfare to work (see Chapter 3). From this it is a small step to more explicitly virtue-based accounts of welfare and wellbeing. In these we find something like the claim that tenants cannot really flourish as 'good' citizens. It then only requires a few more steps before it is regarded as a straightforwardly bad outcome – a violation of the accepted standards of the good citizen, rather than the tragedy of a life unfulfilled.

These illustrations clearly highlight the limitations of subjective wellbeing. But I also wish to highlight another point, directed specifically at the sceptical view of subjective wellbeing – the 'happiness agenda' – as an instance of neoliberal artifice. Lined up next to each other, we have two cases in which an individual is held to be mistaken about their wants. Do we really want to dismiss as 'neoliberal' the finding that social tenants do well, in terms of their subjective wellbeing, because of social housing? Perhaps it would be better instead to defend a right to be a mistaken happy clam, against the assertion that social tenants have mistaken their true selves.

Social policy: wants, needs, and subjective wellbeing

I now offer some guiding comments on the relationship between social policy and the subjective wellbeing of those we might believe to be mistaken about their own wants and desires.

As an illustrative abstraction, the case of the wanton addict draws out two problems that we face in the real world of social measurement using subjective wellbeing. The first is that our addict's euphoria will pass. If we take the response she would give, at the height of her high, as the data we actually use, we will at best have a distorted view of this particular individual. To some degree this is a problem of methodology. This is an empirical limitation that we are unlikely to surmount fully.

The second problem is really a restatement of the objectivist's position: we are assumed (reasonably, in this case at least) to think that such 'positive' results should be discounted. Our addict is right, *a priori*, about her mental state, but not about her wellbeing. Yet the problem takes on a different complexion when set in the context of contemporary social policy debate. The view that our addict is wrong about her wellbeing is, perhaps surprisingly, a contentious one in social policy, especially in housing research, which is beset by an entrenched suspicion of 'paternalism'. A notable exception is to be found in the work of Watts and colleagues:

> Paternalistic interventions – which recognise that vulnerable people are not always able, at least in the short-term, to act in accordance with their 'settled' or 'authentic' preferences – are defensible if they are shown to prevent harms that may otherwise cause irreparable damage to someone's longer-term capacity to act autonomously. (Watts et al, 2018 p 248)

At times this really *is* a problem. Few of us, with the exception of some full-blooded libertarians, will want to deny that there are times when people simply are wrong about what is best for them. At other times we will rightly be very anxious in the face of assertions that someone has mistaken their own needs and wants. But between the moral north and south poles of radical libertarians and ideologues of coercive self-realisation, most of us take it for granted that the subjectivity of mental state metrics will not always be unproblematic.

It is this type of consideration that suggests a need for a more 'objective' account of wellbeing. Objective accounts of wellbeing and happiness have a long history and it is to Aristotle that most contemporary accounts ultimately refer. Aristotle believed that we can only describe someone as 'happy' – a rough approximation of the notoriously hard-to-translate concept of *eudaimonia* – if they are at least seeking to perfect their own essence as a human being. In a strict Aristotelian account this human essence is the exercise of reason and the fulfilment of the self in community, 'man' being a fundamentally social being.

Today we are more likely to see objective accounts that highlight the value of relationships and social interaction, or meaningful life goals, rather than the right use of reason. But what remains fundamentally the same is that wellbeing is judged by external criteria, the norms and values of the society in which the individual is shaped. This applies not just to objective accounts, but also in the discourses of wellbeing and welfare discussed in the following two chapters. Objective accounts of wellbeing therefore continue to play an important role when we think about the welfare state, or, at a more fundamental level, about how we view the values and institutional arrangements of 21st-century society. Wellbeing in this sense thus has a status and place in our shared meanings that is similar to the often unexpressed or unconscious social beliefs that continually influence our interactions with others.

Yet the points in favour of subjective wellbeing remain the same: distortion and ideological manipulation is not inherent to the concept, and we should not abandon a useful tool in the mistaken belief that it is irredeemably tainted.

Measuring subjective wellbeing

My argument is that we can and should treat subjective wellbeing as an indicator rather than the ultimate endpoint in a chain of normative evaluation. Positive or negative mental states may point to desirable or undesirable social states, but the mere fact of a positive mental state is not itself that endpoint. The point is well made from an economist's perspective:

> Economists like to maximise things, and talk about maximising utility and maximising social welfare. But this is just shorthand for saying that we want to choose policies that do best by some criterion. I believe that everyone would agree with that statement: otherwise we could be doing better using exactly the same resources (or, equivalently, doing as well using fewer resources). (Clark, 2015, p 2)

The practical issue, assuming that subjective wellbeing measures do have an important role to play, is how to do more than capture fleeting mental states. Table 2.1 presents the key metrics of subjective wellbeing that have been used in the housing literature to date.

The first entry in Table 2.1 is the GHQ-12. This was developed as a mental health screening instrument. While it was not designed for use by economists and sociologists interested in wellbeing, it nevertheless fits the conceptual category of 'hedonic' or mental state wellbeing, as it is a snap assessment of a person's mood and feelings at the time of the survey. As the GHQ-12 screens for depression it is often treated as a proxy for 'unhappiness', and contrasted to an explicit 'happiness' item in surveys that use the GHQ-12 in combination with other approaches.

Table 2.1: Metrics of wellbeing

Instrument	Purpose	Subjective–objective	Key references
GHQ-12	Self-reported mental health designed for clinical use, but adopted in social research and British Household Panel Survey: Understanding Society	Subjective and experiential, but treated as an indicator of underlying conditions	Peasgood, 2008; Baker et al, 2013; Popham et al, 2015; Foye et al, 2018
Office for National Statistics (ONS) measure of subjective wellbeing	To capture three dimensions of wellbeing: hedonic, evaluative, and eudaimonic	Hybrid: experiential and evaluative	Annual Population Survey, ONS; Hicks et al, 2013
Satisfaction with life	To capture individuals' satisfaction with life at moment of survey	Evaluative, at current moment of survey	Kahneman et al, 2004; Alder et al, 2016; Clark et al, 2018
Control and self-esteem	To assess self-esteem, perceived control, and satisfaction with life	Hybrid: self-reported but reflection. Scaled responses to questions in face-to-face interview	Rohe and Basolo, 1997; Rohe et al, 2007
Warwick-Edinburgh Mental Wellbeing Scale	To capture positive mental health, including aspects of human flourishing	Hybrid: self-reported subjective responses to questions on human flourishing	Tennant et al, 2007; Bond et al, 2012
Capabilities	To assess equality of (real) access to the social goods of human fulfilment	Consensual lists of the basic human goods; objective/external; 'intersubjective'	Sen, 1979, 1992; Nussbaum, 1992; Burchardt, 2004

Note: The ONS reference can be found at: www.ons.gov.uk/peoplepopulationandcommunity/wellbeing/methodologies/personalwellbeingintheukqmi

The inherent limitation lies in the potentially fleeting nature of moods. One way of approaching this is to focus on questions that, by their nature, are evaluative and invite reflection on the part of the respondent. For example, an important and commonly used evaluative question employed in survey research asks respondents to rate their overall satisfaction with life.

More sophisticated ways of doing this are evolving with new methodologies and include the use of vignettes and different scenarios to tease out more reflective survey responses (see Dolan and Metcalfe 2012, Dolan et, 2013; Adler et al, 2016). A notable example is the Day Reconstruction Method. This asks participants to reconstruct their experiences of the previous day, structuring this around episodes, such as the day's commute, domestic chores, or a social engagement (Kahneman et al, 2004).

One criticism of the current wellbeing measures is that they have a tendency to measure deficits, rather than a positive sense of wellbeing (Tennant et al, 2007). This is certainly the case for the GHQ-12 survey, which is one of the three key variables I later examine in my analysis of the BHPS. This is in one sense simply a function of different purposes: the GHQ-12 is designed to detect depression and anxiety, and in a clinical setting this may trigger a helpful intervention. But the point does have some force, especially when we are using such measures sociologically, or as a guide in policy development. We may for example find that social housing does not have a negative effect on wellbeing (and specifically on the mental health metrics of the GHQ-12), but in a sense this pathologises the issue, applying standards of illness, rather than 'wellness'. From this wellness perspective we might find that social housing is in fact positively good for you.

Such insights motivate an alternative assessment of wellbeing: the Warwick-Edinburgh Mental Wellbeing Scale (WEMWBS), which has been developed and applied in a number of fruitful studies of wellbeing in a neighbourhood context (Tennant et al, 2007; Bond et al, 2012; Baba et al, 2017). This scale includes both hedonic and explicitly eudaimonic items ('personal development, competence and autonomy') and was developed by drawing on similar consensual techniques to the consensus approach to poverty touched on in Chapter 1. The WEMWBS, as we shall see, shares some similarities with the metrics developed in some of the capabilities literature, which (in some variants) adopts a consensual list approach. Both proceed from the assumption that some are some universal human needs (most obviously material needs such as food and shelter) but that these needs take on different local meanings – and make different distributive demands – as we move to notions of higher needs. A key reference point for all these accounts is Maslow's famous 'hierarchy of needs' (Maslow, 1943; Maslow, 1981 [1954]), proceeding in five steps, from basic material needs, to social needs of belonging, to self-esteem and, finally, at the apex, the pursuit of self-actualisation (Maslow, 1943; Maslow, 1981 [1954]).[2]

Research in the US has also used items on self-esteem and sense of control, though this approach has not been adopted in the UK. Using data from a Baltimore-based programme to extend ownership among low-income households, Rohe and Stegman constructed a longitudinal survey panel in which participants were interviewed once before they bought a home and then again 18 months later. A control group that remained in rental accommodation throughout was also recruited, and Rohe went on to test the longer-term validity of their findings with follow-up interviews three years later (Rohe and Basolo, 1997; Rohe et al, 2007). As seen in Chapter 5, in these studies Rohe and colleagues find that owners are indeed more likely to be satisfied with life than renters, but no more likely than renters to report higher levels of self-esteem or perceived control.

The dynamics of welfare institutions and wellbeing

Figure 2.1 presents a stylised model of the relationship between wellbeing and the cultural and institutional influences that shape both the meaning of wellbeing and individual outcomes. As the book progresses, this model is redrawn to explicitly represent the relationship between housing tenure and wellbeing.

The arrow at the bottom of Figure 2.1 represents a line from objective accounts of wellbeing on the left, to the most subjective, on the right. Life satisfaction sits between the two, as it is assessed subjectively but with implicit reference to external social norms and standards. The right-hand side is presented as 'happiness' as a shorthand for mental-state criteria of wellbeing, capturing mood and feeling at a particular time. The obverse is the 'unhappiness' of depression, captured by the GHQ-12.

It should be stressed once more that the GHQ-12 was not designed within the conceptual context of philosophical debates about hedonic wellbeing, or its eudaimonic counterpart. But the aim of my stylistic presentation is to capture the broader contours of the relationship between wellbeing and

Figure 2.1: The dynamics of institutions, culture, and wellbeing

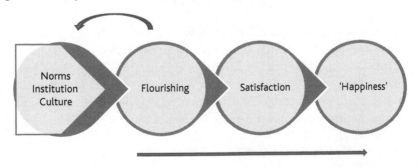

institutions. Norms, institutions and culture are represented on the left-hand side, feeding into the 'flourishing', which is the most 'objective' of the three concepts of wellbeing in the graphic. The social constructivist perspective of my approach takes the institutional influences to be historical and mutable products. The wider cultural context includes deep-seated beliefs about human agency and related concepts of human virtue. But the direction of influence is not linear: deep-seated conceptions of virtue shape our beliefs about the rightness and legitimacy of institutions, which in turn influence discourses of virtue. This loop is represented by the topmost arrow.

In later iterations of this model I focus on different aspects of wellbeing, in particular the relationship between life satisfaction and happiness, and present potential feedback loops between these two wellbeing metrics. The key question I pose later is this: Do lower levels of satisfaction with life lead to lower levels of happiness? This becomes an important policy question when we consider the possibility that housing tenure may have an impact on one but not the other; if lower levels of satisfaction with life does not feed into lower levels of happiness (or higher levels of depression) this will have a bearing on how we view future policy directions.

Capabilities and human flourishing

Over the past two decades there have been sustained attempts to bring such conceptions of flourishing to the surface of public policy debate, under the banner of the 'capabilities approach'. In view of my own emphasis on flourishing, the capabilities approach therefore warrants closer attention. Ultimately I argue that the capabilities approach does not deliver on its promises, but the process of exploring these promises helps to further clarify my framework of analysis.

The concept of capabilities is most closely associated with Amartya Sen (1993; 1999), and has taken on increasing importance in social policy debate over the past decade. It has already generated a large literature across a range of academic disciplines. To avoid the controversies increasingly associated with even basic characterisations of the concept, I turn first to one of the leading commentators on the 'capability approach':

> Despite some philosophical disagreements about the best description of the capability approach, it is generally understood as a conceptual framework for a range of normative exercises, including most prominently the following: (1) the assessment of individual well-being; (2) the evaluation and assessment of social arrangements; and (3) the design of policies and proposals about social change in society. (Robeyns, 2011, p 2)

Robeyns' concession to 'some philosophical disagreements' is something of an understatement. However, in order to avoid undue complication at this stage of my argument, I do not engage with any of these disagreements, focusing instead on a skeleton account of the capabilities approach, with some brief comments on how it relates to the key arguments of this book.

The language of the capability approach revolves around three central terms: 'beings', 'doings' and 'functionings'. As Robeyns explains: 'Functionings are "beings and doings", that is, various states of human beings and activities that a person can undertake'. Positive examples of 'being', derived from Sen, include being well nourished, educated, and embedded in social networks (Robyns, 2011). Negative examples of 'being' would include the absence of these goods. These 'beings' give the person the wherewithal, if the opportunities are present, to engage in 'doings'. Examples are again positive and negative. Here we can take a positive example: we may be able to exercise our being as an educated person in a highflying job (a 'doing'), but we may be prevented from doing so by social or institutional barriers.

Such barriers could be based on degrees of prejudice. This could include, for example, racist name spotting in the selection of interviewees for legal pupillages, or perhaps the glass ceiling faced by women in the workforce. Or a society may go to great lengths to offer us all the same 'being' opportunities but, more innocently, overlook things that a majority take for granted but which systematically prevent some people from exercising their being in a 'doing'. High pavement curbs and step-only access, for example, prevent wheelchair users from accessing a whole range of opportunities in everyday life (for discussion of disabilities and the capability approach, see Burchardt, 2004). So it is only with this recognition, and exhaustive changes to pathways and access points, that we are able to say that the wheelchair user in our example is better able to exercise her *capabilities*.

We can therefore characterise the capabilities approach with the following simplification: a person's capabilities consist of who they are able to be, what they are able to do, and the opportunity structures that allow them to fulfil this potential. Hartley Dean, a capabilities sceptic, distils this nicely: 'Sen's argument has been that equal inputs do not necessarily give rise to equal outputs because human capabilities – the real freedoms that people have to fashion their own way of living – may be objectively constrained' (Dean, 2009, p 262).

At this point we do not need to enter the subtleties of interpretation and refinement in the capabilities literature. As indicated in the case of disabilities, the capabilities approach has some great merits. But there is a risk of theoretical overkill. And similarly, it helps to set the concept of capabilities in some historical context.

Contextualising capabilities

Two things now stand out when we place the capabilities approach in its own historical context. First, the development of capabilities occurred at a time when a number of prominent theorists and philosophers were seeking to bring virtue and human flourishing into accounts of distributive justice, rather than pushing them aside as a potential threat to liberal neutrality. While Rawls has not directly figured in my argument, his Kantian account of distributive justice is inescapably in the background of any theoretical discussion of justice and the welfare state.[3]

Second, this movement towards virtue was also implicitly historicist: central to the movement is an emphasis on the variability of belief about the constitution of human flourishing in different historical contexts, and this will change over time within different cultures. This context is important for the development of capabilities as a concept, and helps in considering the relationship capabilities of capabilities with other wellbeing perspectives.

As Dean asserts, it is in the early stages of the Rawlsian debate that Sen started to develop his account of capabilities. Set against this background, capabilities 'is a concept that transcends a narrow hedonic and utilitarian calculus in order to embrace the essential "virtues" that, morally, define humanity' (Dean, 2009, p 264).

There are two components in Dean's statement that are of direct interest to us now. The first is the rejection of 'a narrow hedonic and utilitarian calculus'. Notably, in terms of my argument in this chapter, Sen was reacting to the limitations of utilitarianism, in particular the kind of 'narrow hedonic' measurement of subjective wellbeing that I have argued should not be ruled out of court. Rawls was also explicitly reacting to the failings of utilitarianism. But Sen takes the critique further and, to some degree, directs it at Rawls's own theory. The explicit criticism is that Rawlsian justice does not pay sufficient regard to the diversity of individual wants, needs and circumstances – hence the need for a capabilities framework I sketched in the previous section. Even with a generous distribution of material resources, accompanied by strong formal rights, there are people who will not be able to access the goods that we consider to be part of a rich and rewarding life. But diversity does just sit within the individual and does not simply refer to the variety of barriers that individuals may face in practice. Running throughout Sen's work there is also an increasing emphasis on the variety of cultural norms and expectations, both within and across different societies. Viewed from this perspective, Sen can be counted as part of a broader movement of political thought that stresses the limitations inherent in the search for a universal standard of distributive justice. These concerns coalesced around the way in which Rawls – and others writing in the Kantian tradition – invites us to think about how we construct the rules of justice. This thought is conducted through the device of the Original Position. In this we are all to check in our beliefs and values at the door, and imagine a scenario in which we design a system of justice with no knowledge of where we ourselves would end up in the imagined society.

The wealthy architect, surgeon or successful performer *may* be in a similar position in this new society – but there is a good chance that they won't. Instead they might switch roles with their immigrant office cleaner. No superior education following us through life, no privileged social networks or inherited wealth, and no guarantee that we will be born with the same skin colour. Considering this risk, what kind of society would we want? The rough answer is that we would likely choose something like a strong, decommodified welfare state, providing everyone with a right of access to considerably more than the basic material necessities of life. Social housing is this world would not be distributed by need, if this criteria creates the kind of stigma that we sometimes see today. For Rawls, such a system would undermine the 'bases of self-respect'.

Further to this we would also want to ensure that we are able to pursue our deeper commitments to the ethical and moral traditions that we are born into, or go on to adopt more reflectively. Integral to these commitments will be some conception of human flourishing. But, again, we do not know what these commitments might be. They too are checked in before we enter the Original Position. So we once more hedge our bets, and opt for a system that allows the greatest range of possibilities. This system is one that, in the language used in the theoretical debate, gives precedence to the 'right' over the 'good'. Rather than seeking a consensus about the true nature of human flourishing (the good), we instead agree to a system of rights and institutions (the right) that allows us all to pursue different and sometimes profoundly held beliefs about what constitutes human flourishing. In one way this is a restatement of the classic liberal principle that the state is there to allow and regulate diverse views and ways of life; it has no business weighing in on the validity of any of these claims, so long as they do not restrict others from pursuing their own views and ways of life.

But this means that criteria for human flourishing do not have a legitimate role to play in our assessments of social justice: the 'good' cannot enter debate as a measurable metric, or, more generally, as a guiding distributive consideration.

It is this exclusion that Sen, along with other key critics of Rawls, finds problematic. It is not that Sen seeks to impose a particular conception of the good on others, or that the critics of Rawls did not share the worry that state-sanctioned accounts of virtue may carry the risk of moral authoritarianism. The objection is instead that a blanket exclusion of virtue leaves us with a universalism that is just too sparse to be of use in thinking about real issues of distribution, justice and measurement. Rawls' procedural account of justice achieves universal truths at the price of having too little content, but the broader objection is that such universalism is ahistorical, denuded of the rich social material from which meanings – and the goods we distribute – emerge. In this, Sen holds much in common with MacIntyre (1985), Taylor (1992) and Walzer (1983). For Sen – if not all advocates of the approach – the capabilities in question are therefore a product of time and place. In this respect, Sen is again in the same company as MacIntyre and colleagues.

Not all capabilities advocates share the same view: Martha Nussbaum, in particular, stands out for her attempts to derive, *a priori*, a list of capabilities that are universally valid and essential for human flourishing (2006). But generally, despite the many points of nuance visited within the literature, there is a consensus that any 'list' debate should be about the best means of deciding what to include on it (see Burchardt, 2004; Alkire, 2005). So, for Sen, capabilities are in part a corrective to the austerity of the Rawlsian account. This corrective is part and parcel of the criticism of 'resourcist' approach to social justice, which is intended to provide the resources that people need in order to pursue what they consider to be a life worth living.

The limits of 'resources'

My purpose in highlighting the early development of the capabilities approach has been to stress the double-edged sharpness of Sen's critical reaction to a Rawlsian view of distributive justice (including the assessment or measurement of actual distributions). With one edge, Sen does greater justice to our intuitions that 'wellbeing' must ultimately be about human flourishing in a given social context. But, with the other edge, the potential of capabilities of a metric is limited; there is a trade-off between richness and precision.

Yet if we treat the capabilities approach as a normative *critique*, rather than as an empirical metric or sociological concept, it has a great deal of force. This is especially the case when we return to a resourcist view. We may, for example, provide a wheelchair user with ample monetary resources. The further question is then one of access, not just in the very simple sense of unthought-of practicalities (though we continually learn of quotidian nuisances such as hand-dryers in accessible toilets being place at the wrong height), but also more subtle social processes and signals that need a bit more work – and help from the affected parties – to uncover. In the case of the wheelchair user, the transformation in the UK (such as it is) came with recognition not just of freedoms curtailed by an impossible transport system, but of barriers blocking access to more complex cultural goods. London's South Bank is easier for the wheelchair user to access now because it is a deeply held belief that the arts are of great human value; we believe the creation and appreciation of the arts is an exemplar of human flourishing. It is in this kind of case that the capabilities approach has been able to add something that other ways of thinking (particularly the more technical theories of justice) had failed to fully appreciate.

By the same logic, the quality and affordability of social housing is not all there is to wellbeing. Indeed, one of the strongest results in my empirical results (Chapters 5 and 6) is the great importance of neighbourhoods and social cohesion. This will include measurable factors such as the quality of services and transport links, but neighbourhood and locality are also constituted by social relations. This can come with negative social relations – patterns of stigma and hierarchical social status – as well as positive opportunities for interaction and flourishing. And for all the resources that may be available to social tenants, a capabilities critique will correctly point to the residual debilitating effects of these social structures.

One contribution of the capabilities approach is that it offers important new ways of discussing human flourishing in an actionable policy context, providing a bridge between different traditions of thought, analysis and normative argument. A more distinctive contribution is to give clearer and more finely grained empirical content to human flourishing as a useful and substantive concept in policy design and evaluation, taking us down a level from the broader strokes of historical and theoretical treatments of virtue and human flourishing.

However, it is unlikely that the capabilities approach can do more than provide analytical and normative guidance in a policy context. To do more than this has become a central ambition within the capabilities approach, with a very wide-ranging attempt to apply it directly to specific policy goals and outcomes (Burchardt, 2004; Alkire, 2005). This has come with the attempted development of the capabilities concept as an empirical metric, rendering it somehow into a mode of measurement able to assess the impact of policies on an individual's wellbeing (Burchardt and Vizard, 2011). There are a number of critical responses to these attempts, including from some capabilities advocates (Hick, 2012). But critique, as I have argued, is as far as the capabilities approach can really take us.

The question is: how *do* you measure flourishing? Well, you could ask people if they are flourishing, or you could tick a list of behaviours or actions. We could include in this list visits to art galleries, fulfilling employment and active political participation, perhaps through democratic social housing management. We have determined already that these are indeed forms of human flourishing in our society, and we have sought out the barriers that need to be brought down to prevent all people exercising these virtues, should they wish to. A metric measuring something like this is possible: the number of people in a group facing some kind of barrier to participation, set alongside the numbers in those groups who do in fact manage to access these goods, compared with the general population.

Yet in all this we would not really be measuring individual flourishing but, rather, a proxy indicator of the number of people participating in potentially enriching activities. The potentiality of this is important: all things considered, we may only say that access to the goods in question is an encouraging sign and something to welcome. But the 'all things considered' caveat is important. The human complexity that falls under this caveat is just too rich to be reduced to a usable 'metric'. The attempt to do so risks being as crudely reductionist as the hedonic account of subjective wellbeing, or, conversely, could lead to the frightening world of objective standards of human flourishing – virtues and excellences that are judged in some form of perfectionist tribunal or moral arbitration, as seen in the preformation history of Western Europe, and in the more recent history of totalitarian states. The historical comparison serves as an important reminder of the liberal intellectual tradition that Sen was both working in and reacting to: a tradition based on a fear of the state's arbitration of what counts as human flourishing. This is precisely why Rawls gives priority to the right over the good.

Another problem re-emerges when capabilities are treated as a metric. We could (and should) use the insights of the capabilities approach as a way of assessing the overall impact of access policies, but in doing so we are measuring in *aggregate*: groups, classes and cohorts *within* which we may reasonably surmise an average increase in flourishing. If we were worried, for example, about the rate of minority Black and ethnic individuals accessing the legal professions or elite universities, an increase in the proportion of minority Black and ethnic people in the law and in university is a sound indicator of progress.

Nevertheless, there are limits to how far the use of aggregation can be endorsed by capabilities advocates. Further steps in this direction will at some point bring us back full circle to one of the two fundamental objections to utilitarian calculation – that aggregation amounts to homogenisation – that both Rawls and Sen are so keen to avoid. In Rawls' phrase, it would be a form of metric that failed to respect the 'separateness of persons' (Rawls, 1971, p 27). This is not a problem if we are to stick to the original motivations of the capabilities approach, which was primarily concerned with the exclusion of whole groups from the goods needed for human flourishing. But it does suggest that moving beyond capabilities as a guiding framework would reintroduce some potentially profound normative problems.

Conclusion

This leaves us in a similar position to our starting point in this chapter. I have stressed throughout this that conceptions of virtue and human flourishing are inescapably part of welfare and wellbeing discourses, and exert a powerful influence on narratives of social housing and dependency. To ignore or exclude the contested field of flourishing from the ways we view the nature of welfare provision in social policy debate is to miss something of central importance. Yet this does not mean we can or should 'metricise' flourishing or virtue. Conversely, as we have argued, subjective wellbeing approaches should be part of a system of metrics. This is not because such approaches are normatively superior in any way, and it is not without recognition of its inherent limitations. But subjective wellbeing is a well-developed empirical indicator, to be used, with caution, to inform less reductive discussion of welfare and wellbeing.

3

Discourses of dependency: social housing, welfare, and political debate

In Chapter 1 I introduced the concepts of residualisation and feedback loops, in which policy shapes beliefs and attitudes, and these in turn shape policy. Part of the story of residualisation is the way in which the meaning of social housing evolved from being something that was for the 'respectable' working class, to a type of housing only for the 'needy' and – for some observers – the 'undeserving'. I also outlined the key reasons for this evolution. These include the rising popularity of owner-occupation before social housing had become a mainstream option, the wide availability of mortgage finance from the late 1920s, and perceptions of poor quality within the social housing sector once it did become a more widely available housing option. This forms part of the institutional context of the evolution of the meaning and purpose of social housing. But there are also other important influences, which in turn can, over time, shape the evolution of institutional context. Political discourses and media representations of social housing exert a strong influence on our views of the meaning and value of social housing, even when we are in radical disagreement with these representations.

The primary purpose of this chapter is to draw out the underlying assumptions and normative implications of these competing discourses. At this stage I do not offer robust empirical adjudication of the assertion that social housing creates dependency (see Chapters 5 and 6). Although I highlight the misuses of sociological evidence on the relationship between social housing and life chances, it is not my aim to 'myth bust' false narratives of welfare dependency, or to directly challenge the apparent benefits of ownership. I do, however, draw an important distinction between different kinds of 'fact'.

This distinction, between 'strict' empirical fact and social or political fact, becomes increasingly important as we explore competing interpretations of the meaning and purpose of social housing. This exploration leads us into the 'discourses' and 'narratives' of housing. Within the range of such discourses, it is the discourse of social housing and dependency – a specific crisis narrative – that is the dominant theme of this chapter. However, some prior theoretical articulation is required. In the following sections I therefore present a basic outline of contemporary academic usage of discourse as an analytical tool. Closely related to this are variants of 'social constructivism' and the belief that notions of truth and reality are, broadly, products of the way we collectively think about the social world and communicate within it. We can then turn directly to discourses (and constructions) of dependency and social housing, relating these to the concepts of path dependence and feedback loops.

The final piece of my constructivist picture is the construction of social scientific criteria of success or failure, the 'metrics' that are used to evaluate the impact of housing policy. Three such constructions are of particular importance for the development of my argument: the sociological concept of life chances, expectations and evaluations of behaviour, and of course the impact of housing on individual wellbeing.

Theory, meaning, social fact: the social construction of housing discourses

One of the central purposes of this chapter is to explore the social construction of housing as a good. For this purpose I locate myself in the hermeneutic and interpretivist tradition, by which I mean that particular meanings or goods (for example, 'social housing') are understood with reference to other meanings, and that the relationship between these goods is constantly reinterpreted as socially constructed meanings evolve.

There are a number of ways of making sense of social construction as a guiding principle in social policy debate. There are also a number of historical sources and traditions that could lay claim to 'social construction' as a concept, though in social science it is generally attributed to Berger and Luckmann's seminal book, *The social construction of reality* (Berger and Luckmann, 1991 [1966]). The point to stress here, regardless of finer theoretical controversy, is the contingency of socially constructed facts. As human artefacts they are a product of time and place. The same view of the world as a human artefact also applies to the way in which we conceptualise and name the social goods that societies regulate and distribute (Walzer, 1984), including the goods of social housing and ownership.

One way of making sense of the idea of social constructivism is to adopt a well-known approach, developed, primarily, by Bacchi, summarised as 'What is the problem represented to be?' (Bacchi, 2009). This approach unpacks the ways in which certain behaviours or social facts (for example, the rise of the single-parent family) are defined by policy and political elites in terms of 'problems', while other social facts or behaviours may go entirely unnoticed (Bacchi, 2009). Why, for example, is the dependence of a social tenant on the state a problematic dependence, while the buyer of a state-subsidised starter home escapes such notice?

This approach has recently been used to draw out the ways in which the coalition government of 2010–15 channelled its austerity programme through a construction of the 'problem' of worklessness (Pantazis, 2016).

Housing researchers have also applied this type of analysis to a range of issues within social housing. These include constructions of lone mothers as a problem group (Jacobs et al, 2003) and a strong emphasis on constructions of virtuous versus anti-social behaviours among social tenants on housing estates (Franklin and Clapham, 1997; Goodchild and Cole, 2001; Flint and Nixon, 2006) and, more recently, narratives of 'welfare ghettos' following the English urban riots of 2011 (Hancock and Mooney, 2013).

Much of this research has focused on the evolving norms and assumptions of management discourse (Clapham, 1997; Goodchild and Cole, 2001; Flint, 2003; Flint and Nixon, 2006) as they construct and address these behavioural norms, with significant early contributions on the marketisation of management discourse (Marston, 2002) and on the local constructions of social housing allocation processes (Saugeres, 1999).

Within this body of work there is often a strong Foucauldian emphasis on discourses as a form of unstated and often unconscious social control or 'discipline'. This approach has yielded significant research on discourses of anti-social behaviour in social housing and the ways in which social tenants are presented in policy and political discourse (Flint, 2003; Flint and Nixon, 2006). The Foucauldian notions of surveillance and control can be particularly salient in this context, where surveillance may be literal, for example in the use of CCTV monitoring (Clapham, 1997), or where contractual relations between landlord and tenant are based on strong behavioural requirements (Goodchild and Cole, 2001; Flint, 2003; Flint and Nixon, 2006).

Foucauldian-inspired discourse analysis has also been applied to homeownership. It has, for example, recently been used to good effect in work on homeownership that draws on 150 qualitative 'narratives' that delve into the lives and lived experiences of homeowners (Smith, 2008). With greater emphasis on the Foucauldian notions of surveillance and discipline, it has also been argued that 'tenure is imbued with a disciplinary power which normalises homeowners in the same way that Foucault's inmates, orphans and soldiers are normalised' (Gurney, 1999, p 66). This, in my opinion, stretches theory too far and is a case of the tendency, observed by King, to apply particular theories to domains that they were not designed for (King, 2009). McKee offers a similar observation on a tendency for Foucauldians (though not Foucault himself) to neglect or downplay the 'multiple, overlapping and at times contradictory forms of rationality' that may coexist within governmental programmes and strategies (McKee, 2009., p 474).

By the same token, for all its merits, I do not use the language and tools of governmentality. Where Foucauldian analysis works best is in a very fine-grained understanding of particular practices or modes of thought, either in uncovering the underlying moral assumptions and values of a tradition (for example, Foucault's own genealogy of psychiatry), or in evolving institutions or social norms. My own purpose, however, is less fine-grained. I seek to explore social housing, but in a way that highlights the interaction of discourses in this sphere with the meanings and practices of other spheres. This approach is no less able to accommodate the demands of a rigorous discourse analysis, and, I believe, allows a wider view of the relation of different discourses to an ideological 'whole'.

Nevertheless, the theoretical framework I have sketched shares much with the Foucauldian canon, which has become dominant across housing theory. In view of this dominance my divergence from this approach calls for some explanation.

First, some brief comments on the limitations of the main body of discourse analysis just mentioned. One of the limitations we have observed stems from the selection of *a* theory rather than a more promiscuous identification with a broader tradition or set of conceptual family resemblances, as implied in the case of Gurney's treatment of ownership, which I suggest stretches Foucault's 'disciplinary power' too far.

I have also touched on a second limitation that applies to the more general use of discourse analysis in housing research. The great merit of such discourse analysis is its capacity for richly textured representations of particular practices within a given domain of enquiry (for example, the management of social housing). However, the same granularity has sometimes led to the criticism that the focus of discourse analysis in housing research has been too narrow, excluding important forms of discourse that lie outside of elite policy formulation (Hastings, 2000; Watt, 2008). This could in principle be corrected by complementary research drawing on a more balanced range of sources, going beyond policy discourses and document analysis to explore discursive practices more ethnographically (for example, see Percival, 2001).

But my contention is that the discourse analysis that has developed in social policy – and in particular the strain that is strongly influenced by Foucault – is less well suited to an understanding of how different discourses shape one another. In terms of the Weberian-Walzerian metaphor of 'spheres', the body of work I have briefly reviewed provides a superior means of understanding meanings and practices *within* spheres, but is not the best means of understanding the ways in which these spheres interact and shape one another.

Discourses of dependency and the constitution of the independent self

The discourse of dependency and crisis is not confined to narratives of social housing. We could in fact describe the case of social housing as one thematic strand in an overarching discourse of crisis with – and attributed to – the welfare state. With this in mind it is helpful to first consider the earlier genesis of 'welfare dependency' as a term of moral judgement within welfare debate. For this I turn to an important account of the development of 'dependency' as a 'key term' in the US (Fraser and Gordon, 1994). This account consciously employs the Foucauldian language of genealogy and explores the evolution of different meanings or 'registers' of the concept, but nevertheless explicitly diverges from Foucault in aiming to 'contextualise discourse shifts in relation to broad institutional and social-structural shifts' (Fraser and Gordon, 1994, p 311). This approach is consonant with my own preference for spheres of meaning, which are shaped in part by institutional structures.

While Fraser and Gordon are concerned with the specific context of a highly stigmatised post-war welfare system in the US, their genealogical search takes them much further back, first into pre-industrial England and then through the major historical-economic epochs that followed. What we see in these transitions is a slow evolution of 'dependence' from an economic to a moral-psychological category. Thus, in the pre-industrial period, relations of economic dependency were essential, embedded in unquestioned and assumptions and beliefs (sometimes referred to a *doxa*) that knowledge systems must presuppose as a condition of coherent discourse and investigation: 'dependency was, therefore, a normal, as opposed to deviant, condition, a social relation as opposed to an individual trait' (Fraser and Gordon, 1994, p 131).

Subsequent registers of dependency flow from deep, structural social and economic transformations that shift the locus of 'dependency' to the individual, in which individuals may be classified not only as dependent or independent, but as *appropriately* so *vis à vis* their social status in defined social hierarchies; as, for instance, in the social relations of a paternalistic landowner over his land workers. Fraser and Gordon's depictions of earlier registers of dependency have some clear resonances in the early development of social housing in the UK. It is evident, for example, in the tradition of Octavia Hill, for whom paternalistic control was a means of moral improvement within a state of dependency, rather than a demonstration of moral improvement by the learnt ability to become independent.[1]

However, the final stopping point in Fraser and Gordon's historical genealogy is the highly residualised welfare apparatus of the US in the 1980s and early 1990s. Here we see a familiar picture of judgement and stigma, the world of the Reagan era 'welfare queen' and Murray's underclass, underpinned by a two-tier welfare system. As we have seen, this has been mirrored in the UK and, indeed, has been a recurrent theme in the history of welfare and of social housing. The following sections explore the most recent and contemporary manifestations of dependency discourse in the UK. But first I highlight two further observations from Fraser and Gordon, all of which will later help to direct my developing argument.

The first is an important analytical distinction between empirical dependency claims and normative dependency claims, judging dependency to be a psychological failing. A great deal of contemporary debate is, I have suggested, restricted by an overt focus on empirical dependency claims, missing the opportunity to challenge the normative assumption that dependency is morally pernicious. As Fraser and Gordon show, there are many historical examples of what was considered 'good' dependency. Though such examples are unpalatable or offensive to contemporary sensibilities, it is a mistake to rule out the possibility of 'good' dependency *a priori*. Doing so, I shall later argue, restricts the range of normative argument in a way that makes it harder to argue for rather than against the value of social housing and the welfare state.

The second observation is that Fraser and Gordon's account is not just a genealogy of dependency but, crucially, of the self as well. A key moment in this is the 17th-century emergence of Reformation ideals of individuated and autonomous selves, leading to a radicalised Protestantism that 'elaborated a new positive image of individual independence and a critique of sociolegal and political dependency' (Fraser and Gordon, 1994, p 315).[2]

The significance of these observations lies in the way we approach issues of autonomy and agency in the UK today. How and exactly why we have arrived at this position is beyond the remit of this book. But a few further comments are, I hope, helpful at this point. Fraser and Gordon's reference to the emergence of sociolegal and political independence points to a *process* of conceptual and normative expansion, in which we have come to assert the value of independence in an ever-increasing number of spheres. We can see this in a journey that moves from independence of individuals from religious prescription, the independence of some men from economic lords and masters, and then, much later, the independence of women from a domestic patriarch. These changes can all be characterised in terms of freedom and autonomy – 'ideals of individuated and autonomous selves' – and all will be rightly regarded as positive.

But there is also a trap that we often fall into, one that is driven by the same enlightenment assumptions of progress towards a wider and more complete independence. The normative terminus of this assumption of progress is an endpoint that we should approach with caution. If we think that all dependence is bad, we arrive at the same kind of atomised individualism that we find among advocates of welfare retrenchment, particularly within the theoretical and normative assumptions of neoliberalism. Complete independence seems very similar to detachment or isolation, and if we are aiming for this state it is hard to know how we should interact with others, and even more difficult to construct an account of what we owe to each other. So my suggestion is that there must be a point along the line of positive historical development that becomes pathological, where independence is destructive. Paul Hogget expresses this clearly:

> There is nothing necessarily constructive about agency and we should be aware of smuggling normative assumptions into our thinking here, as if agency is good and absence of agency is bad. Just as we can be destructive agents so also at times we can be constructive in our dependency and powerlessness … we need a model of self as object as well as self as agent. (Hoggett, 2001, p 43)

A similar argument is developed by Taylor, who advocates a view of wellbeing that, like mine, is pluralist and wary of binary distinctions between hedonic and Aristotelian accounts of wellbeing (Taylor, 2011). In this kind of account we should be wary of 'independence' because we know, from human experience, that we are all vulnerable at different points in our lives. All of us need to be dependent at some point. Once we recognise this the fear or shame of 'dependence' should dissipate. The crucial challenge we face is one of differentiation. What is *wrong* with dependence? These questions should be approached with a view to the broad context of the spheres in which they arise. As Taylor states: 'If we take a relational view of wellbeing, the issue is: which type of social relationships are constitutive of which kinds of wellbeing for any individual in different contexts and over their life-course?'(Taylor, 2011, p 781).

Finally, we should ask what motivates empirical dependency claims. Here there is a final distinction to add to the claims that, first, some people *are* dependent, and, second, that this comes from a moral failing or weakness of character. The third claim I have in mind is that you *should* be dependent – and that this is the right order of things, the world as it should be. It is probably this last claim that most of us would want to reject. The basis for doing so is that this claim is hierarchical and segregating, classifying whole groups in an inherently conservative social order of higher and lower classes.

Welfare reform in the UK: crisis reimagined

Discourses of dependency and of crisis have gone through repeated iterations at various points in the history of the British welfare state. Throughout this there have been different layers of discourse, from abstract philosophy, to sociological argument, to policy and political rhetoric. But the place of social housing in this discourse has not always been as explicit as it is today. Many of the iterations were, rather, directed at neighbourhoods and classes, at 'slums' and their inhabitants (see Welshman, 2007). But with the emergence of social housing built specifically with the intention of rehousing the populations of slum neighbourhoods, it is easy to see how social housing came to be associated with an 'underclass' – and a short step from this to narratives of social housing as a cause of welfare dependency. In this section I explore one of the most recent manifestations, starting with the political rhetoric and policy prescription of the 2000s and 2010s.

At the same time, however, there has been a parallel discourse that heads in a different direction, away from claims that social housing creates welfare dependency. This discourse was largely developed through Conservative Party policy thinking in the 1960s and 1970s and revolved around the issue of 'fair' rents in social housing. In this discourse, the Conservative Party portrayed council tenants not as workshy and needy, but as affluent and privileged (Jacobs et al, 2003).

This debate has re-emerged in recent years and presents practical and normative challenges that should be taken seriously (see Chapters 7 and 8). Taken at face value and as part of an ongoing debate about housing finance, the key point at issue is the efficiency – and fairness – of continuing to provide sub-market housing to social tenants if their finances improve to the extent that the private market is no longer inaccessible. From this perspective, the shift from privileged to workshy tenant looks, at first sight, to be a dramatic change of narrative. In both narratives, however, the underlying assumptions are based on normative criteria of desert: the weight given to 'fairness' is greater than the weighting of 'efficiency'. The underlying premise is that the state – and the voting taxpayer – is subsidising the living costs and lifestyle of an undeserving client of a bloated welfare state. The key point of difference is that, in the 'fair rents' debate of the 1960s and '70s, we do not yet see the full force of the 'dependency' narrative in Conservative housing policy.

How these two discourses interact in current housing debate is a theme I return to in Part III. But it is the dependency narrative that is now dominant, and must take precedence here.

One of the most dominant discourses of the past 20 years is the narrative of a 'broken Britain', a phrase first associated with the former Conservative Party leader, Iain Duncan Smith. There have been a number of commentaries on the emergence and rapid success of this discourse (Flint and Powell, 2012; Hayton, 2012; Jenson, 2014; Pantazis, 2016). One commentary that stands out is Tony Slater's (Slater, 2014), which highlights the re-emergence of an earlier narrative of problem families, expressed in the more contemporary idiom of 'intergenerational worklessness'. Slater quotes in full the following passage from Iain Duncan Smith's Preface in a 2008 report from the Centre for Social Justice (CSJ), *Housing poverty: From social breakdown to social mobility*:

> I have no hesitation in claiming that Britain is broken. This claim is factual. During the last five years my think-tank, The Centre for Social Justice (CSJ), has presented evidence of the entrenched poverty that traps millions of people, in the world's fourth largest economy. ... Our recent *Housing Poverty* report concluded that Britain's social housing estates, once stepping stones of opportunity, are now ghettos for our

poorest people. Life expectancy on some estates, where often three generations of the same family have never worked, is lower than the Gaza Strip. (CSJ, 2008, cited in Slater, 2014, p 962)

A central component of Slater's characterisation of this statement as ideological is its claim to 'truth'. The force of Slater's argument is not theoretical but, rather, in his argument that the CSJ intentionally distorts evidence in a way that contributes to a broader 'production of ignorance'. It is important to note that this manipulation broadly takes place within the framework of accepted social scientific practice and research; it is a case of breaking the rules, not changing the rules of the game itself. Indeed, Slater observes that the presentation of the CSJ case is explicitly launched with tacit homage to the New Labour mantra of 'evidence-based policy'.

Slater convincingly describes the evidence presented in the case of 'broken Britain' as 'rigged'. This is shown in analysis of CSJ's apparent evidence demonstrating widespread family breakdown: 'When consulting the methodological appendices to the report, which detail some of the survey questions asked of a "representative sample" of 2166 people, the evidence was never going to show anything different with respect to the supposed causes and prevention of "family breakdown"' (Slater, 2014, p 951). This is by no means an isolated example of empirical sleight of hand, as we shall see when we explore the discourse of life chances and social housing in greater depth. But it is clear that the case of social housing is part of an overarching narrative of crisis – that Britain is 'broken' in many places, and it is broken because, as David Cameron declared in a 2009 Conservative Party conference speech, "government got too big, did too much and undermined responsibility".

In embedding this perception, Cameron was greatly helped by the press, whose role in the creation and acceptance of crisis narratives has been particularly strong in the UK. The seminal sociological study of this phenomenon is Golding and Middleton's account of the 'scroungerphobia' led by the printed press in the 1970s (Golding and Middleton, 1982), with colourful depictions of Derek Deevy, the cigar-smoking, high-living 'King Con' who was convicted for benefit fraud in 1976. The force of the story is not the undisputed fraud, but the wider moral extrapolation: 'Deevy was immediately enthroned as King as a teeming population of scroungers and spongers' (Golding and Middleton, 1982, p 63), inviting readers to write in and confirm the suspicion that this was just the tip of the iceberg of sponging. The offence in question was no longer fraud as such, but the vices of laziness and greed, living it up at the expense of others.

A similar narrative has re-emerged in the last decade. A number of commentators have taken up the case of Mick Philpot, who in 2013 was convicted of the manslaughter of six of his children (see Jenson and Tyler,

2015). The exemplar is the infamous *Daily Mail* headline: 'Vile product of welfare UK: Man who bred 17 babies by five women to milk benefits system is guilty of killing six of them' (Dolan and Bentley, 2013). The explicit assumption was that the welfare state had been responsible for the formation of Philpott's vices. Notably, his dependency vice was also attributed to social housing, with the familiar trope (albeit with an unusual gender twist) that children are conceived as a means of accessing social housing, or a larger 'council house' in Philpott's case. As in the case of Deevy, criminal and simply unethical behaviour was tacitly elided – and holistically blamed on the welfare state.

There are also some grounds for the argument that poverty and (apparent) welfare dependency are increasingly treated as a form of entertainment, particularly in the televised 'poverty porn' that has become popular in the past ten years (see Jensen, 2014). Popular interest seems to be particularly strong when dependency is identified with place and 'culture' – typically the 'sink estates' and 'ghettos' of large post-war council estates.

There was also a striking spike in tabloid coverage of dependency as the discourse of a 'broken Britain' filtered into public debate at the turn of the 2000s. From tabloid to broadsheet to current affairs magazines, a crisis of dependency is declaimed: 'Britain's benefits ghettos: Report reveals growing number of estates where half those of working age are dependent on handouts' (Williams, 2013); 'Rush-hour silence in a welfare ghetto' (Gilligan, 2010); 'Spectator exclusive: Britain's welfare ghettos' (Howker, 2010), the last of these providing a table of rankings.

These headlines are of course the product of social construction. But this is not to say that they are conjured up without any regard for truth or fact, even though the evidence may be grossly distorted from a social scientific perspective. An important mediating mechanism in this context is the role of think-tanks and a range of domain-specific policy advocates. In the creation of discourses of dependency, think-tanks on the right of the political spectrum have situated their narratives of crisis on the boundaries of popular opinion, the pragmatic yet also ideological demands of party politics, and the 'facts' of history and social science (for broader discussions of the role of think-tanks, see Crockett, 1995; Peck and Tickle, 2007).

Wellbeing, work and paternalism

We have seen that there is a strong and historically persistent strain of dependency narratives in social housing discourses. I have also touched on traditions of paternalism in social housing. At this point there is another theme to bring to the fore: the explicit turn to individual wellbeing as the objective of welfare reform. Here we see a form of 'tough love' that, ostensibly, is driven by a concern for the wellbeing of individuals who have been sapped of their will and aspiration by an enervating welfare system.

In an apparently seamless transition from New Labour to coalition government, and from Tony Blair, through Gordon Brown, to David Cameron, Lord David Freud presents a series of speeches and statements in which, for example, 'the heart of this issue [is] the lost human potential' (Freud, 2011). 'Quite simply good work is good for you.'

> Housing Benefit is a case in point. In some situations the State was supporting people to live in homes with such high rents that they had no realistic chance of earning enough to cover the rent independently and to escape benefit dependency. And in many cases those homes were more desirable than those afforded by low income non benefit claimants. (Freud, 2011)

Three years later the theme is has reached a point of almost sublime epiphany in Freud's thinking, as he presents to his audience the concept of 'salutogenesis' – doubtless prompting a fever of furtive smart-phone googling among his audience – and tells us that the concept captures a sense of 'a purpose in life – what [Aaron Antonovsky] called coherence – [is] crucial to understanding human health and well-being' (Freud, 2014).[3]

Within all this apparent sophistication, however, the message is still this: 'Helping people get into work gives them a purpose and meaning to life that may have been lacking' (Freud, 2014).

For the most part the connection to social housing runs in the subtext, though a later speech to the Chartered Institute of Housing praises social housing for its efforts to support tenants into work (Freud, 2016). As we have seen, there is in fact a high concentration of worklessness in social housing. This naturally leads to the assumption – so ingrained that it is sometimes unspoken – that the welfare to work agenda has a special resonance in social housing discourse and policy.

Moreover, there is indeed strong evidence that work is, all things considered, 'good for you' (Waddell and Burton, 2006). But note the caveat: all things considered must include the quality of work, security and pay, and must also be set in the broader social and economic context. At the top of the list there are very tangible and well-known problems with housing affordability and the cost of childcare. Work is manifestly *not* good for you if it requires trade-offs that lead to a negative effect on wellbeing in other areas of life. Moreover, the stress of zero-hours contracts, with the need to constantly navigate the pitfalls of a notoriously unresponsive benefits system, represents a serious and increasingly well-documented threat to wellbeing and mental health (Curchin, 2017).

Life chances: from sociology to politics and psychology

One of the most important conceptual vehicles of the transmission of social scientific into political discourse is the sociological language of life chances, which was developed as a statistical framework with which to measure the likelihood that an individual's circumstances at one point in time will influence their later circumstances; the probability, for example, that he or she will have good employment opportunities or positive health outcomes. Although the sociology of life chances has a much longer pedigree (first associated with Max Weber at the turn of the 19th century), we can see the emergence of this concept in social policy debate in the early late 1990s and early 2000s, when New Labour developed and then rolled out Sure Start early years centres. This was a clear instance of the evidence-based policy imperative, and was motivated by data showing that social and economic equalities began to have a negative impact on pre-school children throughout their lives (see Bamfield, 2007). But the immediate point of interest for us is the mediation of the concept into political discourse, and then into narratives of social housing and welfare dependency.

The wider political context at this point was also being reshaped, as we have seen, by the emergence of centre-right think-tanks such as the CSJ and Policy Exchange in the mid-2000s. With the journey of life chances from sociological to public discourse already underway, the language of life chances was available for rhetorical use and conceptual refashioning. Further contextual layers provided the resources necessary for this kind of refashioning. These include a host of related discourses under the overarching language of dependency. Of particular importance is the evolution of narratives of unemployment and worklessness, accompanied by the development of active labour market policy, first by New Labour and then enthusiastically reclaimed by the Conservative Party in opposition. But the sphere in which life chances really came to life was in the social housing debate of the mid- to late 2000s, and in particular a suggested relationship between social housing and cultures of worklessness.

Life chances and social housing

The event around which the life chances debate took shape was the 2007 publication of *Ends and means: The future roles of social housing in England* (Hills, 2007). This review proved to be highly influential, but there are two important qualifications to enter before we discuss this influence. The first is that the influence of the review does not extend to Scotland, Wales and Northern Ireland, and housing policy in Scotland, in particular, had by this point already started to diverge from England. But the divergence should not be overstated, as the problems (as well as the positive points) highlighted in the review took shape before devolution. The second qualification is that I am not in the first instance judging the review in terms of its empirical rigour, or, indeed, the motivations or beliefs of the authors. My concern is instead with impact and influence.

Ends and means was commissioned by the Department for Communities and Local Government at the start of Labour's third term in government. Significantly, this was the period in which Labour policy development increasingly focused on broader welfare reform, which in practice meant active labour market policy and greater conditionality in the benefits system.

The review was therefore commissioned by a government concerned with 'worklessness', and specifically with concentrations of worklessness in social housing and deprived neighbourhoods, many of which have historically been associated with large social estates. It is in this context that the review reported that there has been a dramatic decline in the level of employment among social tenants: whereas in 1981 a full 67 per cent of working-age householders were in full-time work, by 2006 this had fallen to 34 per cent. Moreover, this did not appear to be a simple selection effect; in other words it was not the unsurprising result that there are more unemployed social tenants following the adoption of an allocations system in which those excluded from the labour market may be considered in greatest housing need: 'Even controlling for a very wide range of personal characteristics, the likelihood of someone in social housing being employed appears significantly lower than those in other tenures' (Hills, 2007, p 5).

In 2008, as newly appointed housing minister (a position based in the department that commissioned the Hills review), Caroline Flint announced in her first major speech that she was considering the introduction of 'commitment contracts' for social tenants, for whom active job search would be a condition of their tenancy: "Social housing should be based around the principle of something for something." In an accompanying interview with *The Guardian*, Flint went further and began to elaborate a more sociological position, suggesting a neighbourhood effect: 'If you are in a family, an estate or a neighbourhood where nobody works that impacts on your own aspiration. It is a form of peer pressure' (Wintour, 2008).

As in my discussion of dependency, we can see a complex mix of empirical and normative claims – and the lynchpin of 'life chances' is not yet explicit. It becomes so in a second important publication on the relationship between social housing and a range of socioeconomic disadvantages, including the disadvantages associated with persistent and long-term unemployment (Feinstein et al, 2008). In this study, life chances are the central concept (and the dependent variable), and the focus on life chances continues in a follow-up study (Lupton et al, 2009). Unlike *Ends and means*, these studies were not commissioned by the government and were explicitly social scientific in purpose and design.

The basis of the evidence is four British birth cohort studies that have tracked a selection of individuals born in 1946, 1958, 1970 and 2000. The data include a very wide range of characteristics, judged by the authors of the research to be sufficient to separate out characteristics that led an individual into social housing in the first place from characteristics then associated with social housing itself. Crucially, the cohort studies allow a comparison between different tenures, allowing us to draw some tentative conclusions about the impact of social housing on individuals and their risk of poverty. Just as importantly, the study design controls for the fact that disadvantaged individuals are more likely to be 'selected into' social housing in the first place. As the authors stress: 'Separating effects of housing from the factors that lead people to reside in social housing requires clear conceptual foundations and very good data' (Feinstein et al, 2008, p 2).

Some of the results are very striking. For those born into social housing in 1970 the study found the following characteristics (Feinstein et al, 2008, p 10):

- By the age of 30 they were 11 times as likely to be outside education, employment and training as those born into other tenures.
- They were nine times as likely to live in a workless household, to hold no qualifications (to level 4), or be a single parent.
- They were twice as likely to suffer from poor physical or mental health, twice as likely to be dissatisfied with their life and four times as likely to suffer from drug or alcohol abuse.
- But for the cohort born into social housing in 1946 there was no statistically significant disadvantage associated with social housing.

This last point is of crucial importance. It tells us that, over time, something has changed in the relationship between social housing and life chances. At first sight this is an obvious conclusion. We shall see, however, that this is not the conclusion drawn by the most influential think-tank interventions, and this in turn leads to Conservative Party policy that also suppresses the contingencies of the life-chances evidence. And without this suppression we are still left with a complex entanglement of overlapping and competing causal explanations of the changing pattern of social tenants' life chances. In the following section I explore the first of these issues: the use and abuse of the life-chances evidence by one right-of-centre think tank and the subsequent transmission of these distortions into policy and ultimately legislation. It is to be noted, however, that I do not suggest that the process I describe is representative of the wider body of right-leaning political thought and policy advocacy.

Policy Exchange: essentialism and dependency

In 2010 Policy Exchange published a report – *Making housing affordable* (Morton, 2010) – that argued that social tenants are effectively victims of the welfare state:

> Current social housing policies are driving unaffordable levels of welfare reliance and increasing poverty for social tenants – evidenced by an 'unexplainable gap' between social tenants' much lower rates of employment when compared with similar individuals outside the sector. This is caused by the appalling incentives that social tenants face. (Morton, 2010, p 5)

Morton goes on to further assert that:

> Though the effects are getting worse, social housing has always damaged equality of *opportunity. Studies show those born in 1958 and 1970 who grew up partially or exclusively in social housing have done significantly worse than otherwise identical individuals* (adjusting for factors ranging from income to parental attitude to learning and so on) across a host of factors. (Morton, 2010, p 52, emphasis added).

In these passages it is clearly implied that the 'unexplainable gap' is identified as an issue by the authors of *The public value of social housing report* (Feinstein et al, 2008), which Morton employs in the second passage, and on which much of the general thrust of his argument depends. Notably, this is not a phrase found in Feinstein and colleagues' report; less trivially, the central conclusion of the Policy Exchange position is that the gap is indeed explainable, as we see in the invocation of 'appalling incentives'. But the conclusion is only possible because a whole cohort is missing from this analysis – the first (1946) cohort, for whom there is no social disadvantage associated with growing up in social housing.

At this point it would be tempting to dismiss the Policy Exchange view of social housing. The suppression of the 1946 cohort of social tenants gives us ample reason to do so. But there is more to it than this. In the context of narratives of social housing the issue is not just social scientific veracity. My analysis is also concerned with the discursive contexts that either curtail or allow the creation of social fact. In this case the context is one in which essentialist claims (social housing has *always* created dependency) resonate with the historical and contemporary assumptions of a dominant strand of discourse that runs deeper than the politics and anxieties of the past two decades, as we have seen in Chapter 2, as well as in my discussion of the 'genealogy' of dependency earlier in this chapter.

This was expressed, politically, by David Cameron, with a clear allusion to 'life chances':

> Generations of families are trapped in social housing, denied the chance to break out or to buy their own property. I don't want a child's life story to be written before they're even born, and a responsible housing policy which helps people up and out of dependency can help rewrite that story. (Cameron, 2009)

Progress: contingency and dependency

We have seen that narratives of welfare dependency and social housing are embedded in right-of-centre political discourse. But I have also touched on an apparently similar narrative in the Labour governments of the 2000s, in particular Caroline Flint's assertion that "[s]ocial housing should be based around the principle of something for something" (BBC News, 2008). Flint's intervention was intended to be controversial, and can reasonably be described as being on the right of the Labour Party. But it was by no means an unorthodox view within that section of the party, or indeed in the history of the party. Narratives of social housing and dependency were soon part of an internal debate and were given clear expression in a series of articles published by the 'Blairite' think-tank, Progress. In one we find Frank Field asserting that a there was a breakdown in the moral order of social housing allocation, followed by Liam Byrne setting a 'something for something' corrective:

> The system Clement Attlee adopted paid out benefits based on individuals' contributions. Welfare was very largely awarded on the basis of contributions and public housing was allocated to those who had waited longest and who were best-behaved. (Frank Field, cited in Philpot, 2011, p 158)

> That is why Ed Miliband has said we should explore the way we reward those who do the right thing, for example by looking again at the way we allocate social housing … your place in the queue is affected by whether you are doing the right thing, getting a job, paying taxes, being a good tenant and neighbour, and so on. (Liam Byrne, cited in Philpot, 2011, p 140)

Frank Field continued to play a prominent role in policy debate once Labour was no longer in government, leading a review – *The foundation years: Preventing poor children becoming poor adults* (Field, 2010) – on behalf of the new coalition government when it sought to reposition itself in the poverty debate. In this we can see the clear co-option of the language of life chances and its incorporation in the 'broken Britain' narrative. Field now presents a wider cultural and sociological view of the structure of poverty and social disadvantage, attributing much to poor parenting and the breakdown of traditional family structures. In this, he argues, social housing plays a clear and identifiable role:

> Post-war housing policy has also enjoyed more than a walk-on role. Mega developments, sweeping up communities, shaking them around, and scattering them onto new estates, often on the periphery of the towns where they had long established roots, also played a major part in the break-up of the extended, matriarchal family hierarchy and in so doing destroyed the support that this informal network provided for couples as they began the process of starting a family. (Field, 2010, p 18)

This direct engagement with the Conservative Party and coalition government inevitably strengthens the position of commentators who believe that Field and his colleagues – or indeed the 'Blairite' wing of the Labour Party – are indistinguishable from the mainstream Conservative consensus that the welfare state creates dependency. In the case of social housing there is a significant degree of consensus between some on the 'right' and 'left', or at least one particular branch of the left.

However, there are some significant differences, with important implications for how we view the purpose of social housing. The key to this difference lies in the contingent nature of the failings that the Progress statements attribute to the welfare system and social housing. The most important contrast is evident when Frank Field points to a time when social housing worked well, whereas Policy Exchange asserted that social housing 'always' failed because of the 'appalling incentives' it creates.

This distinction allows the Progress position to be highly critical of welfare dependency but still strongly advocate the intrinsic value of more social housing, and this is indeed the policy recommendation of these interventions. The aim is not to scale down social housing to a residual social service for the most vulnerable, but to expand it with the active support of the state while introducing greater conditionality. Moreover, while a significant role is attributed to implied negative incentives in the social housing system, this is not actually an endorsement of the neoliberal model of agency motivation. Thus, on the one hand, we can see clear reference to the value of a less needs-based allocations system. On the other hand, however, there is a paternalistic element of 'tough love', focused on improving the lives of individual social tenants. With the right support and conditions social housing, in this view, could in fact be a source of social stability and individual independence rather than part of a problem of welfare dependency. In both respects there is a strong historical precedent: concern with moral hazard, evident from the very start of social housing in the 19th century, together with faith in the power of social hierarchy, redolent of Octavia Hill's paternalistic management of her social housing.

Conclusion

In this chapter I have taken a close look at discourses of social housing and dependency. In this we can see the ways in which different assumptions about the purpose of social housing feed into negative discourses of dependency, from the tabloid and broadsheet press and popular TV entertainment, and in the speeches and announcements of a number of politicians, a majority of whom come from the centre-right of the political spectrum. But these discourses also interact with more social scientific discourse, which is often introduced into political discourse and policy via think-tanks. Sometimes, as we have seen, this is a process in which the facts and evidence of social science are misinterpreted, perhaps wilfully at times, but I have also argued that this is not simply a case of distortion for ideological ends. It is an inherent characteristic of social discourse and the evolution of social meanings – part of the process in which social facts emerge. As we shall see in the following chapter, there is also potential for similar distortions in pro-social housing discourses.

4

Counter-narratives: dependency, culture, and the myth of worklessness

We have seen the ways in which social scientific evidence can be subverted and transformed into powerful social facts. In this I have engaged with narratives from the right of the political spectrum, and in particular from the discourses of social housing and dependency. These narratives, we have seen, are sometimes based on straightforward misrepresentation of the evidence, and in some cases on simple abuse of this evidence.

Nevertheless, it would be a mistake to think that the selective use of evidence is confined to one side of the argument. In this section I argue that there is a similar pattern in some of the pro-social housing narratives found in the academic literature and, more widely, in the counter-narrative of worklessness and cultures of dependency as 'myth' rather than reality. In making this argument I do not simply seek to demonstrate balance. The wider aim is to argue that the 'myth busting' approach to assertions of welfare dependency is counter-productive. Paradoxically, it concedes too much. I start first, however, with two illustrations.

My first illustration takes us back to neighbourhoods, and in particular the role of 'culture' in discussions of neighbourhoods and worklessness. This brings us to the idea of a 'neighbourhood effect'. Like the idea of a tenure effect, this hypothesizes that living in a certain type of neighbourhood further disadvantages an individual, even controlling for individual factors such as skills and education, and structural factors such as the local economy and the strength of public services. The 'effect' of neighbourhood here is something over and above identifiable individual or neighbourhood characteristics. My attention is focused on an explicit counter-narrative to the discourse of 'cultures of worklessness'. I argue that, at times, the counter-narrative misrepresents this evidence, potentially dismissing a significant phenomenon that requires greater attention. Moreover, by seeking to debunk a 'myth', and by treating 'culture' as an inherently suspect concept, these counter-narratives effectively cede to their opponents the right to set the terms of debate. We should instead acknowledge the role of culture, but in a way that gives due regard to structure and does not (over)attribute outcomes to individual agency. In this way we can reorientate the debate away from the judgemental language of welfare vice and virtue.

My second illustration is the development of discourses of democratic participation in social housing management. This narrative has two overlapping strands. The first is the positive value of democratic participation as a form of management structure. The second strand is more explicitly articulated as a reaction to the overbearing management practices of large social landlords, typically based on the historic 'landlordism' and paternalism of post-war council housing. Both strands are grounded in an assumption of the value of democratic social housing management for individual wellbeing, at times hinting at an almost Rousseau view of human flourishing.

Neighbourhood effects and the underclass

The seminal research that sparked the long-running debate about neighbourhood effects comes from the US, which continues to dominate research output on neighbourhood dynamics and poverty. William Wilson's 1987 book, *The truly disadvantaged*, explored concentrated poverty in American cities, particularly in African-American 'ghettos' (a term I adopt from Wilson's own usage), and argued that the social isolation of these neighbourhoods systematically disadvantaged residents (Wilson, 2012 [1987]).

There are a number of reasons why this could be the case. Spatial isolation from good services, including health and education services, as well as from suitable jobs, are obvious structural causes of disadvantage. But Wilson went further than this:

> Social isolation deprives residents of inner-city neighbourhood's not only of resources and conventional role models, whose former presence buffered the effects of neighborhood joblessness, but also of the kind of cultural learning from mainstream social networks that facilitates social and economic advancement in modern industrial society. (Wilson, 2012 [1987], p 642)

The hypothesis is that a lack of positive role models makes it easier for anti-social or negative social norms to be spread through group influences, with an early study finding that concentrated disadvantage increases the likelihood of teenage pregnancy and dropping out of schooling (Crane, 1991). Education is clearly an important factor in an individual's life chances, and it is equally clear that if area deprivation is also associated with underfunded and otherwise unsatisfactory schooling there will be a knock-on impact. Whether or not there is an 'effect' over and above this is an issue I seek to address in the next section of this chapter.

The influence of American scholarship has been felt in the UK with the adoption of the concept of 'social capital' (Halpern, 2005). The two key concepts within this are 'bonding' and 'bridging' capital. In the case of bonding social capital we would expect to find tight community bonds, and possibly strong evidence of individuals helping one another through neighbourhood networks. This is clearly a positive feature, though it may sometimes actually reinforce negative neighbourhood effects, as cultural norms and individual expectations may not be challenged by outside influences (Green and White, 2007). But bridging social capital may help to compensate for this by connecting individuals in deprived communities with people with different life experiences and expectations, potentially counteracting 'negative' local influences. This has been studied by a range of researchers and the tentative conclusion is that those who have contacts outside the neighbourhood ('bridging capital') tend to be less influenced by any negative neighbourhood characteristics (Ellen and Turner, 1997; Buck, 2001).

There could be quite straightforward ways of accounting for this. The person with outside contacts may have better opportunities in the job market, for example. But the more important possibility, in terms of the search for an 'effect', is that there is some form of internal social dynamic at work that shapes individual expectations and behaviour. In recent policy discourse this kind of process has often been described in terms of 'peer effects' (Blume and Durlauf, 2001), with at least a tacit expectation that higher-income households within a mixed community will help to positively shape the social norms of a neighbourhood. In the UK, as we have seen, this discourse and policy expectation has been dominated by a preoccupation with 'worklessness' in social housing, with a policy of mix driven in part by the hope that working households will have a positive influence on those for whom (it is assumed) worklessness has become normalised.

However, the evidence supporting this expectation is inconclusive, at least in the UK context. British studies have mostly been based on qualitative case studies, and these have found little evidence to suggest that mixed-tenure communities have a positive impact on labour market activity outcomes for workless people (Tunstall and Fenton, 2006). Qualitative research in the UK finds little impact of mix on employment outcomes, and little evidence for a 'peer effect', with some studies suggesting mixed communities actually fail to mix across the tenures, negating the idea of a peer effect (Tunstall and Fenton, 2006).

Larger-scale quantitative studies, looking more specifically at unemployment, do find an effect, but are not explicitly framed in terms of 'peer' effects. For example, a well-known Swedish study found that at a certain point concentrations of unemployment within an area itself seemed to have a causal effect, finding that 'the risk that a person unemployed in 1991 would still be unemployed in 1995 and 1999, is only 16% if that person lives in an environment with only 0–2% unemployed people, whereas that percentage would double to 32% if he or she lives in an environment with 14–16% unemployed' (Galster et al, 2008). In France and Germany there have been similar findings (Dujardin and Goffette-Nagot, 2005; Bauer et al, 2011).

Conversely, we could just as easily line up a number of studies that look for but do not find a neighbourhood effect. Within France, the author of one of the reports finding a neighbourhood effect finds none in another (Dujardin and Goffette-Nagot, 2010). Other analyses also find no effect (for example, van Ham and Manley, 2009).

When we turn specifically to the evidence from the US there is an interesting change in perspective, as much of this evidence is based on a 'natural experiment', with a human control group. Under the Moving to Opportunity programme introduced in the early 1990s, public housing tenants were randomly selected into three groups, with each given different housing opportunities. This was based on a voucher system, allowing one group only to move to or within low-income areas, while allowing another to move to a more affluent area. Early results seemed to be the same as the pattern that emerged in England; positive effects on liveability, satisfaction and quality of life, but no clear impact on labour market outcomes (Sanbonmatsu et al, 2011; Ludwig et al, 2013).

This debate will continue for some time before there is any resolution. My own intuition is that significant neighbourhood effects are likely to exist. But even if there are no such effects, this does not necessarily imply that large mono-tenure estates are desirable, either for those who live on them or for policy makers concerned with a wider set of social outcomes. If concentrated social housing does not somehow contribute to diminished life chances for social tenants, we may well still think that they have a right to live in a more mixed and socially integrated environment, and, moreover, we may believe this kind of mix to be an important social value for all of us.

At this point it is helpful to pause and look back at one of the key questions of Chapter 1: would you feel comfortable living next door to social housing? In both the previous section and the next the evidence and arguments advanced point to the role of character and individual virtue. In the previous section this is not quite explicit, but just beneath the surface of the idea of peer effects. What stands out in these discussions is that the spotlight of judgement is shone on those at the bottom of a presumed social and economic ranking. Presented as such, the language of peer effects – and the normative assumptions underpinning it – is strikingly hierarchical and one-sided. The 'peer' has every appearance of social superiority.

Yet, as I have argued elsewhere, it is on this type of person that we can and should direct our judgement (Gregory, 2015). We should do so because there is no one group in society – if there are any – towards which we should direct our ethical gaze. If some wish to draw on the language of vice (idleness, sloth), or to frame policy as a vehicle for raising people up to the virtues of industry and independence, I wish to point to the virtues of humility and compassion. For those who find themselves higher up the economic pile, greater experience of what life is actually like for those lower down the scale may well lead to greater compassion and a more authentic engagement with the point at issue – the kind of social housing and welfare state we want and need. My own interpretation of this comes later, in Chapters 7 and 8, with a renewed discussion of social mix and the virtue of compassion.

The myth of intergenerational worklessness: Yeti or decoy?

A selection of recent studies set out to test and refute this claim. Macdonald and colleagues undertook an in-depth qualitative study in Glasgow and Middlesbrough in which they sought to find ten families in each location consisting of three generations in which no-one has ever worked (Macdonald et al, 2014). In introducing this research they say they 'believe that ours is the first study to put the idea of "three generations of families of where no-one has ever worked" to the empirical test' (Macdonald et al, 2014, p 200). Even with extensive effort the researchers could not find any families that met this description, and they draw on contemporaneous quantitative work finding that the number of families in which three generations had never worked was statistically insignificant (Macmillan, 2014). From this, Macdonald and colleagues conclude that the household where three generations have never worked is a mythical 'Yeti'. These findings – qualitative and quantitative – also play an important role in Slater's critique of the narrative of 'broken Britain', discussed earlier (Slater, 2014).

There are many points of interest in this research, and it should also be stressed that the empirical search for three generations of worklessness was set in the context of the concept of 'cultures' of worklessness. Yet the 'ever worked' standard is absurdly demanding and the myth of the Yeti is perhaps too easy a target, distracting us from what may still be a very big problem. While Macmillan does not find three generations of worklessness, she does 'find a moderate relationship in spells out of work across generations for the UK' (Macmillan, 2014, p 886). 'Sons with workless fathers are 14.9 to 17.3% more likely to spend a year or more out of work than sons with employed fathers from leaving full time education to age 23', though the chances of the son never working are very low (Macmillan, 2014, p 879).

This is still a significant disadvantage that should concern us. In a recent analysis of social housing and its relationship with labour market activity, Judge finds that there is a much smaller employment gap between social housing and other tenures, once we fully control for the characteristics associated with the needs-based allocations system. Yet she also comes to something like my own normative conclusion:

> All in all, it would be remiss to use the raw employment gaps between social renters and those in other tenures as a reason not to build more homes in the social sector. But it would be equally wrong to reject

concerns about rates of work out of hand. It's time we had a less polarised, more evidence-based conversation on the topic. (Judge, 2019)

Culture and character

My suggestion here is not that the authors do not have this worry – indeed, it is very clear from their body of work that this is not the case. Macdonald and colleagues also provide a subtle account of the potential role of culture in transmitting norms of worklessness. They find, as does a significant body of literature, that individuals and households falling under the cloud of suspicion typically express a strong desire to work, and are not motivated to rely on the benefits system. This is supported by a range of other studies that draw out instead the deeply entrenched institutional and structural barriers to work: the complexities and failings of the benefits system, the lack of childcare, the deskilling of older cohorts of industrial workers, and the simple fact there often just few too jobs to apply for.

So Macdonald and colleagues do in fact acknowledge the role of culture and 'would not wish to substitute a simplistic, one-sided, structural explanation in place of the idea of cultures of worklessness' (Macdonald et al, 2014, p 215). Here they point to the seminal work of Wilson in the US, which describes the phenomenon of social isolation and cultural adaption of 'ghettos' to the external socioeconomic forces of modern America, coming to believe that there are no opportunities to pursue (correctly in many cases) and developing behaviours that contribute to neighbourhood deprivation. These could range from the extreme cases of gang-based economies in the US, to a far more prosaic normalisation of economic inactivity. We may also employ the language of adaptive preferences, describing the way in which the constant disappointment of expectations leads not just to a lowering of expectations, but to a belief that they did not really want whatever they cannot have in the first place. This could, in principle, include things such as employment and education.

This suggests an important distinction between two interpretations of culture: the 'lifestyle choice' description of cultures of dependency, and a 'horizons' view of culture. On the one hand we have a view of culture that is really just an aggregation of individual choices and is ultimately based on conscious agency. This was the view of George Osborne in 2010 when, in an interview with the BBC journalist Nick Robinson, he declared that "if someone believes that living on benefits is a lifestyle choice, then we need to make them think again". The logic here is that of the neoliberal mind – change the choices or 'incentives' and the rational human will respond. On the other hand we have a more structural view of culture, as a human construction but one that outstrips individual agency and may not be visible to us.

In terms of the social housing debate and, indeed, in broader debates about welfare dependency, I therefore suspect that the Yeti hunt is in fact symptomatic of a deeper problem that besets those of us who want to defend the value of social housing and a strong welfare state. The Yeti begins to look suspiciously like a decoy – or, in the metaphorical spirit, a wild goose chase – when it sets the terms of an argument that seems to be closed once the most obvious fallacies have been dismissed. This may well be motivated by an understandable instinct to correct the 'myths' of tabloid lore, but in practice is cedes the field to those who seek to characterise social housing and the welfare state as a cause of dependency and moral indolence: we have given them the idea of 'culture' to do with it as they please.

An idealised democracy?

There is a rich tradition of democratic discourse in the history of social housing, stretching back to tenant activism in the 1920s and the emergence of tenant associations (Ravetz, 2001, pp 146–150). A resurgence of community-based housing associations in the late 1960s and 1970s added another dimension to this. A number of these housing trusts were established, initially, to improve rather than replace existing housing stock, as in the case of the Glasgow Housing Trust, founded in the early 1970s in an area where 25 per cent of all homes had no inside toilet (Lund, 2016, p 241). Notting Hill Housing Trust in London, founded in 1963 with a handful of houses, and against the backdrop of Rachman housing and racial tension, was one of a number that began to grow with a funding regime introduced in 1974 that allowed housing associations to compete for the same central development subsidy that was available to local authorities.[1] Although such organisations would come to grow into large-scale housing providers, their genesis as community-based housing associations still represents powerful ideals of community, voice and tenant participation.

My first concern in this section, however, is with a specific strand of democracy discourse in social housing – the ideal of democratic accountability exercised through the ballot box of local government. The illustration I use here comes from the debate on the nature of Large Scale Voluntary Transfers (LSVTs) that took place from the late 1980s but accelerated in the later 1990s and early 2000s. This debate foregrounded two specific democratic questions: first, the simple question of choice, namely the vote for or against transfer; and, second, the more normative question of democratic legitimacy, framed in the specific terms of ballot-box accountability through local elections.

Stock transfer, participation and accountability

The context is the Housing Act 1988, which built on a provision in the Housing Act 1985, allowing tenants to choose to transfer the management of their homes from the local authority to an alternative landlord, and promoted the powers of transfer as the right 'escape council control' (Pawson and Mullins, 2010, p 35). The specific transfer process was contained in the Tenants' Choice provision of the Act, which was intended to encourage private landlords to take on (with tenant consent) segments of council housing stock. In practice very few homes were transferred – fewer than 1,500 homes in England and Wales over the seven-year duration of Tenants' Choice, and fewer than 2,000 in Scotland, where the policy lasted a further three years (Malpass and Mullins, 2002, p 675).

However, the precedent set by early transfers later transformed the social housing landscape. The Housing Act 1988 was intended to appeal to private landlords, but it also contained important changes in housing association finance. Borrowing by associations for capital investment was to be 'off balance sheet' for government accounting purposes and this precedent took on great importance with the new Labour government of 1997. Labour in 1997 faced a physical legacy of badly maintained social housing stock, along with a political legacy of perceived public aversion to tax-funded capital investment. The transfer mechanisms, combined with exclusion of housing association borrowing from the national balance sheet, provided the solution.

Expansion of housing associations could therefore proceed without appearing as state spending and access to funds to improve existing council stock (under the Decent Homes programme of 2003) could be realised through one of three ways: through a joint public–private redevelopment partnership, through the creation of an 'arms-length management organisation' that was independent of the local authority, or through transfer of the housing stock to a housing association. By 2008 over 1.3 million homes across the UK had been transferred from local authority to housing association control and approximately 250 new housing associations were created to help achieve this (Pawson and Smith, 2009, p 411).

The transfer in question was of council housing stock to ownership and management by a housing association. These were in principle voluntary, as transfers required over 50 per cent of affected tenants to vote in favour. Controversy arose because the terms of new investment in existing housing stock – investment needed to correct years of neglect and occasionally appalling quality – came with conditions. One of the ways in which funds could be released was by voting for a transfer, and in this respect we may detect a degree of soft coercion. Yet the way in which the process has sometimes been presented in academic debate is as potentially misleading as the more commonly observed distortions of centre-right discourses of dependency.

In an influential essay arguing that stock transfer is a privatisation of council housing, Ginsburg states that: 'The advantages of council housing are its relatively low rents (reflecting low borrowing costs) and its democratic accountability to local politicians, which gives tenants a sense of security as part of the public realm, rather than being subject to the risks of private consumption' (Ginsburg, 2005, p 118). This claim is presented in the context of council tenant attitudes, and draws on data from the 2000 British Social Attitudes Survey. Yet a close reading of the survey shows the democratic impulse described is the author's own interpolation. Notably, the survey itself does not mention democratic accountability. In fact 'democratic' and 'accountability' simply do not appear in the survey document. What it says is this:

> Of course, people may not always be able to rent accommodation from their preferred type of landlord. So, irrespective of who they would most prefer as a landlord, would people take up a council tenancy if they were offered one? To assess this, we asked those who are not currently council tenants how strongly they agreed or disagreed with the statement 'I would like to live in council housing if I could get it'. A clear majority (75 percent) would not like to live in council housing and disagree with the statement. Only 13 percent agree. (Kemp, 2000, p 141)

So, it is correct to say, as Ginsburg does, that housing association tenants would on balance prefer to be local authority tenants. But, Kemp remarks, 'it remains the fact that almost half of all council tenants do not think council estates are generally pleasant places in which to live. ... In fact, if they had a free choice, the great majority of people (including most tenants) would rather not rent at all and would choose to buy their home' (Kemp, 2000, p 140). Finally, it is instructive to consider the BSA author's own comments on the narrative of council housing 'privatisation':

> Interestingly, opponents of the transfer of council housing in Glasgow to community housing associations have, in an attempt to discredit the proposal, described the transfer as being one of 'privatisation' to private landlords. This perhaps reflects longstanding folk memories of 'Rachmanism' in which 'unscrupulous' private landlords are said to have exploited tenants by charging 'exorbitant' rents for slum property. (Kemp, 2000, p 147)

A more nuanced account of democratic control is provided by Smyth, who notes that '[a] central argument advanced by those who oppose stock transfers is that the tenants will lose control of their landlord, as elected councillors will be replaced by an unelected board' (Smyth, 2013, p 48), and then presents research on tenant attitudes that shows that 'the notion that simply being able to vote out councillors meant tenants could exercise control, was not strongly identified'(Smyth, 2013, p 48). Smyth correctly argues that the ballot box is not the only form of democratic control, and finds that tenants may be sceptical about ballot-box power but have more faith in 'a form of "every day" accountability that was exercised based on the mandate of local councillors and their ability to exert pressure on and control over local authority officers' (Smyth, 2003, p 46).

Context or ideology?

How the prospect of transfer was viewed also depended on local context, including the ways in which the transfer was 'sold' to tenants, the level of engagement, and the nature and extent of any proposed regeneration of existing stock (for a nuanced discussion, see McCormack, 2009). Moreover, there does not seem to have been a clear pattern of votes based on satisfaction with local authority landlords. In some cases dissatisfaction seems to lead to a vote in favour of transfer, whereas, in others, the same dissatisfaction led to a paradoxical vote *not* to transfer. The logic is explained by Daly and colleagues in a comparison of transfer votes in Birmingham and Glasgow (Daly et al, 2005, p 337):

> Unlike in Birmingham, where the low regard of tenants for the City Council and its housing department led tenants not to trust the pronouncements on the benefits of stock transfer, Glasgow's tenants did see benefits in moving away from the local authority precisely because of a loss of faith in the effectiveness of its housing services.

Within this national and local variation there was plenty of scope for cynical marketing, motivated by profit or ignoble political calculation, and there are doubtless examples of such practices. But, equally, we can cherry-pick from a limited – and far from impartial – record to make either case: that tenants were duped into transfer, or that they exercised their well-developed agency (or, in some cases, class consciousness) to forge ahead in a brave new world of post-council housing (for a flavour of this, see Hodkinson and Robbins, 2013). Thus, in their measured comparison of Birmingham and Glasgow, Daly and colleagues point to one of the positive reasons behind the vote to transfer in Glasgow: 'there was a strong emphasis on community ownership and empowerment, building on a tradition of community-based housing associations that existed since the early 1980s' (Daly et al, 2005., p 338).

What we do not see in any of these accounts is evidence of a widespread faith in the 'democratic accountability to local politicians, which gives tenants a sense of security as part of the public realm' (Ginsburg, 2005, p 118), though we do find this sentiment among activist and political groups. The most notable of these is the campaign group, Defend Council Housing, which produced a range of written outputs, as well as engaging in active protest. A relatively late addition is a compilation of essays from a range of MPs, local politicians, tenants and union representatives. The following argument, from the late Gerald Kaufman, then Labour MP for Manchester Gorton, is broadly representative:

> Local authorities are democratically elected. Any councillor can walk into the director of housing's office and demand explanations. The only people with the right to do that with housing associations, at present, are Housing Corporation staff – but there's only 24 of them; not exactly a Sword of Damocles. (Gerald Kaufman, cited in Defend Council Housing, 2006, p 32)

There is also no shortage of more rhetorically charged statements, as when the founder of Defend Council Housing, Alan Walter, asserts that: 'Council tenants are being mugged. Behind all the fine words of "choice", inclusion and "empowerment" government is trying to take away our security, lower rents and democratic tenure' (Defend Council Housing, 2006, p 88). Similar rhetoric is also found in some of the more academic literature:

> Despite its historic links to council housing and the tenants' movement, the Labour government continued the neoliberalization process, pushing along marketization processes set in train, or introducing new market-based solutions to address the contradictions of previous neoliberal policies. ... In line with Blairism's deep antipathy towards municipalism à la New Right, the focus of Labour's privatization policy was on accelerating the demunicipalization of social housing through 'stock transfer' to housing associations, and expanding the role of private providers and finance. (Hodkinson and Robbins, 2013, p 63)

Regardless of rhetorical tone, there are two fundamental flaws in the arguments against stock transfer. This does not necessarily mean that there are no valid arguments against transfer, or that transfer was always a good idea. There are certainly many cases in which both the process and outcome were poor, and some of these failings are discussed in Part III. The immediate issue, though, is with the form of argument I have highlighted.

The first flaw lies in a problem of attribution – of who holds the beliefs and opinions adopted. This problem is inherent to all qualitative research (especially the use of interview data), as much to the original material I present in Chapter 5 as it is to the stock transfer controversy explored here.

The most basic challenge is our personal filters and biases. Few researchers will claim to have fully filtered out their biases, and it may be doubted that the ideal of strict objectivity is realistic or even desirable.

Nevertheless, in some cases the risk of cherry-picking is greater than in others. In anti-transfer discourses the great problem is that there is no single pattern, and a great range of nuance in the attitudes of tenants balloted in different times and places. In this context it is particularly easy to tune into what we want to hear. There will be something for everyone in this respect, pro, anti or neutral. I have sought to present only a glimpse of this selective filter in the anti-transfer discourse: the expectation that the point of contestation is *democratic representation* through the structures of local government.

As I have argued, there is little evidence that this sentiment formed a wide consensus among social tenants. This leaves open the possibility that those who did not vote at all were either unaware of the importance of the issues at stake, or that those who did vote in favour were not given full and accurate information. In either case, there is a fundamental dilemma. On the one hand, advocacy of tenant power and control rests on the assumption that tenants have the requisite will and agency to exercise such control. On the other hand, however, anti-transfer discourses often rely on the claim that votes have been determined by disinformation campaigns and cynical manipulation.

Both of these claims can be true. Agency is complex, and we can all be misinformed and, as argued in Chapter 2, we can simply be wrong about our best interests, even when we are fully informed.

Yet there is a particular tension when, as in the case of the anti-transfer narrative, we hold strongly to these two positions: first, that there we are uniquely placed to best know our wants; and, second, that there is an ideal outcome or correct choice. For the extreme libertarians I discussed (and dismissed) in Chapter 2, this problem does not arise; whatever is decided is right for the individual, *a priori*. The second position never comes into play, so there is no dilemma. However, there is a correct answer in the anti-transfer position, and hence a need to navigate the relationship between these two positions. How are we to explain that those who vote against transfer are mistaken about their real needs? Is this a case of false consciousness? There have certainly been advocates, recent as well as more distant, of a self-consciously Marxist view of the class interests of social tenants (Hodkinson and Robbins, 2013).

This dilemma sits within a broader history of democratic discourse in social housing. Early calls for democratic voice and control stretch back to at least the 1920s, when some of the first tenant associations were formed. And although much of the post-war period of council housing management is notable for a paternalistic disregard of tenant voice, the power and importance of tenant participation – particularly in estate regeneration – became part of 'conventional wisdom' by the 1990s (Ravetz, 2001, p 215). The expectation here was much broader than specific lines drawn of democratic consent and accountability in the transfer process. The ideal was that tenants would engage in an ongoing form of democratic participation in the control and management of the local community. In practice there seems to have been little appetite for this.

My intention in this analysis has not been to suggest that there is a deficit of agency among social tenants, or that they are somehow less able than (for example) the ostensibly virtuous owner to assess and process the complexities of management. But *why* would we expect *anyone* to want to manage their own housing? This is a very strong normative ideal – and one that potentially distorts the debate about the role and value of social housing.

Meaning and purpose: historical projection

Throughout this chapter I have argued that the purpose and value of social housing reflects the meanings that we attribute to it as social good. How we actually distribute social housing also influences our views of social housing – of what it 'is' as much as what we might like it to be. This is a constructivist position. Yet it is anchored in the more prosaic historical record of facts, dates, and documents. We do not need to seek a definitive truth in these. But historical record does constrain the range of permissible interpretation, and whether or not democratic participation *should* be part of the purpose of social housing, there is little in the record to suggest that it has been broadly conceived in such terms, outside of an important but small sub-strand of housing discourse. It is an ahistorical idealisation to claim that democratic participation is inherent to the purpose of social housing. The following assertion from Jeremy Corbyn in 2015 encapsulates this distortion: 'there is a problem with housing associations. Initially set up to provide decent homes for people in need, many are developing into businesses that sell or rent at market levels. We need more democracy and accountability, and a return to their original purpose' (Corbyn, 2015, p 6).

While there are some housing associations that were founded to serve this 'original purpose', they have in reality been very few in number. Nor would there necessarily have been much sympathy for these ideals. Council officers were often poor champions of social justice and, indeed, could be notorious for excluding applicants who did not fit the mould of the white working-class family (Rex and Moore, 1967; Ravetz, 2001). Sometimes the 'accountable' local councillor was directly in control of allocations, able to use council housing to pursue a kind of political clientelism, dispensing favour along lines of party political allegiance (Cullingworth, 1969). In the case of the early housing associations – which for many years were far more significant than local authority housing – even the most fair-minded management would have been aghast at the notion that their tenants were able to take charge of the social structures of housing and management. Paternalism was not then a dirty word; democracy, for many of the political and social elite, was.

Conclusion

In this chapter I have offered a critique of two counter-narratives to the dominant discourses of social housing and welfare dependency. In both cases I have argued that normative preference influences the interpretation of empirical evidence.

In the case of worklessness, I have been critical of a myth-busting approach because I believe that it minimises a real (though vastly overstated) problem that we should approach without moral judgement. I have also argued that by dismissing 'cultures of worklessness' we cede the concept of 'culture' – the sociological equivalent of cutting off the nose to spite the face.

For the second counter-narrative I took the case of organised opposition to LSVTs. I have focused not on the relative merits of transfer, but on the dominant argument against, namely that transfer leads to a loss of democratic accountability. I have been particularly critical of this second counter-narrative, as I believe it is a distortion of history, and that it presents an 'original purpose' that limits our shared power to reshape the meaning and practice of social housing as a more universal social good, extended to a much wider range of people.

This is the kind of housing vision I outline in Part II. In this outline my own normative prejudices come nearer to the surface. Inevitably I too run the risk of distorting evidence and empirical 'fact' to fit the mould of my own moral and political intuitions. In some crucial respects, however, the policy prescriptions I favour are based on assumptions that are shared by many of the critics of the transfer process. The market has indeed been too dominant in housing provision; private developers have too often been allowed to cynically manipulate their planning obligations to help to provide affordable housing; and we have allowed housing provision in the UK to be hijacked as a global asset class that favours only a tiny minority of our citizens or permanent residents. Where I will differ is in how we should respond to these challenges.

PART II

Social housing, wellbeing, and experiences of the home

Experiences of the home: place, identity, and security

Discourses of ownership: tenure as a social fact

In Part I, I stressed the importance of social construction in the creation and evolution of social housing as a good. I now apply this specifically to the concept of housing tenure. This exploration of 'tenure' is to help us understand the special place that social housing has occupied in contemporary welfare debates in the UK and its culture more broadly. From this perspective we are better able to understand the assumptions and normative ideals that underpin the housing debate in the UK, and in particular the negative meanings attached to social housing.

Tenure has an ambivalent status in housing debate. On the one hand, it is clearly of great importance in politics, policy, and culture. Though the term itself may not be often used in these contexts, it is only just beneath the surface of any housing discussion, or controversy, in the UK. The role of housing tenure in the messier world of social fact was well captured by two Americans, Rossi and Weber, over 20 ago years ago, when they point to: 'a vast surplus of sentimental and hortatory writing on those topics [ownership, wellbeing and behavioural outcomes], as is typical in areas involving widely held social values. A wide variety of sources extol the benefits of ownership to households and to society' (Rossi and Weber, 1996, p 1).

These social values can also be presented in terms of the ideology of property-owning democracy (Jackson, 2005; Ronald, 2008; Gregory, 2016) and it is easy to trace in the political cultures of a range of Anglosphere countries, from the US and UK, to Australia and New Zealand. Owner-occupation has become well established as the cultural norm in such societies (Gurney, 1999) and, more extravagantly, posited as a condition of 'ontological security' (Saunders, 1990; Giddens, 1990, 1991).

On the other hand, however, within the more academic literature, tenure is often treated as a chimeric concept, impossible to pin down in a way that is useful for social scientific research (Zavisca and Gerber, 2016; see also, for example, Montgomerie and Büdenbender, 2015). This, in part, reflects the treatment of tenure as a social construct, highlighting the social and historical context of tenure, both as a concept (for example, Barlow and Duncan, 1988) and in terms of the effective legal framework within which they operate (Bright and Hopkins, 2011). Bright and Hopkins, in particular, show just how constrained property rights often are in the real world. But this does not necessarily diminish the importance of tenure as a core term of discourse and as a 'social fact' that shapes not just housing in the UK, but society more broadly. Taking a step beyond Rossi and Weber's observation, I suggest that the social fact of tenure – representing a set of underlying beliefs and assumptions about the nature of property and social order – is more important than 'tenure' as an empirically observable category.

I start by further clarifying tenure as a concept, before briefly revisiting the political ideal of owner-occupation. Following this I review the academic literature on ownership and civic virtue, and go on to compare this with the asset-based welfare agenda, focusing on the concept of an asset effect. Later (in Chapter 8) I revisit this discussion through an analytical distinction between what different housing tenures can do 'for' someone, versus what it may do 'to' them.

Tenure and dwelling revisited

Tenure as chimera

In academic debate it cannot be taken for granted that housing tenure has the degree of importance I attribute to it here. In order to clear the ground for the argument to come, I therefore address this issue first. There are two common objections to the use of 'tenure' as an empirical category in sociological research, both of which are well-founded but overstated.

The first concern is that the 'twin rights' of ownership (exclusive use and unfettered transfer) are in practice quite elusive. Few owners in the UK – including those covered by the separate law of property in Scotland – possess these rights in an unqualified way. In England, for example, a common form of owner-occupation is possession of a leasehold (in effect renting the land on which their home is built) and owners may technically be regarded as leaseholders rather than owners (see Bright and Hopkins, 2011; Cowan et al, 2018). The freeholders owning the land can, and often will, exercise ownership rights. This may include restrictive covenants on the right to sell; for example, setting a cap on the price the home can be sold at, or retaining a right of first refusal before the home goes on the open market. In some housing associations such restrictions are the norm for shared owners.

The second objection is a by-product of the first. We accept a great diversity of ways in which people can be said (in common parlance) to be homeowners or owner-occupiers, and this raises the subtleties I have just discussed. But we should not lose sight of the most important fundamental difference – the distinction is between outright owners and those buying with a mortgage. Much has been made of this distinction, in particular since the financial crisis of 2008 (see Montgomerie and Büdenbender, 2015). In the US the fragility of so many mortgaged owners became particularly evident and, among other related influences, reflected the great reach of deregulated mortgage markets of the US (Schwartz and Seabrooke, 2009). A similar but less extreme story can be told in the UK (Smith et al, 2009).

These complexities have therefore led some social scientists to conclude that tenure, in particular the 'title' of ownership, is in reality too varied to be of significant use as an empirical category, especially when comparing different national housing systems (Zavisca and Gerber, 2016). As previously suggested, these concerns can be overstated. But the more fundamental response is that 'tenure' is not exclusively an observable empirical category. The crucial question is: do doubts about the value of tenure as a social scientific variable change the view of social housing from the perspective of owner-occupation? The answer, historically at least, is 'no'.

Discourses of flourishing: the transformative potential of ownership

Towards the end of Chapter 3 I highlighted the growing importance of narratives of property-owning democracy and began to draw out a distinction between conservative and neoliberal inflections in these discourses. In Chapter 1 we took an in-depth look at the development of the closely related discourses of social housing and welfare dependency. I shortly turn to another important strand of discourse – the academic and social scientific literature on the relationship between owner-occupation and a range of individual outcomes. There we will see that much of this evidence base is methodologically flawed and leaves the question of a tenure effect wide open. First I briefly revisit the evolving political discourse of property-owning democracy.

Contemporary political narrative of property-owning democracy; ideology or expedience?

In my discussion of the 2008 'broken Britain' report in Chapter 3, we saw that Iain Duncan Smith linked ownership to the 'responsibility of maintaining one's own assets', arguing that 'in the long run this will transform our estates' (p 6). We also saw that David Cameron asserted a causal link between social housing and dependency, further asserting that the chance "to break out or to buy their own property" will help social tenants "up and out of dependency". And once in government, Cameron repeatedly returned to the fundamental value of owner-occupation, as stated in an interview with the *Daily Mail* in 2015: "That's the most natural instinct in the world. Owning your own home – I'll never forget the moment I got the first keys to my flat and walked through the door" (cited in Chapman, 2015). With

Theresa May as Prime Minister we saw slightly less emphasis on ownership, but a subsequent reaffirmation in the new Boris Johnson administration:

> 'As Conservatives we know that owning a home is not just about the four walls around you, it's about investing in your family, saving for the future and putting down roots in a community. We are on the side of hard-working people who want to play their part in our property-owning democracy.' (Robert Jenrick, Secretary of State for Housing, Communities and Local Government, cited in Conservative Party, 2019)

A note of caution is required here. Cameron's calls for more ownership was electorally strategic, while also providing political cover for the thinly disguised fiscal Keynesianism of the belated response by George Osborne, then Chancellor of the Exchequer, to an emergent recession in 2013. Measures such as Help to Buy pumped money into a faltering economy and into a very fragile building sector. But, to a degree, the language of property-owning democracy offered a convenient veneer of ideology. The same sense of political positioning is also present in Jenrick's 2019 pronouncement (Conservative Party, 2019) and, indeed, in some of the earlier New Labour co-option of property-owning democracy. Thus, in 2005 the then Chancellor Gordon Brown promised "a further major extension of Britain's home-owning, asset-owning, property-owning democracy".

There is perhaps more candour than we find from either Brown or Cameron when we consider a restatement of core Conservative values in a 2019 publication for the Institute of Economic Affairs (Rees-Mogg and Tylecote, 2019). *Raising the Roof: How to solve the United Kingdom's housing crisis* explicitly calls for a revived property-owning democracy, linking homeownership to core Conservative values. In their statement of these values, the authors refer to our 'shared understandings of what constitutes good behaviour'. These have been shaped by 'a relatively strong emphasis on private property rights and freedom under the rule of law' (Rees-Mogg and Tylecote, 2019, p 20), to which the authors attribute the UK's early (and apparently superior) economic development. This sets the context in which the authors discuss declining homeownership rates, leading 'to another generation of renters, prevented from joining our property-owning democracy' (Rees-Mogg and Tylecote, 2019, p 39), and the conclusion that: 'Our failure to build is already harming our children and grandchildren' (Rees-Mogg and Tylecote, 2019, p 39).

There may be a temptation to dismiss these statements as theatrical bluster. But the values and beliefs expressed here run deeper than the surface froth of the authors' rhetoric. This will become clear when we turn to the sociological concept of 'ontological security'.

Ontological security, identity, and the home

So far we have reviewed the relationship between housing tenure and the ways in which an owner may develop as a citizen. Now I turn to ownership as a more personal development good, specifically to the concept of 'ontological security'. My aim here is to first introduce the concept. It has been described, with some charity, as 'vague and deep' (Kearns et al, 2000, p 389), and later in the book, in Chapter 7, I address its conceptual failings in some depth.

Nevertheless, the concept of ontological security has been influential in some important housing research, particularly when it is used to think about our experiences of the home and what it provides us in non-material benefits. This raises another distinction, to add to our distinction between tenure and housing. A 'home' is more than both tenure and dwelling, although 'tenure' is ever present in the subtext. It is not just that poor quality is likely to influence feelings about the home; our tenure status can also be part of the social meaning of home. This is encapsulated in the following statement by Susan Smith: 'Owned homes are a hybrid of money, materials, and meanings' (Smith, 2008, p 521). We see this hybridity in the survey data presented in the following sections, as well as in some of the rich interview material to be found in the housing literature, not least in Smith's own research conducted with 150 owners from a range of backgrounds.

Ontological security and ownership

The concept of ontological security is generally attributed to Anthony Giddens, though Giddens draws explicitly, and somewhat heavily, on the psychological work of earlier writers such as Mead (Mead, 1934) and Laing (2010 [1965]). For Giddens, ontological security signifies a deep psychological need for a sense of stability in an uncertain and sometimes threatening world, one that is no longer ordered by the social structures of traditional societies in the 'pre-modern' world (Giddens, 1990, 1991). At times the pre-modern world is treated by Giddens as a more 'natural' environment of routine and face-to-face interaction, in contrast to our 'created' modern world of distance, bridged by technology and the abstractions of the cash nexus.

So ontological *in*security occurs with the loss of the traditional routines and hierarchies, within which people previously found meaning and interpreted their place in the world. Another piece in this account is the adoption by Giddens of Irving Goffman's metaphor of front- and back-stage, albeit with an apparent reversal of the player's locus of self-creation. Whereas for Goffman we create and maintain our sense of self on the stage of public interaction, for Giddens it is in the private realm that this happens in the modern world. The stability offered by the privacy of a secure home therefore gives individuals a domain they can shape and control, allowing them to renew their sense of self-control.

Giddens' conception of ontological security has since been adopted across a wide range of subjects in the social sciences. But the most important use of the concept in housing studies is Peter Saunders' sustained attempt to tie ontological security directly to owner-occupation (Saunders, 1990). In his book, *A nation of homeowners*, Saunders (1990) argues that ownership is the 'natural' tenure, almost universally preferred by everyone – regardless of country and culture – who has the opportunity to own their home. This contention is based on a wide range of sources as well as on primary research consisting of interviews with over 500 individuals in three largely working-class English towns in the mid-1980s. Saunders' aim is to explain the apparently superior status of owner-occupation as a source of ontological security, and to test two possible psychological explanations: natural territoriality and natural possessiveness. Of the two it is the latter that he believes to be borne out by his extended foray into ethnography and evolutionary biology. For Saunders, the ethnographic and biological evidence base provides 'strong grounds for arguing the plausibility of a genetic basis to our behaviour' (Saunders, 1990, p 83). He therefore concludes that 'we may draw the conclusion that a widespread desire for owner-occupation is likely to be fuelled by certain natural dispositions as well as by cultural and economic factors' (Saunders, 1990, p 83).

By the time that Saunders arrives at this essentialist conclusion there is a clear sense of polemic, with an argument driven in part by an overt hostility to a perceived leftist bias in sociological thought and research; a 'leftist cabal' temperamentally hostile to owner-occupation and driven by ideological fervour.

Nonetheless, his earlier engagements with Giddens and ontological security are sophisticated and offer some important insights. These insights are highlighted by Dupuis and Thorns in their empirical study of homeownership and ontological security in New Zealand (Dupuis and Thorns, 1998). For Saunders the important point is that the day-to-day activity in both the modern and pre-modern worlds is routinised and takes place through familiar time-space paths. Unlike Giddens, Saunders can see no necessity for these paths to be 'natural' rather than 'created', and once it is accepted that ontological security can be maintained in the built environment, it is only a small step further to Saunders' proposition that the home is the key locale in modern society where ontological security can be sought. It is to be stressed that this sense of 'security' is not the banal one of being warm, safe, and cosy in a house full of loved ones. It is instead security in the maintenance of identity and selfhood, which could in other historical contexts not require the prosaic security that a safe and stable home (and home life) represents for us. We can now turn to the operationalisation of ontological security.

Researching ontological security: from vague and deep to specific and broad

There have been a number of studies that explore the relationship between ontological security and housing. These have generally focused on lower-income individuals and households, and have often been set in the context of neighbourhood deprivation. Of these the most significant, for my purposes, is a series of studies in and around Glasgow (Kearns et al, 2000; Hiscock et al, 2003; Clark and Kearns, 2012).[1]

This ongoing research takes seriously the underlying issues that emerge in discussions of ontological security, while pointing to some of the inherent conceptual confusion as 'a vague and deep concept' (Kearns et al, 2000, p 389). The depth – as I later argue – is somewhat illusory. But the exercise of adding empirical purchase to the vagueness is fruitful, and leads to the development of a series of survey and interview questions that tap into the way the home is experienced as a fulcrum of identity and selfhood. These have subsequently been adopted by other researchers (for example, Kleinhans and Elsinga, 2010) and have become a crucial tool in ongoing research conducted with colleagues at the Universities of Birmingham and Manchester. For this programme of work we designed an online survey that takes from Kearns and colleagues' five experience-of-home items, pairing these with the four ONS measures of subjective wellbeing used in the Annual Population Survey (see Box 5.1).

Box 5.1: Subjective wellbeing and experiences of the home

Experience of home

- I feel safe in my home
- I feel I have privacy in my home
- I can do what I want with my home
- Most people would like a home like mine
- My home makes me feel I am doing well in my life

ONS subjective wellbeing

- Overall, how satisfied are you with your life nowadays?
- Overall, to what extent do you feel the things you do in your life are worthwhile?
- Overall, how happy did you feel yesterday?
- Overall, how anxious did you feel yesterday?

In the following two case studies I present the results of our survey of social tenants, shared owners and owners who bought on the open market.

Case study 1: social tenants and owners in the South East

The survey was designed with colleagues at the Universities of Birmingham and Manchester and was part of a research project with a large housing association, VIVID, based in the South East of England (Gregory et al, 2018). The survey was conducted online in 2018 and was completed by over 2,000 people: 1,700 social tenants and over 300 owners. Of these, roughly 100 bought their home on the open market, and the remainder were shared-owners. We also conducted 30 follow-up interviews.

Shared ownership has had a relatively long policy history in the UK, much of it problematic. A range of issues have prevented shared ownership from becoming a mainstream tenure, and at present it accounts for roughly only 2 per cent of all homes in the UK. These problems range from a restrictive mortgage market that does not meet the specific needs of shared owners, to unique restrictions on the rights of the shared owner that sharply diverge from the rights we would normally expect as owner-occupiers (for instance, the right to decorate or to sublet a room to a lodger). I return to some of these problems in the final chapter of this book, where I turn from evidence and analysis to real-world policy proposals.

Drawing on data from the British Social Attitudes Survey and the English Housing Survey, the recent White Paper – *The charter for social housing residents* (MHCLG, 2020b) – states that: 'Over 60% of social tenants have said they would prefer to be owner-occupiers if they had a free choice, yet only a quarter currently believe they will ever be able to do so. This gap between ambition and expectation is not right' (MHGLG, 2020, p 71). Part of the proposed solution is a right to shared ownership, with housing association tenants being able to buy as little as 10 per cent of their home, and up to 25 per cent. There is also a Help to Buy route for shared owners, allowing people to buy up to 75 per cent of a home.

Results

There are two striking findings from this study. The first is that there is a significant difference in outcome when we shift from descriptive results to a (probit) model that controls for all the variables included in the survey. These include the following: marital status/cohabitation, responsibility for children or adult dependents, income, age, employment, level of education, financial stress, job satisfaction, and long-term sickness. These are all well-established determinants of wellbeing.

There are a number of conceptual nuances and methodological challenges that we must face in a fuller discussion of statistical representations of housing tenure and wellbeing. Of particular importance is the need to avoid causal inferences based on correlations alone. This warning is unlikely to come as a revelation. But it is worth noting that statistical analysis of social housing in the UK is particularly prone to compositional or selection effects (in which we find, for example, high levels of poor health because this is one of the social housing allocation criteria), owing to the residualised nature of the social housing sector. I address these issues in greater depth in Chapter 6. For the present it is sufficient to bear in mind that these selection effects are controlled for in the survey results outlined here, albeit without the full robustness employed in the modelling presented in the next chapter.

At a descriptive level, we find the following:

- Social tenants on average report higher levels of personal anxiety (by three percentage points more, at 23 per cent) than all owner-occupiers, 20 per cent of whom report high levels of anxiety.
- When we control for background characteristics, for the social tenant the probability of being anxious *reduces* by seven percentage points (compared with the average respondent, at 21 per cent).

Social housing is, in short, good for the social tenants we surveyed. Moreover, with these controls, social tenants are no less likely than owners to say that life is worthwhile. This cancels out a 12 percentage point gap in the descriptive results, in which only 58 per cent of social tenants returned positive scores on the 'worthwhile' question, compared with 70 per cent of all owners.

There is another, equally striking finding. Even though social housing has a positive or neutral effect on some aspects of wellbeing – most notably on anxiety – this is *not* the case for either happiness or satisfaction with life:

- Even with the full range of controls, there is an eight point percentage gap between social tenants and owners in their reported satisfaction with life.

How do we explain this?

Some clues are available in the way that social tenants and owners report different experiences of the home:

- More social tenants in the South East (71 per cent) than owners (64 per cent) say they do not feel a sense of privacy in their home.
- Fewer social tenants in the South East (37 per cent) than owners (46 per cent) feel that they can do what they want in their home.

Crucially, this is not a reflection of dwelling 'type' (for example, houses compared with flats), quality (reported problems) or dwelling size – these are all controlled for in the model – but it does not rule out differences in tenancy rights. Social tenants may be more constrained in what they can do with their home in terms of 'do-it-yourself' or home improvements, or because they cannot sublet their home. But these conditions apply equally to shared owners, who make up two thirds of the sample of owners. In some cases we may find that the restrictions faced by shared owners are actually more restrictive.

Another possibility is that neighbourhood exerts an influence on the ways in which the home is experienced. This would clearly make sense for the privacy and safety items. While the statistical analysis in this case study does not include neighbourhood variables, our follow-up interviews strongly suggest that neighbourhood quality is indeed an important determinant of both wellbeing and the way in which the home is experienced. Further indications of this are present in a companion study, conducted over three years in East Devon (see case study 2).

But what really stands out from the survey results is the disparity between the perceived social status of social housing compared with both shared and open-market ownership. Controlling again for housing quality and type we find that:

- Fewer social tenants (36 per cent) than all owners (45 per cent) feel that other people would like a home like theirs.
- Fewer social tenants than owners say that their home makes them feel that they are doing well in life. Across the whole population of social tenants and shared owners, 36 per cent of respondents felt their home makes them feel they are doing well in life. But when we look just at social renters, the rate falls to just 9 per cent.

Loops and pathways: the dynamics of social housing and wellbeing

In Chapter 2 I introduced a visual representation of norms, cultures, and institutions and their dynamic interaction with the three core components of wellbeing: flourishing, satisfaction with life, and 'happiness'. We can now give this housing-specific content for two of these wellbeing components, namely satisfaction with life and happiness. In my first iteration of this graphic in Chapter 2, 'happiness' is treated as a convenient label for a range of mental state metrics, including mental health symptoms such as depression and anxiety. For the present purposes I concentrate on anxiety specifically, as the relationship between social housing and anxiety proves to be particularly significant in the South East case study.

In Figure 5.1 we can see the relationship between social housing and two aspects of wellbeing. The central line of direction is from social housing to satisfaction and happiness, both of which are lower for social tenants than

Figure 5.1: Social housing in the South East: divergent paths?

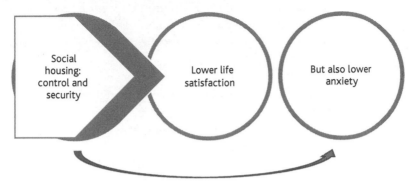

for owners in the South East case study. The central line shows a significant but negative association between social housing and satisfaction with life, whereas the bottom line shows a significant and positive association between social housing and reduced anxiety, which is present even after controlling for the greater prevalence of mental health issues among the social housing population.

We therefore see a divergence of two aspects of wellbeing: the *evaluative* metric of life satisfaction diverges from the more 'hedonic' mental state of metric anxiety. This raises an issue of normative choice: are we equally concerned about the negative relationship with life satisfaction, or do we take the positive relationship with mental health to be the primary outcome? There are equally important empirical questions: why does this satisfaction–happiness divergence occur, and what sociological mechanisms underlie the divergent outcomes?

As the bottom line of Figure 5.1 suggests, there are two mechanisms in play, with two separate pathways. The degree of that separation is also important. Although my empirical data indicates a separation (a finding that is confirmed in Chapter 6), there may be more subtle interactions *between* 'satisfaction' and 'happiness'. I return to this theme at a number of points in the following two chapters. For the present my aim is to highlight the issues to come. Of these, relative social status is one of the more important analytical categories.

Case study 2: social tenants and private renters in the South West

Here I present results from a complementary study, using the same methodology, but over a period of three years (2017–2020) and with a different reference group (private renters rather than shared and market owners).[2] Over three years we surveyed nearly 3,000 people in a study of social renters in East Devon. Of these approximately one quarter were private renters who had applied for a social home. In most respects the core message is the same: social housing plays a positive role in individual wellbeing. This is particularly stark when compared with private renting. The descriptive results are as follows:

- 27 per cent of social tenants report anxiety, compared with 43 per cent of private renters.
- 60 per cent of social tenants say that they are happy, compared with only 45 per cent of private renters.
- 68 per cent of social tenants report that they are satisfied with life, compared with 51 per cent of private renters.
- 74 per cent of social tenants report feeling life is worthwhile, compared with 66 per cent of private renters.

In this study the significance of both neighbourhood and felt experience comes through particularly strongly. Controlling for individual characteristics and dwelling type, we found that the following was true of all renters (private and social):

- People who do not feel in control in their homes are 4.1 percentage points less likely to report they are satisfied with life.
- Those who report a sense of privacy and feel that they can do what they want in their home are 3.2 percentage points more likely to report being happy.
- Those who report a lack of privacy are 3.6 percentage points more likely to report being anxious.

These results bring us closer to the concept of ontological security. Privacy and control are important elements of the home as a place where we maintain and renew our sense of identity and place in the world. The results also suggest that social housing plays a positive role, compared with the private rental sector. Experiences of the home are better for social tenants, and this, in turn, is associated with higher levels of wellbeing. A more complete contrast would require a sample of owners, as it is ownership that is posited as the superior source of ontological security. This comparison was not practically possible in the South West study. But, as we can see in the next section, it is possible that housing *tenure* is not the most significant determinant of wellbeing. Neighbourhood is more important.

Neighbourhood and wellbeing

The South West study found that positive perceptions of neighbourhood – regardless of tenure or dwelling type – are strongly associated with higher levels of wellbeing. Again controlling for background characteristics, the following findings emerge:

• Participants who like their neighbourhood are 13.2 percentage points more likely to report being happy, 8.5 percentage points more likely to report being satisfied with life, and 4.1 percentage points less likely to report being anxious.
• Positive perceptions of neighbourhood cohesion are related to higher levels of wellbeing: people with positive perceptions of neighbourhood cohesion are 4.4 percentage points more likely to feel happy and 7.4 percentage points more likely to be satisfied with life.

Throughout this book I have stressed the centrality of housing and housing tenure to ways in which our thinking about welfare and wellbeing are formed. But housing does not sit in its own hermetically sealed sphere. Multiple and overlapping interactions are integral to all welfare spheres. This is particularly apparent in the case of housing provision. Past planning decisions and broader socioeconomic drivers of inequality have, historically at least, led to overlapping disadvantages for social tenants: large-scale social housing estates in areas with weak labour markets, overstretched health services, underfunded schools, and so on.

In Figure 5.2 we can see that there is a direct line from positive feelings about neighbourhood to higher satisfaction with life and lower anxiety. This applies equally to the social and private renters in the South West sample. A lack of owners in this sample means we cannot draw any conclusions from this study, but the large-scale data employed in the following chapter does include owners and confirms that neighbourhood effectively trumps tenure.

So it is not all about housing. In fact, the results of the South West study suggest that neighbourhood is considerably *more* important than housing tenure for individual wellbeing, regardless of housing tenure. While there are certainly some strong statistical associations between tenure and wellbeing,

Figure 5.2: Neighbourhood, home, and wellbeing

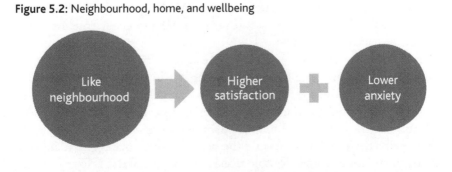

the associations with neighbourhood are markedly more pronounced. This result is again confirmed in Chapter 6. With a full range of controls, and with a nationally representative sample from all tenures and all income groups, data from the BHPS and Understanding Society survey show that neighbourhood consistently emerges as one of the strongest determinants of wellbeing.

Home, security, and control: articulations of the home

There is a strong tradition of ethnographic household research in the UK, and although it is only relatively recently that there has been a specific focus on housing, much of this tradition explores the kinds of experiences and beliefs underpinning the patterns that began to emerge in Chapter 4 (see Lawrence, 2019). The best known of these studies is Michael Young and Peter Willmott's research into family and kinship in working-class communities in Bethnal Green in the 1950s. Of more direct interest, however, is Ray Phal's study of the Isle of Sheppey, conducted over ten years, from 1978 to 1988. The economy at the time was based on a shipyard and the community has been characterised as working-class Conservative (Lawrence, 2019). Despite a majority of islanders already owning their home, this is precisely the kind of demographic that Thatcher's Right to Buy policy was aimed at.

Saunders (1990), of course, presents a range of arguments and evidence for his belief in ownership and ontological security, including over 500 interviews in three large English towns, Burnley, Derby and Slough. Yet, reviewing the interview material that Saunders presents, what is striking is not so much the expression of ideals of freedom and independence, but the wider variety and nuance of feeling and belief. There is certainly a view that ownership is a source of pride, and of freedom in a sense that runs deeper than the rights of ownership, or the instrumental and material advantages typically associated with owning one's home. So we hear the voice of an owner saying, " 'This is ours.' It's what we have achieved" (cited in Saunders, 1990, p 87), and another voice saying, "It gives you pride in yourself. You are not reliant on other people. If I was in a council house I'd feel other people were paying for me" (cited in Saunders, 1990, p 87). This strongly resonates with the normative discourse of ownership and virtue discussed in the first half of this chapter.

But it is not the only, or even the strongest, voice in Saunders' interviews. In a later discussion of the material advantages of ownership, Saunders also draws out a widespread dissatisfaction with council landlords, who tended to be both unresponsive when maintenance needs arose, yet restrictive when tenants wanted to maintain or improve their homes. Ownership was certainly felt to bring the freedom to mould the home to one's needs and identity – and perhaps a deep sense of 'ontological security'. But if this is where we are to find ontological security, there are also more tangible securities: security of tenure (not subject to the property rights of the landlord); greater control of costs and insurance against rent rises; the financial security of minimal housing costs in retirement, after the mortgage is paid off.

All of these different senses of security are clearly present in the interview material that Saunders presents (1990, pp 92–93), and at times his interviewees do little to help his thesis that ownership is a 'natural' preference: "Originally I didn't agree with the idea. I think they ought to keep a backbone of council housing for people who do want to rent. I only bought because of continued rent increase. Otherwise we wouldn't have bothered – we were quite happy as we were" (retired male, Derby, cited in Saunders, 1990, p 107). Similar sentiments are found in Phal's study of the Isle of Sheppey: "I haven't bought so I can say I've bought it. I mean, I've bought it so we can live in it, really, because we ended up with the increase in the price of rents" (cited in Lawrence, 2019, p 190). This sense of financial security also has more complex emotional layers, as we see in another interview response taken from Saunders (1990, p 88): "[Ownership is] a sense of security. And if you've got children you've got something to leave them."

All of these *may* contribute to a sense of ontological security, but they are not reducible to such a concept, and they are not an exclusive or *inherent* characteristic of ownership. This is not to deny that for some people owning their home is associated with the emotions and psychological attachments that Saunders describes as natural. There are certainly signs of this in the interview material presented in the following section. However, it is misleading (at best) to suggest that this is the *dominant* perception of ownership. As Smith stresses, the meanings of ownership are hybrid and complex (Smith, 2008). In the following section I present a spectrum of experiences and emotions articulated by owners and renters in the studies undertaken by the Universities of Birmingham and Manchester in the South East (Gregory et al, 2018) and South West of England.[3]

Virtuous, independent owners

The following passages reveal a strong sense that ownership is considered to be a route to greater financial independence. This is felt in the expression that ownership is a form of investment, which is in keeping with contemporary narratives of virtuous independence from the state, especially in terms of retirement planning. But there are significant references to security of tenure and the ability to predict ongoing housing costs (B: "I like to have my own place. Just personally I like to feel comfortable that no one's going to kick me out or sort of change things or up the price a lot"), and a desire to build a financial legacy that can be passed on to children (B and C).

'Yeah, I think it's sort of always been with me. I've always been sort of a financially minded person, if I'm honest with you. So yeah, I have a sort of mantra of really if I'm going to spend money, do I need it? Is it the right price as such? Or if I don't need it, will I use it? So in that respect I sort of applied that from the smaller purchases right through to the homeownership side of things … do have savings and investments as such.' (A: male open market owner, South East)

'It's just kind of if you can manage to get on the property market I think it's a valuable investment more than anything as well because it's your own space, but also you're sort of investing in something, an asset which hopefully can be handed down to the family as long as they don't bring in things to try and take all your money away, from the government. … So it's one of those things. I like to have my own place. Just personally I like to feel comfortable that no one's going to kick me out or sort of change things or up the price a lot. Obviously there are pros and cons to renting and owning a house, but for us it felt like the right kind of thing to do as long as you can afford it.' (B: female open market owner, South East)

'I just wanted to get my foot on the property ladder. I didn't ever want to be in a position where I was paying a high amount of rent to somebody to pay off their own mortgage, nor did I particularly want to go down the route of renting via the council if ownership was something that I could do, and I could still be in my own property. So that's why I've done it that way. … In the long run it's something that will benefit me. And if I were to ever have children, hopefully owning my own property will benefit for the future as well, so a good investment.' (C: male shared owner, South East)

Virtuous, independent social tenants

A central theme in the housing debate is the relationship between social housing and employment. In the following extracts we see the positive role that social housing can play in *supporting* (rather than discouraging) employment. Both D and E stress the importance of social housing as a stable and affordable home which gives the security needed to enter into and maintain employment.

'If we were private renting we'd be skint. We wouldn't be able to get by. … It might even put us under pressure to be one of those people that don't work and get benefits because if we can't afford to pay the rent working, then you've got no choice, have you?' (D: female social renter, South East)

'I think it's made it easier, I think, in the fact that it's been cheaper for me and it's made me feel more stable. I think the housing's provided stability ... you know, if repairs need doing, they've done it pretty much straight away. So you haven't got to worry if something breaks.' (E: female social renter, South East)

Security, control and stability

Here we come closest to the concept of ontological security. There is a strong sense of the value of security of tenure, which is contrasted by two shared owners (F and G) to the insecurity of the private rental sector. However, this sense of security – and the anxiety of insecurity in the private rental sector – is equally strong among social tenants: "I was renting somebody else's house and there was always that uncertainty of, you know, I could be given two months' notice or a month's notice" (H). For owners there is also a sense of control: "it's just having that security and then having the place as you want it. Like, you don't have to ask for any permission if you want to paint the wall" (F). But we hear the same expressions among social tenants: "I think the number one thing most important for my mental health is that I've got such a long-term contract ... no one's going to kick me out" (I), and: "Private rented houses were fine; our last landlord was very good and the house was lovely, but if rented, it tends to be all magnolia, whereas here we can put our stamp on things" (G).

'I guess it's the security. So not only is it you're ending up with something at the end of it, you don't have that worry that somebody's going to turn round and say "Oh, we're going to sell the house now. You need to move out," or "One of my friends is moving in, so you need to move out." Yeah, it's just having that security and then having the place as you want it. Like, you don't have to ask for any permission if you want to paint the wall or, you know ...' (F: male shared owner, South East)

'Private rented houses were fine; our last landlord was very good and the house was lovely, but if rented, it tends to be all magnolia, whereas here we can put our stamp on things. I thought it was important for the children to choose their own colours for their rooms, as they have a room each now.' (G: female social renter, South West)

'Well, you can't be given notice to vacate the premises. You can't. ... If you have a landlord who wants to get back into the property, I think legally he's only allowed to give you, what, two months' notice? That might not be enough time to find a new place, especially if you have children and you want to find a school in the same … you know, stay in that same school.' (H: female shared owner, South East)

'All the time I was growing up with my mum we lived in the private rental sector and had to move every year … landlords just changed their minds.' [Reflecting over the three years of the study]: 'I think the number one thing most important for my mental health is that I've got such a long-term contract … no one's going to kick me out.' (I: female social renter, South West)

'Things have got harder for people, actually people think I'm really lucky to have such stability and be in social housing and not live in fear of being kicked out by my landlord for no reason.' (J: male social renter, South West)

Neighbourhood

The final set of experiences to consider revolves around the value of neighbourhood. The data arising from the South West study shows a clear relationship between neighbourhood and individual wellbeing, and this is confirmed in Chapter 6. It is equally clear that a poor experience of neighbourhood has a negative impact regardless of housing tenure. We can see this in some of the reported experiences of owner-occupiers in the interviews conducted in the South East. Across both case study areas it is also clear that large-scale spatial design and management matters. Poor planning – and in particular perceptions of segregation – can have a negative impact: "The fact that we've got social housing, owned and then rented in a block in a triangle shape that is the worst thing anyone ever could have done because it has created so much hate" (N), and: "[The housing management] had segregated between shared ownership and fully social housing. So if you're in shared ownership you're classed as … it seems as though you're just left to get on with it" (O). Equally, however, we can see positive reactions to well-planned and managed mixed tenure housing (L).

'It's like being home. The other place [in a rough neighbourhood] I never classed as home because I hated it, but this place I class as home. My mum has a very big house on the other side of Basingstoke and it kind of feels a little bit more like that.' (K: male social renter, South East)

'Well, it's just nice. There're people from all walks of life and it's quite nice to see quite a lot of trades people and people who can … [help out]. So there's kind of a community spirit going on. … So it feels nice to be able to go, "Oh hey, I've got a problem here. Would you be able to help me out?" So that's quite nice. Everyone's quite approachable.' (L: female open market owner, South East)

'The neighbourhood here is amazing. It's a proper community. Everybody is so friendly and likes to help everybody out and yeah, it's really nice. It's a really … I'd have liked to be brought up in a place like this, so I hope my children will have a good childhood because we've got the country park and everything and there's always other children there running around on their bikes, playing football, and everybody just joins in with everybody.' (M: female social renter, South West)

'I hate my flat. The fact that we've got social housing, owned and then rented in a block in a triangle shape, that is the worst thing anyone ever could have done because it has created so much hate. … So many people detest other people from that block, it is ridiculous.' (N: male shared ownership owner, South East)

'[The housing management had] segregated between shared ownership and fully social housing. So if you're in shared ownership you're classed as … it seems as though you're just left to get on with it.' (O: male shared owner, South West)

Discussion: wellbeing and social status

The two case studies presented in this chapter give us ample reason to doubt that there is something uniquely special about owner-occupation. Interview data from both studies also suggest that social tenants are able to view their home as a site of autonomy and control, in marked contrast to the private renters surveyed in the South West, and contrary to the expectations of greater ontological security for owners. There is also strong survey data, particularly from the South East, that suggests a positive impact of social housing on anxiety. This is again supported by the interview material I presented here, chiefly through positive comments on security of tenure in social housing. Such security, it should be recalled, was one of the strongest themes advanced by Saunders (1990) in his argument for the inherent superiority of ownership.

Security of tenure and protection from unexpected rises in the cost of housing provision are clearly fundamental conditions of individual wellbeing. As we have seen, social housing can provide this security as well as owner-occupation. However, this is not the end of the story. The thesis of ontological security runs deeper than these issues, and conveys more than the sense of home as emotional and psychological sanctuary. These qualities are likely, for most people, to form a crucial part of the everyday conditions we need to maintain our sense of identity – of who and what we are.

The 'what' here is important, and central to the meaning of *ontological* security as a concept that is intended to capture the constitution of the 'self' singular, rather than the ways in which individual selves create and express their own sense of identity. If this were all that ontological security meant, we could reasonably conclude that the advantages of one tenure over another are entirely contingent. In terms of housing strategy and policy development, this is the message presented in Part III. Social housing can and should offer the same everyday quality of life associated with owner-occupation. The quality of neighbourhood, regardless of tenure, is equally important.

But there is still something missing. Even though social housing plays a clear role in reducing anxiety and providing a valuable sense of security, in the South East case study there is still a gap between social tenants and owners when we look at 'happiness' and satisfaction with life. In Chapter 6 we shall see that this is not an anomaly based on one case study. A similar divergence can be found in a range of studies (for a discussion, see Angel and Gregory, 2021).

The question is, what is underlying this divergence? One answer is that, even though social housing can meet all of our practical and emotional needs through life, there is a significant status gap. This is unsurprising when we consider the negative discourses of social housing and welfare dependency (see Chapter 4). The stigma attached to social tenants is well covered in the literature (Hastings, 2004), as is the cultural expectation that ownership is a social norm to which we should conform (Gurney, 1999).

There is also a large body of work on the institutional dynamics of welfare provision, in which welfare goods targeted on need create a powerful sense that such goods are inherently inferior (for a full discussion, see Horton and Gregory, 2009). It is these dynamics that can help us make sense of life satisfaction as a function of social status, defined in part by the meaning and purpose of social housing as a low-status good.

This is an intuitively plausible conclusion. Yet it immediately raises more questions, two of which stand out. The first question is the relationship between satisfaction with life and other concepts and metrics of wellbeing. What we do not see in the data is an indication of a causal mechanism from tenure status and lower satisfaction with life to poorer health outcomes. The two case studies presented in this chapter do not come close to the scale and breadth of survey evidence required to address this question. Nevertheless, it is now accepted that social status can directly affect the physical and mental health of individuals on the lower rungs of the pecking order. The basis of this knowledge is formed by two longitudinal studies of civil servants in London (see Marmot and Brunner, 2005). Over several decades these studies monitored in great detail the personal and professional circumstances of staff of all grades, and found that the lowest-grade workers in fact experienced the greatest stress, leading to a greater risk of physical ill health (see Marmot, 2005).

In Chapter 6, however, it becomes clear that the effect of tenure status (to the extent that there is such an effect) does not follow the same pattern. To the extent that there is a relationship between tenure and wellbeing, it does not seem to follow the expected hierarchy, in which social tenants fare worse than private renters or owners. On the contrary, the data point instead to poorer wellbeing outcomes for mortgaged owners, who are more likely to be depressed and dissatisfied with life than either renters (social and private) or outright owners.

The second question takes us back to the concept of ontological security, discussed in more detail in the next section.

Ontological security and status hierarchies

In introducing the concept of ontological security earlier in this chapter I noted that it has been described as 'vague and deep' (Kearns et al, 2000, p 389). To some extent this vagueness is unobjectionable in a concept that was not intended to function as a precise empirical metric. But the risk is that the vagueness allows the concept to be too broadly interpreted, undermining its usefulness even as a framing concept that lies behind empirical investigation. To avoid this we need to set some boundaries around the use of ontological security, and in particular to stress that it is not just the sum of all the parts – tenure security, financial security, and a sense of safety and belonging in the neighbourhood.

For all its vagueness, there are two essential characteristics of the concept that are very clearly presented in the texts of the four 20th-century thinkers with whom it is most closely associated: Mead (1934), Winnicott (2018 [1965]), Laing (2010 [1960]) and Giddens (1990, 1991). The first characteristic, in all of these accounts, is that ontological security is not a static state that can be measured and recorded; it is a *developmental* process – a process of 'being' and 'becoming'. This 'becoming' resonates in post-Kantian philosophy and, later, in the traditions of phenomenology and existentialism. But there is also a strong connection with developmental psychology, in particular Winnicott's account of childhood development, in which the infant learns to make sense of themselves through the external world (Winnicott, 2018 [1965]). Giddens devotes considerable space to this process (Giddens, 1991, pp 39–54) and draws heavily on theories of childhood development. The point to stress, however, is his more general formulation: 'To be ontologically secure is to possess, on the level of the unconscious and practical consciousness, "answers" to fundamental existential questions which all human life in some way addresses' (p 47).

The second characteristic is that ontological security is inherently relational. It describes not just our place in a world of social relations, and 'what' we are as well as who we are, and this can only be known through our interaction with others. With the notable exception of David Taylor (2011), few contemporary accounts of wellbeing – and fewer still in the social policy literature – appreciate the developmental and relational nature of ontological security. As Taylor emphasises, the security in question cannot be reduced to material interests. His account of wellbeing thus 'suggests that the purpose of social policy might be the promotion of *an individual ontological security which goes beyond the traditional focus on redistribution and possession*' (Taylor, 2011, p 779, emphasis added).

In societies where property ownership signals moral, social, and economic status, it is the more abstract good of 'title' that brings ontological status into play, over and the 'more traditional' focus on material redistribution and possession. We can view this in terms of unstated power, as observed by Fitzpatrick and Pawson: 'Modern socio-legal scholars have continued to demonstrate the key role the law plays in constructing power relationships within housing ... and that, crucially, the power implied by these legal relationships "exists" whether it is acted upon in practice or not' (Fitzpatrick and Pawson, 2014, p 603). This sense of unstated power is perhaps best exemplified today by the private renter faced with the ever-present possibility that the landlord will exercise their power to terminate the tenancy. Equally important is the unequal power of contractual enforcement. Few private renters are able to really force a landlord to meet obligations (such as timely repairs) that are ignored or delayed.

A sense of *ontological* insecurity, however, may be better captured by the tenuous rights and status of the lease-holding home owner. Subject to onerous or ambiguous contractual terms, the owners in this case might feel a deeper (not necessarily conscious) disruption of their place in the world – a frustration of their sense of self as 'owner'. This, I have stressed, is a contractual and legal relation. But this is not a case of it 'just' being this, as if we have clarified an error, or avoided a reification. Over and above the power relations described by Fitzpatrick and Pawson, there is also the possibility that legal relations are constitutive of our identity.

This argument is presented most forcefully by Axel Honneth (Honneth, 1996), drawing on the same intellectual resources as Giddens, though with a more overt indebtedness to Hegel. Honneth advances an account of individual development that owes much to Hegel's account of contractual law as a vehicle of mutual recognition, building an account of legal rights as a precondition of self-respect – not as simply as respect that others give us, but as recognition of our status, and equal moral worth (Honneth, 1996). We do not need to follow this level of philosophical abstraction to take the central point: housing tenure may 'only' be a bundle of rights, but these rights can tell us a lot about who we are, and what we expect our place in the world to be.

Being in and being through the home

I now wish to introduce a distinction: it is *through* rather than just *in* the home that we should view the development of the self. This distinction helps us to make sense of the wellbeing divergence that has begun to emerge in this chapter. If there is little or no relationship between social housing and hedonic or mental state wellbeing (and hence little impact on happiness or depression), this might be a function of wellbeing *in* the home. The conditions for this can be attributed to housing or dwelling characteristics that are not intrinsic to any one tenure. Conversely, where we find a relationship between ownership and higher satisfaction with life, this may be viewed from a different perspective of wellbeing *through* the home. Here there is indeed an intrinsic characteristic of ownership that gives it a special cultural and normative status, over and above the everyday securities that are not inherent to ownership.

This type of belief has been described by a number of theorists. Much of it is influenced by Hegelian beliefs about the historicist nature of truth and knowledge. One writer that stands out in recent sociological theory is Bourdieu, who employs the Greek concept of *doxa* – intuitively accepted and unquestioned belief – to be contrasted with the conscious knowledge of *episteme* (Bourdieu, 1977). Others, drawing on the same intellectual history, arrived at much the same place, and generally before Bourdieu. Gadamer, for example, recovers the meaning of 'prejudice' as 'pre-judgement' to capture the same sense of unquestioned belief, setting the 'horizons' beyond which we are unable to see (Gadamer, 2013 [1960]).

In the context of this book, the value that operates in the background as *doxa* is the value of ownership. By this I do not mean the relatively recent historical phenomenon of homeownership, but the value of property more broadly, which is central to the European Enlightenment. But it is more than an ideology or political economy; it is a belief in the centrality of ownership to human identity. In Locke it is human nature to take control of the natural world and convert it for our own use, a process in which 'property' comes into being as we 'mix our labour' with natural resources and thus claim them as our own (Locke, 1962 [1689]). In Kant and Hegel this becomes more explicitly a social process, mediated through the recognition and institutional guarantee of individual property rights, and in Hegel's terms, it is the process by which the 'will' becomes 'actual'. And, as we have seen, it is the same kind of process that is expressed by Giddens' in his use of 'ontological security'.

These are all developmental accounts in which property is essential to the fulfilment of human nature. Comparison with Saunders' assertion that the preference to own is 'innate' immediately suggests a continuity of thought with the aforementioned *doxa*. The bridge between the Enlightenment value of private property and our contemporary discourses of ownership is that ownership is both essential for human flourishing *and* the vehicle through which this flourishing is achieved. It is *through* rather than just *in* the home that we should view the development of the self.

An alternative way of understanding this discourse is to draw a distinction between what home ownership does 'for' you and what it does 'to' you (Gregory, 2014). Asset ownership, including homeownership, could be a means to the end of securing a range of material and immaterial goods: warmth, shelter, security, and family life. Providing these goods is what homeownership does 'for' a person. But it is also taken (by some) to have a transformative effect – to do something 'to' you. Just as ownership is believed to have a positive transformative effect, creating virtuous and independent citizens, social housing is believed to have the opposite effect, creating welfare dependency (for a broader discussion of asset-based welfare, see Prabhakar, 2008). Housing tenure does something 'to' you.

Significantly, the to/for distinction does not just apply to the welfare narratives traditionally associated with the right of centre, or with a normative preference for the 'small state'. The same logic applies to the idea of an asset effect, which is most closely associated with left-of-centre narratives of social inclusion. In the case of asset-based welfare the policy emphasis has been on the value of relatively modest liquid wealth, held in savings accounts, with lower-income savers helped to save with direct matched contributions from central government. Instrumentally, this type of scheme does something 'for' the lower-income saver: it allows the household to smooth consumption in the face of income shock such as unemployment, so that their spending habits and consumption patterns can remain the same. But it is also expected to do something 'to' the saver. This is expressed most clearly by Michael Sherraden, who insists that asset ownership has an independent effect on individuals, over and above the financial and consumption benefits we may assume it to have: 'income only maintains consumption, *but assets change the way people think and interact with the world*' (Sherraden, 1991, p 6, emphasis added).

My point is not that we should accept this view of ownership. But the belief runs deep. It has longer historical antecedents than the contemporary accounts of property-owning democracy discussed in this book, and continues to influence the ways in which we think about welfare and wellbeing. To be an owner is not just to have a certain status and identity in society, but also to develop (and display) a particular identity. This, I believe, helps to explain the powerful grip that ownership has on our political discourses.

This has significant normative implications. Tenure may not have an impact on mental health, but the relationship with life satisfaction may lead us to ask whether binary owner/social distinctions have a bearing on equality of status or respect. If belonging in our society relies on access to most fundamental social goods – the standards of the day that Adam Smith evoked – and if ownership is one of these goods, the case for social housing faces an additional layer of complication. Recognition of this must be at the heart of any coherent account of the appropriate place of social housing in the welfare state, regardless of any substantive final conclusions.

Conclusion

We may want to consciously reject this way of thinking. To the extent that this is possible, my own belief is that we should appraise the legacy as critically as we can. A result of this, I hope, is that we can view the value of social housing differently, and also view the value of ownership more critically.

By this I do not mean the contingent and instrumental value that has, by and large, tended to come with owner-occupation in the UK. Nor is this just a case of repudiating snobbery, or questioning the need to 'keep up with the Joneses'. Rather, the point at issue is how far we view ownership as an integral part of self-development – of 'ontological security' as a developmental process that, in the modern world, requires ownership. This cannot be decided abstractly, or from the normative perspective of what 'should' be the role of ownership in the social world we occupy. Such critical perspectives are important, and we can hope that they nudge the evolution of our shared meanings in certain directions. Yet if ownership confers this meaning as a matter of social fact – if the belief is sufficiently widespread and embedded – we cannot hope to just push it aside, asserting the empirical 'fact' that there is no intrinsic relationship with housing tenure and wellbeing. And if ownership is an embedded part of what it means to belong or flourish in the UK today, this must be recognised in any account of the value of social housing – especially when my purpose is to argue for an expansion of this form of housing, recreating it as more accessible and universal social good.

6

Mental health, happiness, and satisfaction with life

Facts and figures: an analysis of BHPS and Understanding Society data

In the first half of this chapter I present an analysis of subjective wellbeing using nearly 30 years of data from the BHPS and its successor, Understanding Society. In the second half I turn to more limited analysis of the relationship between social housing, employment status, and political engagement.

The primary aim is to provide some detailed analysis of the effect of tenure on the lives and experiences of social tenants, owners, and private renters. This allows us to view the findings of Chapter 5 from the perspective of a wider, national sample. The data I draw on is longitudinal and allows us to control for a very wide range of background circumstances. For each individual we can control for the effect on wellbeing of their overall health, level of education, employment status, income, and marital status. To some degree we can also control for the effect of area and neighbourhood. This too is an important influence on individual wellbeing and the experience of the home. If we can account for the influence of all these factors and still find a significant association between housing tenure and wellbeing, we shall have a good indication of a tenure effect. By this I mean that there is something about 'tenure' that plays a causal role in an individual's subjective wellbeing.

The introduction of causal language should be treated with some caution. There are two more specific caveats. The first is that the data I draw on and the statistical methods used in the analysis cannot account for all potentially confounding factors. Tenure may seem to be the force at work but there could be some other influence not captured in the data. The first model used here greatly reduces this risk and follows the methodologies used by a number of researchers in the housing literature. Moreover, as we are able to follow a person over time we are able to control for some of the most important individual characteristics not captured directly by the data. For example, we are able to take account of, or control for, a range of personalities and dispositions. If we find that owners are happier than social tenants, this will not be because happy people are more likely to become owners in the first place. This is of particular interest when we consider (see Chapter 5) arguments for an innate or 'natural' preference for owner-occupation.

The second empirical caveat is that we are not pinpointing a precise causal point or action in the way we might expect of a medical trial or experiment. The strict 'gold standard' of the randomised controlled trial is neither possible nor desirable. But we do not need this level of precision to see the *direction* of the effect explored in the models employed in this chapter. Although we cannot definitively rule it out, we are unlikely to unwittingly fall into the trap of reverse causality.

Part A: tenure and wellbeing

What is special about owner-occupation?

In Chapter 1 I traced the historical outlines of a property-owning democracy. I also advanced the argument that we need to understand the meaning and value of social housing through the lens of ownership, the dialectical counterpart that defines what social housing is not. A fuller treatment of this argument is offered in Chapter 7. This will take us on to the terrain of ideology and political argument. But there are some elements that help us to understand the more straightforwardly empirical content of the current chapter. As we shall now see, there is large literature that explores this empirically, albeit in the less loaded language of 'civic virtue'. The empirical and conceptual challenge is the same as that in the statistical evidence presented, namely to isolate and test a 'tenure effect'.

Chapters 3 and 5 discussed narratives of property-owning democracy and, in particular, the belief that ownership creates the virtue of responsible independence. However, there is also a strand of thought within this tradition that emphasises political rather than moral virtue. The Conservative politician Neville Chamberlain, writing in *The Times* housing supplement in 1920, asserted that 'every spadeful of dug in, every fruit tree planted' turned another potential revolutionary into a virtuous citizen (cited in, Merrett, 1979, p 43). More recently, Francis provides a detailed account of the development of this line of Conservative thought, drawing out the same sentiment in leading figures, including Winston Churchill. In this earlier strand of property-owning democracy the Conservatives found 'a means of responding to socialism without appearing reactionary or insensitive to the needs of the working classes' (Francis, 2012, p 278; see also Sutcliffe-Braithwaite, 2012).

Property ownership was of course a condition of suffrage prior to 1918, largely based on the assertion only those with a material stake in society should have a voice in its government. But after this there is a subtle shift from property as a formal qualification of citizenship and democratic participation, to the view that owners are *better* citizens, more likely to engage with the political process and more likely to participate in the sub-state structures of civil society.

While largely stripped of these overt assumptions, there is a significant body of academic research that still seeks to demonstrate a relationship between owner-occupation and civic virtue. A key claim is that owner-occupation encourages greater social and political participation, and a more active citizenry, and the contrast is with rented housing, social and private.

Much of the evidence comes from the US, where the contrast with social housing *per se* is less marked, as there is a relatively small social sector. One widely cited review states that '[t]he empirical evidence on the relationship between homeownership and participation in both voluntary organisations and local political activity is both extensive and consistent' (Rohe et al, 2002, p 395)'.

A number of these studies are reviewed by Dietz and Haurin, who note that '[t]he belief that homeownership affects an individual's social standing and political behavior is a widely held tenet of social science and political philosophy' (Dietz and Haurin, 2003, p 427). They report on a range of studies that find homeowners to be more likely to vote for Conservative candidates, to show greater awareness of local issues than renters, to be more likely to vote than renters, and to be more likely to participate in voluntary organisations. Dietz and Haurin do, however, highlight the fundamental weakness of this evidence base, observing that 'most existing studies must be called into question due to the impact of unobserved household characteristics on both homeownership and social behaviors' (Dietz and Haurin, 2003, p 427).

Recent reviews have also noted that the evidence supporting the positive civic value of homeownership has largely found associations rather than causal mechanisms (Zavisca and Gerber, 2016; see also Lindblad and Quercia, 2015). For example, using the US General Social Survey, DiPasquale and Glaeser (1999) tested for a wide range of civic outcomes and behaviours, finding that nearly all the positive effects of owner-occupation disappear once length of residence is controlled for. Using more recent US data from the Current Population Survey, McCabe comes to a very similar conclusion (McCabe, 2016).

One of the few studies to unpack the alternative factors that could explain the apparently greater civic participation of owner-occupiers in the US leaves room for tenure itself to play a role, but also finds that residential stability is a significant factor in accounting for such civic virtue (McCabe, 2013). The same author sounds a rather sceptical note in later work, suggesting that 'homeowners are not always the community-minded, civically engaged citizens we often make them out to be' (McCabe, 2016, p 142). McCabe's data shows that homeowners may be more likely than renters to vote or attend rallies than renters, but that they are no more likely to participate in other political activities. A similar pattern emerges for civic engagement. Owners are more likely to join neighbourhood associations than renters, but no more likely to join other forms of membership group.

In a broader study of social policy and wellbeing, Searle (2008) used six years of BHPS data to track the impact of a range of factors on individual wellbeing. Controlling for background factors there was a clear relationship between wellbeing, physical health, and financial stress, but little independent influence of tenure on wellbeing (Searle, 2008). Following this lead there are three recent studies that use this secondary data to explore the relationship between housing tenure and wellbeing (Popham et al, 2015; Bentley et al, 2016; Foye et al, 2018). In addition to these there are also a limited number of studies that use similar datasets from other countries (Bentley et al, 2016; Liu et al, 2017).

There are also a small number of studies that explore the impact of neighbourhood and residential environment on wellbeing, of which the most recent and sophisticated is Liu and colleagues' (2017) work using data from the 2010 Shanghai Population Census and the 2008 Shanghai Economic Census to explore the relationship between subjective wellbeing and residential environment in Shanghai. The results include some indication that higher-status neighbourhoods have an independent effect on individual wellbeing.

Using the anxiety and life-satisfaction questions in the UK's Annual Population Survey, the 2014 English Housing Survey tested the relationship between tenure and wellbeing in England (DCLG, 2014). Using ordinary 'least squares' regression this analysis found a significant relationship between tenure and life satisfaction and yielded a positive result for social housing: 'After controlling for personal and other housing factors, life satisfaction was higher for both local authority and housing association renters compared to outright owners' (DCLG, 2014, p 6). Tenure is important in this result, but in fact comes second to financial stress from mortgage or rent arrears. The study found no significant relationship between tenure and anxiety, although arrears did again have an impact.

More recent analyses have taken advantage of the GHQ-12 in the BHPS and in Understanding Society. In an epidemiological vein, Popham and colleagues (2015) compare current social renters with former social renters who exercised the Right to Buy their socially rented home. The hypothesis is that there may be a status and health premium for those who went on to own their homes (Popham et al, 2015). Yet controlling for the improved financial circumstances that could have created the opportunity to own, Popham and colleagues find no sign of ownership reducing levels of stress (Popham et al, 2015).

This finding is consistent with other analyses of individual health using the BHPS with tenure as an independent variable. Bentley and colleagues (2016) use both the BHPS and the Household, Income and Labour Dynamics in Australia Survey (HILDA) to address the question: 'Does tenure (being a private renter or mortgagee) modify the effect of housing affordability on mental health in both Australia and the UK?' Given comparable levels of financial stress, the question is whether or not there is some independent aspect of ownership as a tenure that protects owners from the negative mental health effects of affordability difficulties. Results from the BHPS suggest the opposite effect, as the UK data 'indicated that the mental health of home purchasers significantly worsened' as mortgagees struggled to meet housing costs (Bentley et al, 2016, p 217).

Conversely, the results from the Australian research show a greater negative effect on renters when faced with housing unaffordability. The authors conclude: 'Tenure type influences health, but only in some contexts' (Bentley et al, 2016, p 218)..– a result that chimes with the use of wider European data that explores the stress of housing (un)affordability, though not tenure itself (Clair et al, 2016). It is notable, however, that Bentley and colleagues (2016) do not present a sample of social renters.

Finally, the BHPS has also been used to test the hypothesis that the benefits of homeownership come from its status as a positional good, as well as from the absolute benefits it may bring (Foye et al, 2018). This is an issue discussed in Chapter 5, including in my presentation of primary evidence from the South East case study, in which there were some signs of a negative status effect when social tenants were asked how they felt about their home. I do not, however, pursue this theme directly in the empirical models presented here. This exclusion is based on the complexity of the modelling required and the trade-off between such specificity and a more generalised view of wellbeing and housing tenure. There are nevertheless some important insights from the wellbeing literature.

Ownership as a positional good?

In my use of 'positional goods' I refer to the social comparisons that we are all prone to when we value the worth of what we have. The obvious example is the value of designer brands or luxury goods. To some degree these are valued (and priced in the market) to the degree that they are exclusive: a badge of good taste, membership or success (Luttmer, 2005; Clark et al, 2008; Cheung and Lucas, 2016).

This has been studied quite extensively in the wellbeing literature, particularly in the domain of income inequality (Luttmer, 2005; Clark et al, 2008; Cheung and Lucas, 2016). The broad consensus, perhaps unsurprisingly, is that satisfaction with life is lower if we compare ourselves with those who have more than us. Luttmer, for example, finds that living in an affluent neighbourhood can reduce a person's satisfaction with life and, moreover, that this effect is stronger for those who socialise with neighbours rather than with people outside their neighbourhood (Luttmer, 2005).

When we turn to housing tenure, one potential mechanism through which owner-occupiers may experience higher levels of life satisfaction than renters is a sense of relative social status (Foye et al, 2018). This need not be a conscious awareness. In the case of the experience of social renters in the UK it may indeed be internalised as an unconscious assimilation of narratives of shame and stigma (see Chapter 3).

For some owners, a sense of relative higher status could also be in some sense unconscious, where the value of ownership operates at the deep level of *doxa*. But we can also capture a more conscious sense, closer to the vernacular of 'keeping up with the Joneses'. In more theoretical language this is expressed in terms of positional goods, which take at least some of their value from their exclusivity: I may value my luxury branded shoes in part because they mark me out as a member of an exclusive group, a position that relies on the status of the excluded majority. It is this sense of positional status that Foye and colleagues (2018) explore through BHPS data. The status-conferring role of homeownership is driven by comparison with non-owners and this, argue Foye and colleagues, means that the less exclusive ownership is, the less it will increase the subjective wellbeing of owners, as the satisfaction of comparative status advantage is diminished.

Exploring potential explanations of this finding, the authors' analysis then seeks to understand both the extent to which ownership is a 'social norm', and the extent to which exclusion from this norm is detrimental to wellbeing. Of particular concern for the authors is the possibility that increasing levels of homeownership may trigger a form of status anxiety among renters, especially for those whose primary 'reference group' is dominated by homeowners. Defining 'relevant others' as those in the same age group in the same region and with the same level of education, Foye and colleagues (2018) track changes in how individuals rate the importance of owning their home. Their sense of wellbeing is measured by the same GHQ items employed in my models, though these items are pooled in a slightly different way.[1] Their more evaluative sense of wellbeing is based on responses to the same question used in my analysis: 'How dissatisfied or satisfied are you with your life overall?'

Foye and colleagues (2018) find a negative impact on the wellbeing (as measured by the GHQ-12 items in the BHPS) of renters who experience a growth in the proportion of their peers who own their homes. They also find that owners do indeed value ownership less as it becomes more widespread in their reference group, and it thereby loses some of its comparative status advantage. But there is a crucial twist: while there is a significant positional effect on satisfaction with life, there is no such effect on depression (GHQ caseness). Satisfaction with life diverges from more hedonic notions of 'happiness' (for an extended discussion, see Angel and Gregory, 2021).

Another set of intriguing results emerge in an Australian study of the relationship between satisfaction with life, housing tenure, and relationship status (Stillman and Liang, 2010). Using longitudinal data from the Australian HILDA survey (with a similar instrument to the GHQ-12), Stillman and Laing used a fixed effects model to test the idea that higher life satisfaction among owner-occupiers may be influenced by whether or not the respondent cohabits with a stable partner. They find that those owners in a stable relationship do indeed report higher satisfaction with life than owners not in a relationship. Yet they also find that there is no comparable effect on the experiential or hedonic measures of wellbeing, or on mental health outcomes such as depression (Stillman and Laing, 2010, p 2, table 4). There is, again, a divergence between two components of subjective wellbeing. I return to this issue in towards the end of this chapter.

The dependent variable(s)

In this analysis my central concern is with the effect of housing tenure on three related measures of wellbeing. These wellbeing measures are our dependent variables. The first of these is the GHQ Likert, which is treated here as a measure of depression. The second is general happiness. The third is satisfaction with life. GHQ Likert is a score of 0 to 36, with higher scores implying a higher level of depression. Happiness is treated in the analysis as a dummy yes/no response to the statement: 'Have you recently been feeling reasonably happy, all things considered?' Life satisfaction is based on scaled responses (1 to 7) when survey participants are asked to rate their satisfaction with 'life overall'. 1 is 'not satisfied at all' and 7 is 'completely satisfied'.

These variables do not of course represent all aspects of wellbeing. We should instead treat them as convenient proxies for wellbeing. There are other potential metrics that could be used within BHPS/Understanding Society, and there are of course different metrics in different datasets. For example, the Australian equivalent of the BHPS uses the Mental Component Summary of the Short Form 36 health questionnaire, rather than the GHQ. Psychologists will argue the pros and cons of these and other survey instruments, and considerable energy is spent 'validating' the ability of different metrics to capture the underlying empirical phenomenon of a person's mental and emotional state (see Diener et al, 2018). For my purposes, however, it is unnecessary to enter into these debates in order to explore the social policy context of wellbeing.

The independent variable: housing 'tenure'

In legal theory, 'tenure' is a legal status: the form of contract that gives a person the right to occupy their home (Bright, 1998). In the case of renters, this is a contract with the landlord. Owners have a different set of rights. The most important of these are the dual rights of exclusive use and the right to transfer their property to someone else, through sale, or gift of legacy (Ruonavaara, 1993). In reality, fewer owners than we might expect fully possess such rights (Bright and Hopkins, 2011). Mortgaged owners do not fully own their home, of course, but there are also restrictions on the rights of those who own only a leasehold (rather than a freehold) and therefore rent the land on which their home is built. Nevertheless, as I have argued, home ownership is still regarded as a superior form of housing – and still confers the social status of 'owner'.

Tenure is different from 'dwelling'. This is simply a property that is used for accommodation. But it becomes more complex when we turn to dwelling 'type' (for example, a flat or house) and physical characteristics, primarily quality of build and maintenance. These characteristics – or housing factors (Clapham et al, 2018) – are not intrinsic to any tenure and we may, for example, find an owner-occupied home to be a poorer dwelling than a rented home. The fact that, historically, social housing has sometimes been of poorer quality is a contingent housing factor, not a necessary tenure characteristic.

Controlling for housing factors: dwelling and neighbourhood

In my introductory remarks on the search for a tenure effect I drew on David Clapham's categorisation of housing factors (Clapham et al, 2018). It is well established that unsustainable housing costs have a negative effect on both physical health (Pevalin et al, 2008; Thomson and Thomas, 2015) and on psychological wellbeing (Nettleton and Burrows, 1998; ; Bentley et al, 2016).

It is also unsurprising that the quality of place and neighbourhood has a significant effect on a person's wellbeing. A range of studies confirm this (Guite et al, 2006; Kearns et al, 2000, 2012; Bond et al, 2012. For renters, the role of landlords is also important. Responsive landlords have a positive influence on wellbeing (Evans, 2003; Holding et al, 2020), though the evidence for this is largely based on social rather than private landlords. It is, however, important to exercise continued care to control for such considerations in statistical analysis.

It is crucial to control for these housing factors in the models presented here. These models are able to do so by taking into account a person's income and housing costs, thereby addressing financial stress as a potential source of low wellbeing. To a lesser extent we are also able to control the quality and the dwelling itself, as well as the neighbourhood in which the survey participant lives. While there is a good level of information on these housing factors in some BHPS waves, they are not available in all waves. So to some extent we have to extrapolate conclusions from slightly more limited data.

The first wave of the BHPS was in 1991 and comprised interviews with approximately 10,300 people (over 5,000 households across the UK) in the home on an annual basis. A sample from Northern Ireland was added in 2001. At the final wave in 2008 there were just over 8,000 participants. Of these, approximately 6,500 chose to join the first wave of Understanding Society. This sample was first interviewed in the second wave of Understanding Society, and was added to the 40,000 households that participated in the first wave of the new survey. Both models presented in the following sections use 12 waves of data from the BHPS and its successor, Understanding Society. The first wave of Understanding Society was in 2009, when the BHPS closed. In the final wave of the BHPS, participants were invited to join Understanding Society. From both BHPS and Understanding Society we have been able to construct our 12 waves, from 1991 to the most recent Understanding Society wave, 2017–2019.

There are some disadvantages in using the BHPS and Understanding Society as a combined dataset. The main problem is the way in which some variables from the BHPS are dropped in Understanding Society, or are reframed in a way that makes clear comparison difficult. For my purposes this poses particular challenges in controlling for the impact of dwelling quality and the impact of neighbourhoods on wellbeing. The BHPS has rich data on the quality of the home and includes explicit questions on issues such as damp, noise, and space, these are dropped in Understanding Society. For ease of interpretation these issues are controlled for in a separate model (see Appendix A) that does not include any data from Understanding Society.

Causal or compositional: controlling for selection effects

Where the BHPS/Understanding Society really comes into its own is in the depth of data that it contains for individuals, who were followed over time in successive waves of the survey. This kind of longitudinal data allows us to investigate hidden effects that we cannot immediately see in the data. As we have seen, a key issue here is the influence on wellbeing of unseen individual characteristics such as personality. It may, for example, transpire that the more naturally optimistic are more likely to become owners. So if owners are more likely to be cheerful, the worry is that it is this predisposition rather than housing tenure that is driving the results.

In the first set of models I present a fixed effects approach that allows us to address the cheery/miserable disposition problem. The fixed effect techniques used here therefore allow us to control for the unobserved and 'time-invariant' characteristics of survey participants. This will not tell us *what* these characteristics are. But it does allow us to significantly reduce the possibility that we have missed the real cause of any tenure effect we find, and to affirm that the *direction* of such an effect is indeed from tenure *to* wellbeing, rather than the other way round. These results offer the more robust answer to the question: is there a causal process in which tenure itself influences individual wellbeing? My results show there is not.

We can think of this set of results as a view into what is happening *within* people; we look at the same person over time and ask if a particular event has had an effect on their wellbeing. A key example here is the effect that we might see when someone moves from being a social tenant to being an owner (see Popham et al, 2015). Fixed effect models are widely used in recent BHPS work on housing and wellbeing (Fujiwara, 2013; Popham et al, 2015; Foye, 2017). In the housing literature, fixed effects modelling has become the standard approach to panel data and is also used in the German (Zumbro, 2014) and Australian research I later draw on (Baker et al, 2013; Bentley et al, 2016).[2]

But there is also a different question: what types of people live in different tenures, and do they vary in terms of their wellbeing? If we take wellbeing as the starting point and dig into the situation and individual characteristics of people with higher or lower wellbeing, in what type of housing are they likely to live?

This is the compositional question outlined earlier. When exploring the *effect* of tenure we need to be sure that our results control for these outcomes, ensuring that we do not mistake a causal process for what is really a compositional or selection effect; in other words, that it is simply the case that people with (for example) higher wellbeing are more likely to become owners in the first place. Knowing that this is (or is not) the case is crucially important. This is also a central concern in accounts of social housing and employment. If we want to understand social housing and 'worklessness' we need to acknowledge – and control for – the fact that people who are unemployed or economically inactive are more likely to qualify for social housing in the first place. But this does not, in either case, necessarily mean that we should treat a compositional relationship between tenure and wellbeing as 'merely' or 'only' compositional, and that the task is then to show what is 'really' going on. The correct judgement here depends on the question we are asking.

In this case we are now looking at *between* person effects. Here we are interested in comparing the variation of individual characteristics and social contexts that are correlated with housing tenure. Is one type of person more likely to be an owner, or social tenant, than another? I therefore present a second set of results. These are based on a 'random effects' methodology. Often this kind of random effects model is presented before a fixed effects model. It is assumed to be the less robust of the two approaches, and is less able than the fixed effects model to control for factors that may otherwise be mistaken for a tenure effect. In particular, the random effects model does not control for the unobserved characteristics that are of interest when looking for a possible effect of tenure on specific individual outcomes.

However, the robustness of the fixed effects model can also be a weakness, as it can obscure significant statistical associations that may 'only' be compositional but which nevertheless point towards the ways in which tenure interacts with a wider range of social issues and phenomena. Even if we cannot be sure that individual characteristics and outcomes are a *result* of social housing, we still want to know what these outcomes are and, moreover, how they compare with individual outcomes in other tenures.

Results

In the following sections I present a series of tables. Of these, Tables 6.1 to 6.3 are of the most importance to the central theme of this book: the relationship between housing tenure and wellbeing. These three tables present the most salient results of the statistical modelling. Full models are presented in Appendices A to E. There are only three tenure groups named in the tables: owned outright, owned with a mortgage and private rented. The reference group is the social tenant (not listed in the tables). All comparisons are with this group. For example, when we see that the mortgaged owner is more likely to be depressed, we are comparing her to a social tenant. Similarly, when we say an outright owner is no more likely to be depressed, the baseline comparison is again with the social tenant.

Non-housing factors

Notably, health and employment status are significant across the wellbeing variables. This is intuitively unsurprising and fits the broader evidence base. Similarly, financial struggle has a negative impact on all aspects of wellbeing, and in both the fixed and random effects models.

There are also some significant population level divergences (shown in Appendices C to E) across the three wellbeing variables. These are shown only in the random effects model, as fixed effects modelling excludes time-invariant (fixed) characteristics such as gender and ethnicity. What we find in the random effects model is that women are more likely to be depressed than men, men are more likely to be happy than women but, contrariwise, men are also less likely to be satisfied with life. This is again in line with the current evidence base.

The random effects model also shows some interesting variation between ethnic groups (shown in Appendices C to E). Black and Asian British respondents are less likely than White British to be satisfied with life, in contrast to their higher level of happiness, and lower likelihood of being depressed (see Table 6.1). It is particularly interesting to see further variation between Asian British and Black British in terms of satisfaction with life.

Table 6.1: Housing tenure and satisfaction with life

Variables	Satisfaction with life (fixed effect)	Satisfaction with life (random effect)
Age: 25–49	-0.020	-0.177***
Age: 50–64	0.060	-0.069***
Age: 65–79	0.098*	0.148***
Age: 80	0.004	0.113**
Marital status: single	-0.158***	-0.186***
Marital status: cohabiting	0.007	0.007
Household size	-0.029***	-0.018**
Health: excellent, very good or good	0.272***	0.432***
Health: long-standing illness or impairment	-0.079***	-0.132***
Employment: unemployed	-0.205***	-0.212***
Employment: retired	0.088***	0.121***
Current financial situation: living comfortably	0.301***	0.432***
Current financial situation: doing alright	0.184***	0.248***
Current financial situation: quite difficult	-0.220***	-0.299***
Current financial situation: very difficult	-0.524***	-0.643***
Future financial situation: better than now	0.025**	0.037***
Future financial situation: worse than now	-0.032**	-0.070***
Tenure: owned outright	-0.040	-0.022
Tenure: owned with mortgage	-0.090*	-0.074**
Tenure: other rented (privately or from employer)	-0.008	0.040
Number of rooms	-0.001	0.001
Having problems paying for house	-0.127***	-0.144***
Likes neighbourhood	0.112***	0.261***
Constant	4.920***	5.038***
Year dummies controlled		
Region dummies controlled		
Observations	55,028	55,028
Number of pidp[3]	17,927	17,927

*** p<0.01, ** p<0.05, * p<0.1

Here it is only for Asian British that there is a significant association with higher satisfaction with life. It should be noted, however, that the random effects model cannot tell us what is driving these differences, just that they are present and significant.

The importance of financial stability

Although my direct concern in this book is with housing and wellbeing, one of the most important findings in the data is that a person's financial situation is central to wellbeing. People who struggle financially tend to be:

- more depressed;
- less happy;
- less satisfied with life.

This is hardly a revelation. Nevertheless, it bears emphasis for two reasons. First, if we were to ultimately find that housing tenure plays a relatively minor role in wellbeing, this must be acknowledged when considering the place of housing provision in the wider welfare state.

Second, we know that the experience of social housing tenants is one in which their housing situation intersects with a range of other issues and challenges. Many of these experiences are shared by people in the private rental sector and, to a lesser extent, among owner-occupiers. One of the greatest financial burdens of all households are their housing costs, which have a striking effect on poverty rates. Social renters are also more likely than the population as a whole to experience low pay and insecure unemployment, much of it based on precarious zero-hour contracts. In sum, financial difficulties are often also housing issues. In policy terms, a lack of truly affordable housing is one of the key drivers of financial stress, and therefore of lower wellbeing (see Tables 6.2 and 6.3).

Housing factors

There are a number of issues that emerge in the data that relate to housing factors (as distinct from tenure). The first is the number of rooms in the household, adjusted for household size. Here we find the number of rooms is strongly associated with happiness and depression in the random effects model, though the association is less clear in the fixed effects model.

We can treat this as a proxy for adequate housing, though not for physical quality itself. This is harder to control for as the data are not consistent across all waves. Where possible I have used 'space', 'heating' and 'damp' as dwelling quality controls. Only space has a negative effect in GHQ Likert

Table 6.2: Housing tenure and depression (GHQ-12)

Variables	GHQ (fixed effect)	GHQ (random effect)
Age: 25–49	0.164	0.592***
Age: 50–64	0.061	0.408***
Age: 65–79	-0.007	0.088
Age: 80	0.448	0.702***
Marital status: single	-0.273*	-0.348***
Marital status: cohabiting	-0.128	-0.182**
Health: excellent, very good or good	-1.658***	-2.229***
Health: long-standing illness	0.549***	0.770***
Employment: unemployed	1.168***	1.144***
Employment: retired	-0.379***	-0.216**
Current financial situation: living comfortably	-1.150***	-1.470***
Current financial situation: doing alright	-0.795***	-0.929***
Current financial situation: quite difficult	1.594***	1.810***
Current financial situation: very difficult	3.159***	3.543***
Future financial situation: better than now	-0.248***	-0.330***
Future financial situation: worse than now	0.353***	0.491***
Tenure: owned outright	0.095	0.187
Tenure: owned with mortgage	0.280	0.324**
Tenure: other rented (privately or from employer)	0.029	0.061
Number of rooms	0.038	0.049***
Having problems paying for house	0.686***	0.743***
Likes neighbourhood	-0.685***	-1.044***
Constant	12.611***	13.018***
Year dummies controlled		
Region dummies controlled		
Observations	68,420	68,420
Number of pidp	19,172	19,172

*** $p<0.01$, ** $p<0.05$, * $p<0.1$

(depression), and only in the random effects model, and none of the quality controls has an effect on happiness. However, all three have a negative effect on satisfaction with life, but only in the random effects model. These results are to be found in Appendices C to E.

Table 6.3: Housing tenure and happiness

Variables	Happy (fixed effect)	Happy (random effect)
Age: 25–49	0.009	-0.060***
Age: 50–64	0.010	-0.071***
Age: 65–79	0.009	-0.067***
Age: 80	-0.005	-0.090***
Marital status: single	0.008	0.025***
Marital status: cohabiting	0.030*	0.039***
Household size	-0.007	0.001
Health: excellent, very good or good	0.123***	0.155***
Health: long-standing illness or impairment	-0.056***	-0.055***
Employment: unemployed	-0.092***	-0.082***
Employment: retired	0.062***	0.033***
Current financial situation: living comfortably	0.111***	0.113***
Current financial situation: doing alright	0.073***	0.070***
Current financial situation: quite difficult	-0.145***	-0.156***
Current financial situation: very difficult	-0.299***	-0.323***
Future financial situation: better than now	0.038***	0.050***
Future financial situation: worse than now	-0.018**	-0.032***
Tenure: owned outright	-0.004	-0.034**
Tenure: owned with mortgage	-0.027	-0.045***
Tenure: other rented (privately or from employer)	0.022	0.011
Number of rooms	-0.005	-0.005***
Having problems paying for house	-0.056***	-0.048***
Likes neighbourhood	0.061***	0.095***
Constant	2.729***	2.875***
Year dummies controlled		
Region dummies controlled		
Observations	69,048	69,048
Number of pidp	19,218	19,218

*** $p<0.01$, ** $p<0.05$, * $p<0.1$

We can also see an effect of Housing Benefit on depression in the full fixed effects model, and this becomes slightly more pronounced in the random effects model: those in receipt of housing being are more likely to be depressed There is also a relationship between Housing Benefit and lower levels of happiness and lower satisfaction with life, though only in the random effects model. Finally, we can see across all models, and for all three wellbeing outcomes, that whether or not a person likes their neighbourhood has a consistently significant and large effect on their wellbeing.

Housing tenure and wellbeing: 'just' compositional?

In the following results we can see that there are notable differences between the fixed and random effects models. All of these results are based on comparisons with social housing – my reference group in the models.

Fixed effects

With the exception of a weak (but still statistically significant) relationship between mortgaged owner-occupation and lower satisfaction with life, the most important result is the null finding:

• There is no relationship between tenure and wellbeing in the fixed effects model: *when we control for fixed characteristics such as personality and temperament, housing tenure does is not associated with greater individual wellbeing.*

Random effects

In the random effects model:

• Mortgaged owners are still significantly *more likely* to be *depressed* than social renters. But there are no differences in depression when we compare social renters with either outright owners or private renters.
• In the random effects model both outright and mortgaged owners are significantly *less* likely to be *happy* when compared directly with renters.
• Mortgaged owners are also less likely to be satisfied with life than social renters. But there is no difference in life satisfaction when outright owners and private renters are compared with social renters.

Discussion

I earlier outlined a narrative structure in which a random effects model shows dramatic results that disappear when a fixed effects model comes along and shows us what is 'really' going on. It can do so because the model is able to control for the time-invariant or fixed characteristics – a naturally cheery disposition perhaps – that might otherwise be confused for a tenure effect. In this narrative a random effects model is too vague and cannot distinguish between cause and correlation.

When we look more closely at these results there are three notable effects that are not present in the fixed effects model. The first is that when controlling for a wide range of socio-demographic factors and housing quality in neither model do we see an effect of social housing tenure on the GHQ Likert variable. In other words we do not see a negative effect of social housing on depression and mental health. This is an important finding: social housing *per se* is not 'bad' for you, once we have stripped out the influence on housing factors that can be present in any tenure. Although some may not find this surprising, it should be stressed, as I have done throughout my argument, that the political narrative of housing in the UK does indeed run along such lines. The political narrative continues to be reinforced in the ostensibly apolitical sphere of administrative fact, as we shall see in Chapter 5.

Conversely, we *do* see a relationship between housing tenure and wellbeing for mortgaged owners. Compared with social renters, mortgaged are more likely to be depressed. Mortgaged owners are also less likely to be satisfied with life than social renters and less likely to be happy. In a direct comparison of social renters and outright owners, the latter are less likely to be happy, but there is no difference in life satisfaction and depression in this comparison. These outcomes are presented in summary form in Table 6.4.

The finding that mortgaged owners are worse off across all three wellbeing outcomes is striking, especially when we consider that the model has controlled for housing costs and financial struggle: this is not a simple case of financial overstretch bringing down overall wellbeing. It is of course possible that the controls in the random effects model do not fully differentiate the associations with financial struggle and wellbeing from the tenure–wellbeing associations. As stressed in Chapter 1, there is also great socioeconomic diversity among owner-occupiers, and significant variation in housing factors such as quality, cost, and amenity. With the complex tenure stratification described earlier there is a commensurate risk that the models I employ have under- or overplayed the importance of one or another factor.

However, the results summarised in Table 6.4 are supported by recent analysis of UK versus Austrian owners, using a similar methodology to the random effects model presented in this chapter. In this analysis there is no apparent influence of tenure on the wellbeing of social or private renters in either country, but those who own with a mortgage in the UK (but not Austria) are less likely to be satisfied with life (Angel and Gregory, 2021).

Table 6.4: Summary of (compositional) tenure–wellbeing outcomes

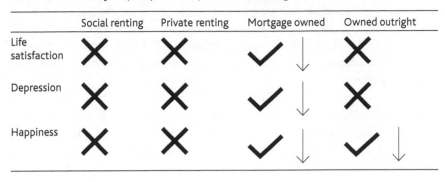

	Social renting	Private renting	Mortgage owned	Owned outright
Life satisfaction	✗	✗	✓ ↓	✗
Depression	✗	✗	✓ ↓	✗
Happiness	✗	✗	✓ ↓	✓ ↓

This conclusion holds regardless of housing costs and is consistent with other studies of tenure and wellbeing using the same data (for example, Acolin, 2020). It is also notable that we do not see the negative influence of housing costs bringing down the wellbeing private renters in the models presented here.

Given what we know about the current complexion of the private rental market (including the overlap with the benefits cuts of the past decade), this is an indication that we should look elsewhere for the sources of lower levels of wellbeing among mortgaged owners. A good place to start is the changing profile of mortgaged owners, which has shifted from a relatively broad base in the 1980s towards a greater concentration of professionals and managers (Wallace et al, 2018). An external observer might conclude that, relative to the groups now excluded from ownership, the new generation of owners enjoy a privileged position. If so, the lower levels of wellbeing of this group remains a puzzle.

But the perhaps the salient reference group is not drawn from their own generation. For at least the past 15 years this group has faced ever-increasing barriers to ownership, and it is possible that lower wellbeing reflects a more subtle sense of unmet expectation created by the experiences of their class peers in previous generations (see Crawford and McKee, 2018, for a development of this kind of argument). For many people born into the middle classes in the 1960s and '70s, it would have been taken for granted that a conventional career progression would be compatible with an unproblematic path to ownership. Yet the reality today is that those in the higher-paid professions – doctors, lawyers, and, even, bankers – will find it a stretch to become owner-occupiers. This does not of course account for intergenerational transfers of wealth – the so-called 'bank of mum and dad'. The comparison is therefore not just within generations, but between them. Compared with their parents, younger owners may feel a degree of relative deprivation.

Nor does it account for intergenerational transfers of wealth, or for a range of potential interactions that are not included in my models. Experiences of the home also vary, even between people whose 'housing factors' are very similar. So we should be wary of overgeneralisation. But there are some wider socioeconomic shifts that would help us make sense of the intuition that the lives and wellbeing of today's (mortgaged) owners are qualitatively different from those of previous generations of owners. Even for the most affluent there has still been a significant disruption of expectations and, for some people, this might even amount to a disrupted sense of ontological security.

Some of the transformations that stand out are: changes in the provision and cost of childcare over the past 20 to 30 years; increasing insecurity of employment and longer working hours; the loss of pension rights; and increased pool of global competition in the property market. In all these respects the UK stands out from comparable welfare regimes across Europe. It has gone harder and faster on welfare retrenchment and labour market reforms, while also leading the way on mortgage market deregulation from the 1980s onwards.

The complexity of these interactions would stretch even the most sophisticated statistical models. We certainly could not sensibly 'control for' all these factors. So my suggestion here is necessarily tentative. The data I have presented only takes us so far, and different statistical methods would also yield different results. In this case, we would also probably see different results across all tenures, rather than just for the group of mortgaged owners. As we have seen, there is no apparent tenure–wellbeing interaction (for any group) in the fixed effect model I present. In the case of mental health (GHQ-12), this is not a surprise: I am unaware of any fixed effects modelling that has found a significant relationship between housing tenure and mental health.

But there are indications of a tenure effect on satisfaction with life in other fixed effects models (Stillman and Liang, 2010; Foye et al, 2018). It is notable that these studies are more specific than my own, as they explore the relationship between tenure and wellbeing for smaller sub-groups, and are designed to yield direct comparisons within tenure. So it is possible that the modelling I employ is too broad-brush to pick up a more subtle status effects. Yet rather than having to decide that one set of fixed effects results is more accurate than another, it is more fruitful to consider how they may be complementary. Of particular interest would be the extension of Foye and colleagues' (2018) line of enquiry across generations: if we take older generations as the reference group will we see signs of lower satisfaction with life among the younger generation of owners?

There are then further questions regarding the relationship between different components of wellbeing. My results indicate that mortgaged owners do worse across the board. But for outright owners there is a curious divergence between happiness, depression, and satisfaction with life.

Outright owners, it seems, are less happy than social and private renters, but otherwise satisfied. This outcome is in some respects anomalous: it does not arise in the wider literature and, unlike the divergence between happiness and satisfaction in other studies, it is hard to think of potential explanations. But the fact there is potential divergence of wellbeing outcomes within tenure groups is not surprising. As we have seen, there are some significant divergences in other studies, and these give rise to some intuitively appealing hypotheses.

Of these, one of the most interesting lines of enquiry is the possibility of a status effect that lowers life satisfaction but does not affect mental health. Under what circumstances does this divergence happen, and does it matter? Our responses to the second question will be inherently normative. Some will feel that the absence of a direct effect on the harder metrics of mental health means that any effect on satisfaction with life is of limited consequence; regrettable perhaps, but not a concern for public policy. Others will feel that a tenure-driven hierarchy of life satisfaction is indeed a matter of social justice, and a primary purpose of a redistributive state to correct or at least mitigate such inequalities. From either perspective, the results I report for mortgaged owners should, at the very least, cause us to reconsider the value – social and individual – of owner occupation.

Part B: tenure and labour markets

There is one more set of results to consider in this chapter: the relationship between social housing and employment status. My treatment of these results is briefer than my discussion of wellbeing. But, as I have argued, the discourses associated with social housing and 'worklessness' are central to ways in which the meaning and purpose of social housing are constructed and contested.

The context of the results presented here is the assertion that social housing creates welfare dependency. This assertion was the subject of Chapter 3. One of the points at issue was the high rates of unemployment and economic inactivity among social tenants. More specifically, the question is whether or not social housing in some way causes these high rates. The alternative explanation is that the high rates of unemployment and economic inactivity simply reflect the fact that people with these labour market characteristics are more likely to be allocated a social home in the first place. Earlier I introduced evidence that suggests that this is not the case. Using longitudinal data going back to 1946, Feinstein and colleagues (2008) found that, even with a wide range of controls, social tenants of working age are still less likely to be working than people in other tenures. It is to be recalled, however, that this was not the case for the cohort of social tenants born in 1946.

Despite the centrality of dependency claims to the social housing debate, there is in fact relatively little in-depth statistical analysis of the issue. For the most part there is a recognition that 'worklessness' within social housing is likely to reflect the allocations process. But the extent of any remaining association – once we have controlled for selection effects – is rarely systematically addressed.

A recent exception is analysis from the Resolution Foundation. Using four years of data (2014–2018), Judge notes a large gap in the employment rate of working-age social tenants, compared with private renters and owner-occupiers (Judge, 2019). Roughly 50 per cent of social renters were working, compared with around 80 per cent of owners and private renters, and a third of social renters were economically inactive – twice the level of economic inactivity among renters and owners. But controlling for selection effects – based on the allocations criterion of social housing – Judge finds that the gap dramatically narrows. With these controls, 67 per cent of social tenants are working, compared with 79 per cent of owners and private renters. As Judge remarks, this is still a large gap and 'should not be waved away or ignored' (2019).

In the following paragraphs I offer a slightly different perspective on the relationship between social housing and labour markets. Instead of looking directly at employment statistics, I consider the relationship between social housing and a stated desire to give up paid work. Once again I present results from both a fixed effects and a random effects model. Table 6.5 shows the following fixed effects results:

- There is no significant relationship between tenure and a desire to give up paid work.
- There is a clear association with financial struggle and the desire to give up paid work, with those finding financial conditions very difficult being more likely to want to give up work.
- There is an association between financial struggle and wanting to start a business: those struggling financially are more likely to say they would like to start their own business, while those who are financially comfortable are less likely to do so.

Table 6.6 shows the following random effects results:

- Asian or Asian British are less likely than White British to want to give up paid work and more likely to want to start their own business. The association is similar for Black British.
- As in the fixed effects model, there is an association between financial struggle and respondents saying both that they would like to start their own business and that they would like to give up paid work.

- In the case of tenure we see that there is only one significant association – mortgaged owners are *more* likely to want to give up paid work than social or private renters.

As we can see in the fixed effects, there is no within-tenure association between tenure and a desire to give up work. Social housing does not create an aversion to work. Equally, there is no fixed effect relationship between ownership and the generation of a greater entrepreneurial spirit sometimes claimed in narratives of property-owning democracy, or by some advocates of asset-based welfare. What we do see is that those who are struggling financially are, regardless of tenure, more likely to want to give up paid work. Indeed, even when viewed from the random effects perspective (Table 6.6) there is nothing to suggest a negative 'tenure effect'. Specifically, there is no evidence that social housing creates aversion to work, even accounting for the greater prevalence of worklessness within social housing. Once again it is in fact the mortgaged owner that stands out: she is more likely to want to quit work if she can.

Wellbeing and future policy: three guiding facts

There are three very clear conclusions that now bear special emphasis. We have seen that financial difficulties have a very marked effect on all aspects of wellbeing in both of the models presented. And with the data on poverty and housing costs, we arrive at two clear policy conclusions:

- There is a direct line from unaffordable housing to lower wellbeing, with a clear impact on mental health as well as on satisfaction with life.
- Of all the tenure groups examined in this chapter, it is mortgaged owners that fare worst across all three measures of wellbeing. Conversely, there is no consistent association between social housing and lower wellbeing.

In my statistical analysis I sought to exclude housing costs (one of the most important 'housing factors') as a potential driver of wellbeing. The intention was to isolate a possible tenure effect that was wholly due to social status, or to something else that is intrinsic to social housing. Here we can see that, if we care about wellbeing, there is a powerful case for the provision of more social housing. This is not just about 'happiness'. It also presents a case for housing intervention on public health grounds.

The same process also established a fundamentally important relationship between wellbeing and a key 'housing factor': neighbourhood. We therefore arrive at a third clear conclusion:

Table 6.5: Would like to give up work or start a business (fixed effects)

Variables	Would like to give up paid work	Would like to start own business
Age: 25–49	1.540***	0.922
Age: 50–64	1.533***	0.715**
Age: 65–79	1.153	0.220***
Marital status: single	0.608***	1.192
Marital status: cohabiting	0.927	1.293***
Household size	0.955	1.040
Number of dependent children: 1	0.952	1.134*
Number of dependent children: 2	0.975	1.020
Number of dependent children: 3	0.841	0.966
Number of dependent children: 4+	0.879	0.718
Education: GCSE	1.027	0.969
Education: A-level	1.215	0.842
Education: degree or higher	1.697*	1.129
Education: other qualification	1.279	1.185
Health: excellent, very good or good	0.804***	0.921
Health: long-standing illness or impairment	1.060	1.110**
Current financial situation: living comfortably	0.885**	0.799***
Current financial situation: doing alright	0.929*	0.850***
Current financial situation: quite difficult	1.065	1.172*
Current financial situation: very difficult	1.350**	1.483**
Future financial situation: better than now	1.047	1.157***
Future financial situation: worse than now	1.314***	0.990
Individual income	1.199***	1.038
Rent including Housing Benefit	1.021	1.039
Benefits: Housing Benefit	0.614*	1.061
Benefits: other	1.002	1.114**
Tenure: owned outright	1.290*	0.935
Tenure: owned with mortgage	1.235	1.048
Tenure: other rented (privately or from employer)	0.802*	0.895
Employment: self-employed	0.667***	0.582***
Employment: retired	1.117	0.505
Job_other	1.328***	0.829

Table 6.5: Would like to give up work or start a business (fixed effects) (continued)

Variables	Would like to give up paid work	Would like to start own business
Year dummies controlled		
Region dummies controlled		
Observations	26,464	15,707
Number of pidp	7,711	4,765

*** p<0.01, ** p<0.05, * p<0.1

Table 6.6: Would like to give up work or start a business (random effects)

Variables	Would like to give up paid work	Would like to start own business
Age: 25–49	2.979***	0.808***
Age: 50–64	4.216***	0.401***
Age: 65–79	1.718***	0.105***
Gender: male	1.030	2.102***
Ethnicity: Asian or Asian British	0.315***	1.841***
Ethnicity: Black or Black British	0.705***	4.126***
Ethnicity: other	0.772**	2.360***
Marital status: single	0.465***	1.206***
Marital status: cohabiting	0.887***	1.548***
Marital status: other than single/married/cohabiting	0.793***	1.124*
Household size	0.908***	1.038**
Number of dependent children: 1	0.909**	1.033
Number of dependent children: 2	0.937	0.909*
Number of dependent children: 3	0.806***	0.860*
Number of dependent children: 4+	0.908	0.789*
Education: GCSE	1.179***	1.366***
Education: A-level	1.145**	1.408***
Education: degree or higher	0.915	1.458***
Education: other qualification	1.195**	1.232**
Health: excellent, very good or good	0.711***	0.852***
Health: long-standing illness or impairment	1.214***	1.115***
Current financial situation: living comfortably	0.623***	0.649***
Current financial situation: doing alright	0.797***	0.733***

(continued)

Table 6.6: Would like to give up work or a start business (random effects) (continued)

Variables	Would like to give up paid work	Would like to start own business
Current financial situation: quite difficult	1.087	1.249***
Current financial situation: very difficult	1.479***	1.941***
Future financial situation: better than now	1.031	1.600***
Future financial situation: worse than now	1.581***	1.267***
Individual income	1.254***	1.054***
Rent including Housing Benefit	0.984	1.034**
Benefits: Housing Benefit	0.582***	0.890
Benefits: other	1.025	0.932**
Tenure: owned outright	1.159*	0.880
Tenure: owned with mortgage	1.350***	1.121
Tenure: other rented (privately or from employer)	1.003	1.119*
Employment: unemployed	0.752	1.498*
Employment: self-employed	0.490***	1.095*
Employment: retired	0.542***	0.437**
Year dummies controlled		
Region dummies controlled		
Observations	83,451	82,688
Number of pidp	40,529	40,345

*** $p < 0.01$, ** $p < 0.05$, * $p < 0.1$

- There is a direct line from positive feeling about neighbourhood to positive wellbeing and mental health, including greater satisfaction with life.

What we build is as important as how much we build – the acute need for more housing must not lead to the later emergence of negative 'housing factors' that depress wellbeing. I first stressed the importance of neighbourhood in Chapter 5. This has been confirmed in my analysis in the current chapter, where one of the strongest statistical results is the relationship between wellbeing and a positive feeling about one's neighbourhood. Place-based policies and planning strategies must therefore be at the heart of any social housing development.

This is not simply a matter of learning from past mistakes. Some post-war mass council housing was poorly planned, both in terms of internal layout, and in terms of connection to surrounding neighbourhoods, services, and labour markets. In the rush to volume in the 1960s there was also a marked decline in the quality of materials, design, and building processes (Dunleavey,

1981). How we manage neighbourhoods is equally important. There is no revelation to report here. The key determinants of satisfaction are well known: good public services and schools, a reasonable state of repair and upkeep across the neighbourhood, perceived safety, and an absence of anti-social behaviour (see Permentier et al, 2011). The political and financial challenges of meeting these conditions are another matter.

PART III

Rethinking the 'social' in social housing: common needs, shared identities

Social housing and welfare spheres

The purpose of this chapter is to draw the broad outlines of a policy framework for social housing in the UK. For the most part, my concern is with the common parameters shared by the nations of the UK. These parameters include the issues and themes discussed in Parts I and II. The overarching commonality that unites the regions and nations of the UK in relation to housing is the rise, and subsequent decline, of mass council housing alongside the longstanding bias in favour of owner-occupation. Between these two main tenures, the private rental sector steadily declined in size and significance, until its remarkable resurgence in the last two decades.

Some of the argument presented in this chapter relies on broad generalisations and typological abstractions. In the first half of the chapter I present a stylised view of social housing and compare it with the NHS. The intention is illustrative and is not to be interpreted as an empirical judgement of the actual state of social housing, either today or in the past. It will be seen that social housing is contrasted, unfavourably, with the universality and popular legitimacy of the NHS. This intentionally represents one aspect of the British welfare state in its best 'Sunday dress', taking for granted the founding claim that we all access the best available health care, regardless of place of socioeconomic status. In contrast, social housing represents the welfare state at its worst. In this I take a liberty with the actual state of social housing as a system, both historically and contemporaneously.

My motivation for this typological characterisation is twofold. First, as highlighted in Chapter 1, the worst of social housing has had a powerful symbolic effect, with negative consequences for the sector as a whole (Dunleavy, 1981; Malpass, 2005). Second, we are now, perhaps, at a crossroads in the story of social housing in the UK. The extent and nature of unmet housing need, across all tenures and for a very wide range of income groups, is at a point where we could reasonably compare current challenges with earlier turning points in the story of social housing. Overcrowding, poor quality, and unaffordability set the context of previous waves of large-scale intervention – the problems that mass social housing arose to meet. The backdrop was market failure, not social housing failure. But, equally, current need invites us to think about what kind of system we would design if we were to build social housing from scratch. So my second motivation in presenting a typological picture of social housing is to provide a form of visual guidance, a very rough compass bearing, pointing to where we might want to go.

Older paths and new branches: post-residual social housing?

Chapter 1 outlined to the growing significance of the private rental sector in the UK. After many years of slow decline, the proportion of people living in the private rental sector has increased dramatically, from roughly 10 per cent in 2003 to 20 per cent today. This pattern was last seen in the 1960s, at a time when the private rental sector came to be associated with poor quality, insecurity, and overcrowding. This was also a period in which massive state intervention allowed large numbers of private tenants to move into social housing. We are now at a point where we need a similar scale of government intervention in the housing market. The private rental market fails to meet the needs of too many people.

I have sought to present a balanced picture of the subsequent social dynamics associated with the social housing of this period. The general pattern was of high quality and amenity. But there were also some poorly planned and built estates that undermined the reputation of the sector as a whole. Further developments – particularly the loss of stock through the Right to Buy – led to changes in the composition of people living in social housing. This in turn has allowed negative caricatures of needy and undeserving social tenants to take hold. As I argued in Part I, it is a legacy that creates institutional and cultural feedback loops, in which a targeted and residual distribution of social housing creates a particular social meaning, namely that social housing is only 'for' a 'needy' – and potentially 'undeserving' or 'dependent' – segment of society. This in turn creates a political environment – discussed in Part I – in which the case for more social housing is harder to make, a process in which 'effect becomes cause' (Pierson, 1993).

Yet there some signs that the trend towards greater residualisation has slowed or even reversed. As shown in Table 7.1, the year after the introduction of the Right to Buy, 47 per cent of social tenants were working. This dropped to 30 per cent ten years later, and has now risen again to 45 per cent. These figures must of course be taken in the broader context. The proportion of retired households also rose significantly from 1981 to 1991. Similarly, the complexion of 'other' is also important, as it will generally refer to working-age people who have left the labour market entirely. The broad trend, however, is clear.

There are also signs of a trend away from income residualisation – the concentration of the lowest-income households in social housing. This has occurred at a time when a majority of European countries have been moving in the opposite direction, with a growing income gap between households in the social and private rental sectors (Angel, 2021).

If this trend is to continue we need to ensure that we break away from the negative feedback loop described earlier. So my task now is to re-examine this dynamic in light of the evidence presented on housing tenure and wellbeing. In the process I offer some limited comment on other welfare

Table 7.1: Economic activity of social renters in England, 1981–2020

Year	Working (%)	Unemployed (%)	Retired (%)	Other (%)
1981	47	8	29	16
1991	30	10	40	20
2006	32	6	33	30
2001	-	-	-	-
2010–2011	32	10	31	27
2015–2016	42	7	28	22
2019–2020	45	6	25	24

Source: DLHC and MHCLG (2021b)

regimes, in comparable countries, as a means of illustrating the nature of some of the policy choices and political challenges that we must confront (for wider discussion of housing and welfare regimes see Torgersen, 1987; Malpass, 2008; Harloe, 2008; Lowe, 2011).

My second task is to examine more closely the sphere of social housing in comparison with other welfare spheres. I do so with reference to an *idealised* and typological representation of social housing, shown in Figure 7.1, which presents the two forms of social distance introduced in Chapter 1: metaphorical and spatial social distance. The aim is to help us think about the kind of housing system we would want, given the opportunity for mass expansion.

It will be recalled that the distinction in Chapter 1 was framed with reference to an important question in the British Social Attitudes Survey: 'In general, how comfortable or uncomfortable would you feel about living next to this [social] type of housing?'

The social distance of experience and imagination

This is the metaphorical social distance felt by the person whose life experiences are disconnected from those needing targeted or means-tested welfare provision. The distance arises in the case of means-tested and conditional income support. It also arises through the needs-based allocation of social housing in the UK. The inability to place ourselves in such a position is a failure of empathy or imagination.

Spatial distance and social separation

This is the literal spatial distance that exists where social housing is densely concentrated and disconnected from other types of housing and from

Figure 7.1: Two axes of separation

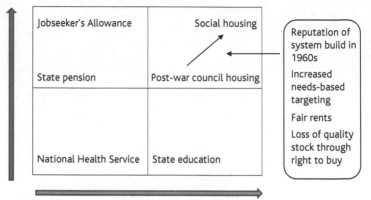

Metaphorical social distance (targeted welfare)

Spatial social distance (place, planning and, services)

surrounding neighbourhoods. The separation is such that there may be a strong visual association between social housing and a needy 'other', and the same spatial separation acts as a barrier to a greater degree of empathy and understanding of the lives and experiences of social tenants.

Metaphorical social distance (targeted welfare and decommodification)

Figure 7.1 represents a stylised contrast between social housing, working-age cash benefits, the state pension, education and the NHS. The vertical axis represents the degree to which each sphere of welfare is targeted. In the upper left-hand corner is Jobseeker's Allowance. This is a means-tested and targeted cash benefit for unemployed people. As we saw in Chapter 3, it is also a conditional benefit, demanding specified actions and behaviour from the claimant. The state pension appears in the same quadrant, but at a lower point. This is because the basic state pension is a universal entitlement but rarely meets living requirements and is therefore widely supplemented by means tested top-ups, currently through Pension Credit.

In the bottom left-hand corner is the NHS, which is the exemplar of universal welfare provision in the UK. We can also treat the NHS as a lifecycle good, meaning that we all draw on it at some point in our lives. Although it is possible to consider a hypothetical individual born with no professional assistance and able to go through life with no medical need, the vast majority of people will have recourse to the NHS at crucial stages in their lives, even if they avoid serious accident or injury. Even accounting for the growth of private healthcare provision, experience of the NHS is a normal part of life in the UK. This stands in contrast to the treatment of social housing as an exceptional remedy, or intervention in a life that has not conformed either to the social norm, or to the expectations of the UK's housing regime.

Social housing sits in the top right-hand corner. On the far right of Figure 7.1 are the key drivers of residualisation as discussed in this book. In the next section I address the position of social housing on the horizontal axis (and hence its place on the right-hand side of Figure 7.1). Its place on the vertical axis, meanwhile, is due to its status as a highly targeted good, distributed on the basis of need. Its status as decommodified good is more complex. It is not free at the point of use for anyone, regardless of their income, and the costs are not fully recoverable.

The vertical axis of Figure 7.1 conforms to the classic comparative framework, which runs along two dimensions. The first is the extent to which different welfare goods are decommodified (being removed from the sphere of market provision and the ability to pay). The second classic comparative dimension is the extent to which welfare goods are either a universal service for all (as with the NHS) or are targeted at a specific group, most often viewed in terms of cash benefits to compensate for loss of income during periods of unemployment (Esping-Andersen, 1990).

Spatial social distance (place, planning, and services)

The horizontal axis of Figure 7.1 represents the extent to which welfare goods are prone to spatial separation. My representation of this form of social distance is less precise than on the vertical axis. Whereas we could (in principle) quantify the degree to which income replacement in the UK sorts people into different categories, the spatial dimension is less precise and more typological. While the NHS is in principle a universal service and distributed evenly across different locations, the reality is a little more complex, with health services not always meeting the needs of some communities, and with some significant variation in the resources and quality of hospital care.

My presentation of education also comes with some caveats. It sits in the bottom right-hand corner because it is a universal good, free to all, but on the right-hand side because of the clear potential for state education to carry the place-based stigma of 'sink schools'. But this is a potentiality rather than a certainty. Equally, though social housing sits on the right-hand side because of history of spatial separation and visual demarcation, I do not claim that is the norm, either today or in longer history of social housing. Yet, as argued in Chapters 1 and 3, the residualisation of social housing has an undeniable spatial dimension, one that still exerts considerable influence on perceptions of social housing and social tenants. This is not a novel observation (see, for example, Hastings and Dean, 2003; Hastings, 2004; Murie, 2016). But there has, I believe, been insufficient attention paid to the interaction of the two forms of social distance addressed in this chapter.

Spatial separation can of course also occur through other sorting processes. These can be cultural, as when immigrant communities emerge and then attract households from similar backgrounds. More importantly, there are also processes of market and income sorting (which can overlap with cultural sorting, as we saw in the case of Sparkbrook, Birmingham).[1] Income and market sorting occurs across tenures and lower-income neighbourhoods are generally mixed tenure. This is equally true of large social housing developments that are now composed of owner-occupied Right to Buy properties, and former social properties that are now currently rented privately.

The argument to come applies as much to these neighbourhoods as it does to those that were (or still are) 'mono-tenure' estates. Both dimensions of social distance potentially coincide where large segments of the population live in areas marked off as 'deprived', or in some respect 'other'.

Figure 7.2 presents the interaction of the two dimensions of social distance. The proposed mechanism is the one outlined in Chapter 1: literal spatial distance and separation potentially feeds or maintains negative perceptions of social tenants, and, I have argued, these perceptions may become attached to broader anxieties about welfare dependency, even where it is acknowledged that claimants are not social tenants. This process is represented at the top of Figure 7.2 by the arrow from the top right-hand quadrant to the top left-hand quadrant. Spatial distance feeds into metaphorical social distance.

I have described this vertical (metaphorical) distance at a number of points in this book. As a residualised and targeted good, the meaning of social housing in the UK is shaped by a process of filtering based on the greatest need, creating a stigmatised and apparently undeserving 'other'. As observed by Bo Rothstein, 'the very act of separating out the needy almost always stamps them as socially inferior, as "others" with other types of social characteristics and needs' (Rothstein, 1998, p 158). This is supported by the literature on social psychology: group demarcation (our 'naming') can create 'moral exclusion' where the poor are not considered to be part of our 'community of responsibility' (Montada and Schneider, 1989; Optow, 1990), and social distance can reduce perceptions of 'deservingness' (van Oorschot, 2000).

There is now another branch of political science to consider, and some further observations from the social psychology literature. In political science there has been a long-running debate on neighbourhood and social capital. This debate was influential in much of the neighbourhood policy developed in the late 1990s and 2000s and played a role in the 'peer effects' discussed in Chapter 4. The key distinction was between 'bonding' and 'bridging' social capital. The former refers to thick social ties in tight communities and the latter to the opportunity to form connections, and hence opportunities, through interaction with a broader range of people. The distinction tiptoes around the concept of culture and localised social norms, but the implication is the same: concentrated poverty constrains social horizons and may thus have a self-sustaining element.

Another stand of debate taken up by political scientists is the relationship between ethnic diversity and a range of phenomena loosely falling under the label of 'cohesion'. Of these the most famous is Putnam's 'bowling alone' thesis (Putnam, 2000). In this he argues that ethnic diversity undermines trust both within diverse neighbourhoods and between these communities and other neighbourhoods. The theme has been taken up by others, who argue that diversity undermines the solidarity needed to underpin a strong welfare state (for example, Alesina and Ferrara, 2000; for a critical discussion, see Banting and Kymlicka, 2006)

Both claims have been disputed. One objection is that the bulk of negative evidence comes from the US (for example, Alesina and Ferrara, 2000), where the history of racial segregation is such that it cautions against generalisation from one culture to another. It has also been argued that the negative case, asserting that diversity undermines cohesion, rests on a weak theoretical framework (Hewstone, 2015). If a strong negative effect is found (and with a full range of controls of the type applied in Chapter 6), we may still not know how or why this arises, or how it varies with context. A direct relationship may be found, but it is the processes underlying this relationship that really matter. Of particular importance is the role of neighbourhood deprivation, which has been shown to have a negative influence on trust and social capital (Letki, 2008). With a strong association between ethnically diverse and deprived neighbourhoods, it has yet to be shown that it is really diversity – rather than poverty – that is driving the negative diversity thesis.

There is also an opposing body of research, finding that contact and interaction within and between diverse communities has the opposite, positive effect (Pettigrew, 1998; Hewstone, 2015). One of the leading exponents of 'contact theory' summarises as follows:

> It is ... now well established that not only the frequency (or quantity) of contact, but importantly, the quality of contact determines the extent to which contact positively affects outgroup attitudes. Further, contact occurs via processes of generalization of positive attitudes from the encountered individual to the wider outgroup ... which are strengthened when group memberships are made salient, and occur especially via affective processes such as reduced intergroup anxiety and increased empathy. (Hewstone, 2015, p 420)

This conclusion offers significant support for the argument advanced in this chapter, albeit with one important difference: the large body of work that Hewstone and others have undertaken is, almost exclusively, concerned with ethnic or religious diversity, with socioeconomic status treated as a control rather as a central object of enquiry. This reflects a broader phenomenon in contemporary sociology and political science. Although there are still niche studies and researchers dedicated to social class, there are many significant domains of enquiry where 'class' only enters as an afterthought, if at all. Ethnic diversity and cohesion is the case in point: why should we not start first with the differences that people construct on the basis of the hierarchy of respectability and the vaunted virtue of 'independence'? There is, as it were, plenty of prejudice to go around – stigma in this case does not discriminate on the basis of race.

Living next door: empathy, distribution, and the virtue of compassion

In contrast to Hewstone and others working on contact theory, my focus is on the 'other' of welfare dependency.[2] Class or social status is the crucial question that lies just beneath the surface of our 'comfort' or discomfort at living next door to a social tenant. The tenant may, of course, identify as an ethnic or religious minority. But it is the social attribution of 'dependency' that creates a toxic view of social housing in the UK – one that is sustained by the spatial distance presented in Figures 7.1 and 7.2.

This brings us to a final feature of Figure 7.2. The diagonal line from the top right-hand to the bottom left-hand quadrant is intended to depict the direction of change advocated in this chapter. If we are able to distribute social housing to a significantly wider group of people – with less of the stigma associated with targeted welfare goods – we can hope to move social housing lower down the vertical axis. At the same time, if we are able to integrate social housing spatially we may also move social housing along the horizontal axis. It would be naïve – and arguably undesirable – to expect social housing to move all the way to the (idealised) status of the NHS, but the representation is typological. The further down the line of the arrow we can move social housing, the further we come to the kind of widely valued welfare good many of us believe social housing should be.

My argument goes further than this. If we bring different people together within the same neighbourhood, it is possible to arrive at the same reduced anxiety and increased empathy that Hewstone describes. This, in turn, may alter attitudes towards the welfare state more broadly, not just towards social housing. Spatial proximity is the structural condition needed for people to make the leap of imagination that reduces the 'other' in metaphorical social distance.

Chapters 3 and 4 considered some of the dominant accounts of neighbourhood and culture. In these narratives there is a negative effect

Figure 7.2: Spatial influences on metaphorical social distance

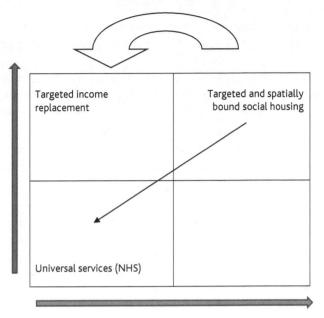

on behaviour and character: concentrated poverty and unemployment is represented by some as a self-sustaining 'culture' – one that suppresses the virtues of independence and self-reliance. Other accounts are softer. These accounts may accept the role of culture (or 'social capital') in sustaining poverty and 'worklessness', but without the same sense of overt moral judgement. The proposed solution is to develop more economically diverse communities, creating positive peer effects that broaden the horizons of those not in work. What we do not find in any of these accounts is ethical scrutiny of the peer who chooses to live in a deprived neighbourhood, or of apparently 'independent' owners who seek to place as much distance as they can – both spatial and metaphorical – between themselves and the underserving poor. But it is to this type of person that we must direct our ethical gaze if we want to bring the language of virtue into a richer, more balanced, discourse of welfare and wellbeing.

In the argument developed here, it is the virtue of empathy that is of primary importance. Elsewhere I have referred to this as the 'compassion thesis' (Gregory, 2015). A very similar account has since been developed, independently, by Sayer (Sayer, 2020).

The intuition I seek to harness in this account is derived from philosophers David Hume and Adam Smith and is based on the natural response of sympathy.

This allows us to shine the light of character appraisal on those we rarely judge in these terms – the owner who would feel uncomfortable living next door to a social tenant. Instead of the vice of dependency, we may concentrate more on the vice of nimbyism, or the character failings of individuals who are unmoved when confronted by the lived experience of poverty, or who unable to make the leap of imagination required to live in another person's shoes.

For this to have practical impact we need to shrink real, spatial difference: we cannot feel the impulse of sympathy if we are not there to see the person trip. This does not, however, require a thick account of democratic participation, or of sustained social interaction. Mix does not imply *mixing*. All that we need – in the model I offer – is the simpler requirement of *proximity*. With this in mind, I now turn to the challenges of bringing us closer to this kind of spatial mix.

Housing, wellbeing, and the welfare state in 2022: key developments

At this point it is useful to draw out the key policy developments and social trends that have emerged over the past decade. In the next, final, chapter I turn to political strategies of reform.

An attempt at a comprehensive review would be burdensome. Where possible I point to further resources, where greater detail and analysis of particular policy strands can be found. I therefore confine myself to five general headings, focusing on the issues that are most relevant to the arguments developed in Parts I and II. Recent policy developments are also considered from the perspective of the two dimensions of social distance set out previously.

The most strikingly obvious development is of course the emergence of the global COVID-19 pandemic and the differential impact it has had on UK households. My remarks here are to some degree speculative and I do not include the pandemic as one of five policy areas addressed in this section. But there are some early indications of what we might expect to find. Internal and external space stands out as one of the key elements of wellbeing during periods of lockdown. Overcrowding is a particular problem in the social housing sector and in some segments of the private rental sector.

This will have a direct impact on the experience of working or schooling from home, and it is likely to emerge as one of the key determinants of wellbeing and mental health. There are also some startling inequalities when we look at external space. Across the UK one in eight households has no access to an outside space. In England there are also inequalities between White British and Black households. The latter are four times more likely than White households to have no outdoor space (ONS, 2020).

A reminder of the facts of housing need also helps to the set the context of the discussion to come. I have previously drawn on the analytical category of decommodification. Later I press the argument that there is no clean distinction between commodified and decommodified housing in the UK. This is especially apparent when we consider the fiscal bias in favour of owner-occupation – a *de facto* form of decommodification.

But my immediate concern here is not with the legitimacy or economic efficiencies of any of these subsidies. Rather, it is with a very direct and uncomplicated empirical fact: there is not *enough* housing decommodification to protect households from income poverty. This applies not just to social tenants, but also to private renters, for whom the gap between before and after housing cost poverty (taking this as 60 per cent of median household income) is ten percentage points, just below a 12 percentage point gap for social tenants. These figures are shown in Table 1.1 earlier, which shows the percentage of working households in the UK experiencing poverty before and after housing costs. A closer look shows that the gap in the proportion of households in poverty after housing costs nearly doubles for private renters, compared with an increase of 50 per cent for social renters.

To this we must add the higher proportion of poor-quality homes (see Harris et al, 2020) and the precarious rights of private renters in England and Wales, where the default rental contract is for six months (with two months' notice), and the landlord has the right to a 'no fault eviction', where no reason for ending the tenancy needs to be given. In a radical departure from this regime, the Scottish Parliament voted for Private Housing (Tenancies) (Scotland) Act 2016, and since 2017 private renters in Scotland rent under an open-ended contract that can only be terminated for specific, codified reasons (see Marsh and Gibbs, 2019).

Income poverty is one of the key metrics discussed Chapters 1 and 2. In these chapters I also discussed the relativity of poverty, and of the evolving meaning of what it is to be poor in any given society. As Adam Smith observed, standards of poverty must be understood with reference to social norms, and account for the goods which we all need if we are not to feel shame in our society. I return to this theme later in the chapter. In the following sections, however, I outline the five central housing issues that should be addressed.

The right to a home and the discharge of local authority duties

Since devolution the countries of the UK have been able to pursue different approaches to allocation. Here, again, we see a marked divergence between England and Scotland, marking very different normative orientations to the purpose and meaning of social housing. In Scotland, the Homelessless etc. (Scotland) Act 2003 created a distinctive social commitment to provide all homeless people with social housing as a right. This became a legal right, rather than a policy aspiration or goal, with the Homelessness (Abolition of Priority Need Test) (Scotland) Order 2012.

England has moved in a different direction. One of the most significant provisions of the Localism Act 2011 allows councils to discharge their homelessness duties by housing a homeless person in the private rental sector. Previously an applicant was able to refuse this option and wait for a social home. Now there is no longer a right of refusal – and some households inevitably have to face the insecurity and financial pressures of an often dysfunctional market.

From April 2012 social landlords in England have been able to offer new applicants 'flexible' rather than secure tenancies, potentially offering only a two-year contract. This is in principle a highly significant change from the lifetime tenancies introduced in the Housing Act 1980 (the same Act that brought in the Right to Buy), though in practice few social landlords opted to use these tenancies and many are reverting to the offer of a full lifetime tenancy (Curry, 2019).

The rhetoric behind these reforms plays on an ambiguity that, at first sight, may be interpreted as an attempt to re-legitimate social housing. By shifting the system away from a needs-based system, and by allowing councils give greater priority to applicants in full employment, the Localism Act 2011 was at times presented as a way of creating greater social mix within social housing. But the dominant narrative was one of an underserving poor, from whom good citizens would wish to maintain a healthy social distance, both metaphorically and spatially. This is made explicit in 2012 government guidance on social housing allocations: 'For years the system for social housing has been associated with injustice – where rewards are reaped for those who know how to play the system best' (MHCLG, 2012).

Social rent, supply, and 'affordable housing'

In 2010 the government introduced a new affordable rent tenancy, in which housing associations can let homes at up to 80 per cent of the open market rent, reduced to 60 per cent in London. This contrasts with the more traditional 'social rent', which typically does not rise above 60 per cent of market rates. The difference can be seen in the mean rent of a one-bedroom flat, which in 2017/18 was just under £100 a week for social rent, and just over £160 for affordable rent.

This innovation came at the same time as massive cuts to the capital subsidy available for the construction of new social homes, leaving social landlords more reliant on cross-subsidy from private developers (see the section on planning and the market), while also making the greater revenue available from affordable rent more attractive – from a financial perspective – than social rents. What remained of the tax-funded capital subsidy was also subject to new restrictions, with a presumption that capital grants be used for affordable rent or affordable ownership.

The idea of a wider affordable rent could, in principle, play a valuable role. Wider options in a broader social housing system could do much to break down the vertical distance of a targeted system, introducing something like a progressive universalism. This is the route now being taken in Scotland, and one that I advocate in my own outline.

But the reality of implementation is very different in England, and must be viewed in terms of real-world outcomes. Despite the label of 'affordable' rent, there is near-unanimous agreement that it is not. How we define affordability is a little more contested, but there is some consensus emerging around a cost-to-net-income ratio of one to three. By this measure, a recent affordability study finds that 16 per cent of social renters and 51 per cent of private renters in England live in unaffordable housing (Affordable Housing Commission, 2020, p 68).

In 2021 a new five-year Affordable Homes Programme was announced, in which £11.5 billion will be made available in capital subsidy. The indications are that half the budget will be for affordable ownership, mostly shared ownership, but with provision for a new First Homes scheme, which replaces Starter Homes. There has also been a loose promise of funding for social rent as well as affordable rent, though it remains to be seen what this will entail in practice.

Research on housing need and supply, based on population data from 2015/16, predicts a need for 380,000 new homes a year across the UK. This figure is based not just on new household formation, but also a backlog of unmet need, with approximately 4.75 million households with unmet housing needs. In England alone it is estimated that 1.6 million households would have needed social housing if their needs were to be adequately met, at an affordable price (Chartered Institute of Housing, 2021, chapter 2). Although net annual additions have increased significantly over the past decade, there are fewer than 250,000 new additions a year in England, which is forecast to need 340,000 new homes a year. Scotland, however, is ahead of the game, with supply outpacing projected household growth.

One of the consequence of inadequate supply is overcrowding. Figures from the 2019/20 English Housing Survey show that 8.7 per cent of social homes and 6.7 per cent of private rental homes in England were overcrowded, compared with 1.2 per cent of owner-occupied homes (Wilson and Barton, 2021a). There is has been a long-term trend of increasing overcrowding in both rental sectors. In part this reflects rising housing costs and broader market trends, coupled with decreasing social housing supply. But overcrowding has also been driven, specifically, by the cuts to LHA, as discussed in Chapter 1 (Crisis, 2019; Clair, 2021). Higher prices and lower purchasing power can lead to forced downsizing – or to spatial displacement (or both).

Follow the money: the spatial impact of a residual housing allowance

I have argued that there is a neglected spatial effect on attitudes to means-tested cash transfers. Of these, Housing Benefit has been one of the most important, and one of the greatest government expenditures. In 2008 a new system for calculating entitlements was introduced for private renters: the LHA. Prior to this maximum Housing Benefit for renters was assessed on a case-by-case basis, by a council rent officer.

When first introduced in 2008 LHA covered 50 per cent of local rents. This was then cut to 30 per cent in 2011, followed by a freeze on LHA rises from 2016 to 2020. At the same time, however, there have been average increases in private rents of 7 per cent, across the UK, from 2015–2019. At present, the Housing Benefit bill is roughly £22 billion a year – dwarfing the capital subsidy available for new social housing.

The policy language behind the development and launch of the LHA has a familiar tone (see Chapter 3), being couched in terms of incentives and as part of New Labour's programme of welfare reform: 'In some areas, Housing Benefit can support customers to live in accommodation that many people in work cannot afford. This makes it harder for customers to come off Housing Benefit when they move into work' (DWP, 2009, p 7). Shopping for value in the open market was also presented as a form of economic and moral tutelage: 'Customers can then make more informed choices about their housing needs and clear comparisons about the levels of support which is available towards their housing costs. It also provides greater personal responsibility by, in most cases, paying benefit directly to the customer.' (DWP, 2009, p 10).

In this early iteration there is a repeated stress on the value of mixed communities. Yet, at the same time, the belief that the Housing Benefit system was unfair (and that it encouraged welfare dependency) was stated explicitly – just the kind of thinking that underlies the metaphorical social distance outlined earlier. This language becomes stronger – and the fairness/dependency message more strident – with the arrival of the coalition government in 2010. But the process was already well underway. The development of LHA has also had a direct impact on spatial distance, which, in turn, feeds into the metaphorical social distance that 'fairness' and efficiency both appeals to and maintains.

LHA in 2018/19 was not sufficient to cover the rent of a single person, couple or small family in 92 per cent of areas in the UK. Renters in England are worst hit and excluded from 97 per cent of areas, while Scotland is significantly less restrictive, with 67 per cent of areas not covered (Crisis, 2019). In the London boroughs of Hackney, Islington and Tower Hamlets, only 2 per cent of the market was in reach for small families needing a two-bedroom property.

Data on the extent to which this kind of exclusion has led to spatial displacement is scarce – in contrast to a host of studies that demonstrate a relationship between LHA shortfalls, overcrowding, and increased material deprivation. Some displacement will be avoided by emergency budgeting strategies (going without material necessities) and/or overcrowding, sharing housing costs. But the effect is likely to be comparable to – and probably far greater than – the displacement of social tenants as a result of urban regeneration projects. One calculation puts the figure of regeneration displacement, in London alone, at 55,000 households since 1997.[3]

This raises two further policy questions. The first calls into question the merits of a system that, despite the vast cost, does not increase the supply of affordable housing, and instead helps to sustain an unchecked private market that can be part of the problem. The second question is the potential use of rent caps to restrain inflation and thus to ease pressure on the benefits bill, while stabilising rent increases for private renters who do not qualify for Housing Benefit.

Such measures remain controversial, as a sustained decline in the supply and quality of private rental housing was driven, in part, by an inflexible rent-capping system in the 1960 and '70s. This is generally thought to have altered the financial balance in a way that discouraged private landlords from carrying out potentially costly repairs, and encouraged many landlords to leave the market (Donnison, 1967; Merrett, 1979, pp 51–53). For many years this anxiety formed the consensus view in policy circles. In one respect the response to this dilemma is quite obvious. Instead of regulating the market, the state should be *in* the market, offering an alternative at such a scale that there is a positive impact on market dynamics. In the following sections I sketch a view of this kind of intervention. The push is towards a state presence that reduces the metaphorical and literal spatial distance outlined earlier.

A note of caution is needed, however. Although there is a temptation to view the landlord as the net winner in the new private rental market that has emerged in the past two decades, we should acknowledge the parallel decline in pension security, or the same narrative of independence that encouraged people to build private assets for their retirement. Helping one group achieve security should not simply displace insecurity, pushing anxiety and hardship elsewhere. This does not, of course, rule out a very different approach to the use of residential properties as a global asset class (see the next section) or a wider evaluation of the taxation of wealth and pensions provision in the UK.

Ownership and the Right to Buy

Scotland has again pursued the boldest path, scrapping the Right to Buy entirely in 2016, in direct contrast to a highly politicised English revival in

2015. Running with the 'right to' leitmotif, there has even been a recent promise of a 'right to shared ownership', in which all housing association tenants would have an automatic right to part-buy their home, starting with a 10 per cent share but with the right to later buy the home in full.

Yet the English revival of the Right to Buy is in some respects more symbolic than real. Although discounts were increased (up to £103,900 in London or £77,900 in the rest of England), the target population did not have the same financial resources as those who bought their home in the 1980s, so in practice the new Right to Buy has not seen significant take-up (Pattison and Cole, 2020). A similar conclusion can be drawn from the attempt to extend the Right to Buy to housing association tenants.

Where we still see a real distributional impact is in the direct and indirect subsidy of owner-occupation in the open market. Some of this subsidy flows directly to individual households. Help to Buy, introduced in 2013 to stimulate the UK-wide housing market, is the most familiar example, with variants of the scheme in all the devolved nations. The scheme gave buyers access to interest-free loans for five years, the main condition being that the loan must be used to purchase a new-build home. In practice a majority of those using the scheme were not first-time buyers (NAO, 2019).

These direct housing subsidies should also be viewed in a broader political economy context. In 2019, VAT exemptions on construction costs and the sale of new builds amounted to £16.1 billion of foregone tax, while the capital gains exemption on main residences cost £24.9 billion. As the housing commentator, Jules Birch, observes: 'To put them in perspective, that CGT exemption is worth more than the pensions tax relief paid to individuals and costs about the same as Housing Benefit' (Birch, 2020).

The unequal distribution of housing wealth is also important. In 2018 the net value of residential property in the UK rose above £7 trillion, a rise of 34 per cent over ten years (Savills, 2018). But the rewards of this are heavily skewed regionally, with hugely disproportionate gains in London. Outright owners in 2018 held £2.5 trillion of housing wealth – doubling their equity in ten years.

In this mix there is also a significant proportion of overseas investors. The *Financial Times* has covered research suggesting that 1 per cent of all residential properties in England and Wales are owned by overseas buyers (*Financial Times*, 2021). In number this amounts to 250,000 homes, up from 88,000 ten years ago. Two details stand out. First, it is estimated that a fifth of the owners are domiciled in countries considered to be tax havens. Many more homes are sold to Asia (often off-plan). The second detail is the location of these properties. Overseas investor-buyers may be associated with the wealthiest areas of London, in particular, but there new homes are also being bought in the less affluent boroughs, including Newham and Tower Hamlets. The same trend is also evident in Manchester and Liverpool.

Equally, however, we should not forget the lessons of tenure stratification (see Chapter 1). A number of owners – both outright and mortgaged – struggle financially and may live in accommodation that fails below the standards of social housing. Some will also have relatively weak ownership rights, as we saw in the case of leasehold some properties. At present there is some movement towards strengthening these rights in England and Wales, with a Leasehold Reform (Ground Rents) Bill scheduled for further parliamentary debate.

The longer-term legacy of the post-2000 boom – with many standardised flats built to questionable standards and in concentrated, spatially disconnected blocks – remains to be seen. The comparison with the social developments of the 1960 and '70s is tempting.

Planning and the market

Since 2010, one of the central assertions of Conservative Party housing policy has been that planning policy is too bureaucratic and state-centric, constraining a free market that would otherwise flourish, providing a sufficiency of homes for all. The key target is Section 106 the Town and Country Planning Act 1990 in England and Wales. This allows (but does not oblige) local authorities to require developers to provide a number of social housing units. In Scotland essentially the same mechanism falls under the Town and Country Planning (Scotland) Act 1997. The loss of Section 106 finance is a threat to the future of social housing. In 2018/19 half all affordable homes built in England were financed in this way (for useful discussions, see Jones et al, 2018; Crook and Whitehead, 2019).

A recent White Paper – *Planning for the future* – has finally set out the government's vision for a new regime: 'Reform will enable us to sweep away months of negotiation of Section 106 agreements and the need to consider site viability'. One headline proposal, since dropped, was to increase the size of developments to which Section 106 agreements can apply. At present Section 106 agreements can be applied to developments of ten or more private homes. The proposal was to raise this to 40 or 50. Ostensibly this was to encourage smaller builders into the market, as it would allow them to develop on a larger scale without the burden of planning obligation.

Although the government's own modelling suggests that this policy would reduce funding for affordable housing by 10–20 per cent, its confidence in market forces is such that a significant rise in private housing supply will balance the scales. Notably, a similar logic was in evidence when LHA was introduced. This too was expected to affect the housing market, with less generous housing allowance forcing landlords to reduce rents. As we have seen, there has been no such effect.

The significance of the proposed planning reforms goes beyond the issue of housing supply viewed in terms of volume. The real failing of the Section 106 regime has not been that it discourages developers from building at all. The problem, rather, is that the system has evolved in such a way that it can encourage them to build badly. Contrary to the suggestion that developers are disadvantaged by a planning negotiation process, the more common scenario has been a kind of gaming, in which private developers seek to pare down the cost of affordable units, particularly units for social rent.

There has also been a tendency to segment the design of developments, with social tenants spatially separated from owner-occupiers, having to walk through separate 'poor doors' to access their home. The extent of such practices is actually hard to verify. In some cases the existence of separate entrances is the result of difficult financial compromises. The symbolism, however, is apt. Regardless of the stated reasons for separate entrances, the image of poor doors is powerful because it is true to the underlying reality of social separation and status ranking.

Planned spatial segmentation is particularly problematic in regeneration projects, where old social housing stock is demolished and replaced with mixed-tenure developments. There have been several high-profile cases in which social tenants were moved ('decanted') for the duration of the project. One of the most notorious examples is the redevelopment of the Heygate Estate in London. It has been estimated that just one in five social tenants were able to continue living in the same postcode (see Lees and White, 2020).[4] The regeneration of the Heygate has also led to a real loss of social housing, with fewer than one in three planned or completed homes being affordable (at 80 per cent of market rate) and still fewer let at a social rent.

But this is not always a fair judgement. Much of the redevelopment of the surrounding area comes closer to the kind of mixed development (and mixed economy) I argue for, and can be part of a broader view of social housing. The neighbouring Aylesbury estate – the site of one of Tony Blair's first major speeches as Prime Minister in 1997 – also loses social homes, but with the addition of more private homes increases the total available housing stock.

It is not my intention to adjudicate the facts of any particular case. As in the case of post-war council housing developments, there will be extremes of good and bad, with many variations in between. What we can do is to take the worst and best cases and use these as templates of what we should aim for, and of what we must not allow to happen again.

Conclusion

The challenges outlined in this chapter present a compelling case for more social housing, built at scale and available to a wider range of income groups. What form this takes, however, is a more complex question. A simple return to mass social housing provided by the state is unlikely to meet the more complex housing needs of today's population, and a single 'social' tenure may not be suitable, or desirable, for some people. More fundamentally, a housing system that has only one form of social housing invites binary distinctions between social and private. The reality is that there is surprisingly little housing, in any tenure, for which we could not say is subsidised by the state.

One political approach to this would be a vocal articulation of the distributive facts of housing subsidy, pointing to the contradictions of a contrast between 'dependent' social tenants and 'independent' owners. This should be part of the argument. But it risks blurring the more fundamental fact that good housing is central to everyone's wellbeing, including those who have a lower income but want to own, as well as those who might want to carve out a portion (or all of) their life course in a high-quality private rental sector.

My argument is that social housing – whether provided by the state, local authorities or housing associations – could do a lot more to meet these diverse needs. This is not just about the massive financial investment that can only be delivered through the power of the state. It is also a much more fluid approach to the relationship between state and market. I do not advocate another dose of marketisation. The case, rather, is for the state to take control and be more active in the market, at times a direct player – with all the might this brings in the competition for custom of 'market share'. The following, final, chapter sketches the shape of this system and its possible place within a broader account of wellbeing and the welfare state.

8

Rethinking the 'social' in social housing: common needs, shared identities

The two principles driving this policy outline are, first, that housing need is wider and more diverse in its form than it has been for most of the post-war period, and, second, that individual needs and preferences are far less fixed than they have been in the past. Housing associations play a key role in creating this new offer, building for the open market as well as social rent. Often this practice has either been condemned as neoliberal or viewed at best as a necessary means of cross-subsiding social housing. This chapter thus builds on the previous chapter to make a principled case for a 'hybrid' housing model, taking us towards a more mixed housing model that combines state and market in a way that prioritises social over commercial value (for discussions of hybridity, see Mullins and Pawson, 2010; Mullins et al, 2012; Mullins and Jones, 2015).

In some respects this hybridity is similar to the early development of social housing, when charitable trusts such as Guinness and Peabody developed limited-profit housing, designed for a working class whose needs were not met by the private rental sector. By the same token, we should recognise that much of this housing was out of the reach of many working households, just as some 'affordable' housing is today.

There is also historical precedent in the more recent history of local authority housing. Local authority housing in the post-war period was part of a mixed economy and, at times, came close to a more activist role for the state *in* the market, rather than running alongside it. Councils both developed homes for sale (see Murie, 2016) and lent to would-be buyers who would otherwise be unable to access mortgage finance. The Birmingham Municipal Bank was created in 1919 and from 1923 launched a scheme intended to help council tenants buy their home, albeit at full market value (Murie, 2016), which ran in parallel with a growing council housing sector.

One historical analysis shows that over 10,000 homes were built for sale by local authorities in England and Wales between 1961 and 1967 (Murie, 2016). This is in keeping with a longer-term principle that, if not dominant at all times, has had a strong presence in the normative underpinnings of social housing policy in the UK. Another analysis of mortgage lending in the 1970s found that local authorities in England and Wales provided around 16 per cent of all mortgages in this decade, often with strict criteria based on unmet housing need, but extending to first-time buyers locked out by the retrenchment of mortgage lending during the financial crises of the 1970s (Bassett and Short, 1980).

None of this compares with the sheer scale of council-built social housing prior to 1980. And despite glimmers of a renaissance (for an account of developments in England, see Morphet and Clifford, 2020), we are far removed from the political and institutional context in which the state was expected to, and largely did, deliver mass social housing. If we were able to repeat this scale of building, however, my position would remain the same. Direct capital support for the full range of tenures – rather than an opaque tax bias favouring owners – is both necessary and desirable: necessary if we want to bring social housing into a more universal welfare state, necessary if we want a functional private rental system, and desirable if we want a more transparent and flexible way of supporting would-be owners.

Social identity in a hybrid system

We saw in Chapter 3 that the housing and welfare policies of the Conservative Party have successfully co-opted the language of life chances, and in some instances have distorted the evidence of the relationship between social housing and life chances. A 'tough love' paternalism has also been used as rhetorical cover for a form of welfare conditionality that suppresses the reality of our labour market, which at the lower end is precarious, underpaid, and unrewarding. A similar colonisation of concept and practice has taken place in both the planning reforms discussed earlier in this chapter and the category of affordable rent. It is important to reclaim the principles that are used rhetorically as a cover for outcomes that are detrimental, not just to the future of social housing, but to the housing system as a whole.

The stated principle of affordable rent was that it was meant to provide a wider range of social housing options within a broader strategy to make 'social housing more responsive, flexible and fair' (DBIS, 2010). In practice, however, it has achieved none of these objectives. Instead it has been used to supplant rather than complement social rents, and the majority of households allocated affordable rent housing would previously have paid social rents – precisely because they could not afford a higher rate. So affordable rents were not used for the middle or (relatively) higher-income households that a genuinely more flexible social housing system would be seeking to attract. If they were used in this way, we might hope to maintain social rents for the large group that need them, while also making social housing provision more universal in scope. As with the ostensible 'tough love' paternalism of welfare to work (see Chapter 3), it is difficult to take the claim for flexibility at face value, rather than treating it as a piece of political rhetoric.

But if we do want a more universal social housing system, we must embrace a more fluid approach to social rents. There is a large population that is struggling in the private rental sector, but could (unlike the current affordable rent population in England) afford a rent that is closer to market rates than social rents. A genuine attempt to offer an affordable rent could bring many more people into the system. Something like this is being developed in Scotland, with a new mid-market rent programme. This falls under its overarching More Homes Scotland initiative (launched in March 2016) – a tenure-wide strategy to increase supply for owners and private renters as well as social renters. Where the mid-market rent differs from affordable rent is in the fact that it is grant-funded, albeit aimed at middle-income households who would not qualify for social housing. Mostly provided through housing associations, early evidence suggests that it is a popular form of housing, and that it could present private landlords with real competition (Marsh and Gibb, 2019).

If landlords were to operate in this way there could be greater opportunities for households to move between tenures if and when their circumstances change. Overstretched owners might become part-owners or social tenants, or perhaps intermediate renters. Social tenants who want to own may have similar opportunities to move between tenures. Shared ownership may be particularly valuable, if the problems outlined in Chapter 5 are overcome. I have argued elsewhere that we may be able to 'shape a policy narrative around shared ownership in such a way that a positive story is told about its hybrid nature, bridging the often binary distinction between "independent" owners and "dependent" social tenants' (Gregory, 2016, p 18).

Flexibility, or insecurity? Principle and practice

An extension of the hybrid logic would be some form of flexibility based on income changes. This type of policy can be highly contentious, as it raises fears of strict means testing and threats to security of tenure. The threat to security of tenure has re-emerged in England over the past decade, first with the Localism Act 2011, which permitted housing providers to offer tenancies of between two and five years, and then with Housing and Planning Act 2016. The latter was intended to compel reluctant social landlords to take up fixed tenancies, but this was effectively dropped in 2018, when Theresa May took office as Prime Minister.

A 'Pay to Stay' policy was also included in the Housing and Planning Act 2016, though this was again quietly dropped shortly afterwards. Under this policy, as the name suggests, social tenants whose income increased were required to pay more – or lose their home. There have been a number of well-publicised examples of this, with outrage expressed over the fact that highly paid public figures (such as the late Frank Dobson, and ex-Labour

MP, and the union leader, Bob Crow, former General Secretary of the National Union of Rail, Maritime and Transport Workers) had continued to live in subsidised housing.

In its original formulation, the Pay to Stay policy was flawed in nearly every respect. Not only was it presented in highly emotive terms, it also introduced a perverse incentive not to increase income, and would in any case have raised very little money. However, the dilemma is very real. Do the rights of existing social tenants always trump the rights of those who are waiting for social housing, sometimes in conditions and life circumstances that are worse than the typical social tenant? What should be the status of affluent social tenants, and of those whose circumstances might have dramatically improved? (For further discussion, see Stephens et al, 2008; Fitzpatrick and Pawson, 2014.)

The counterpoint, of course, is that the opportunity to live in a social home improves the circumstances of many social tenants, and they should not be penalised as a result. To take away the home that enables success feels perverse, even if we could be confident that we would not be sending households on a path back to difficult circumstances. It also feels wrong to say that anyone should be made to move out of social housing if their income is considered too high.

The social and individual consequences of this are undeniably hard to justify, even in the rare cases of Dobson and Crow. Social housing in the UK is already so tightly constrained that there are many people who are in dire need but will still fail to reach the top of the waiting list. To bump more people off the list, in pursuit of mix as a social ideal, would be dogmatic. But at this point I would like to suggest an ideal towards which we might progress.

Historical comparison again shows that there is precedent, and that some form of flexible rent is not necessarily associated with small-state or right-of-centre concerns. The case in point is a system of rent pooling (see Malpass, 2005; Lowe, 2011). The Housing Act 1935 required local authorities to draw together all housing debt and expenditure into a single Housing Revenue Account (still in use today). This permitted and in theory encouraged a system of local authority rent pooling, which allowed local authorities to average out rent across all their properties. This, in combination with a system of rebates, effectively meant that higher-income social tenants could subsidise those on lower incomes.

The further question, of course, is how rent would be pooled and then redistributed. If we are to ask what council tenants should pay, we need a method of determining this. Means testing is not new in social housing. But the reasons for means testing, as well as the way in which such tests are conducted, vary in some significant ways. The most basic question of motive is the intended result: is the intention to release more resource in order to widen and strengthen social housing provision, or is the ultimate aim to encourage exit? The latter signals a different view of the purpose of social housing and, in the terms set out in Chapters 1 and 3, creates (and sustains) negative meanings of what social housing is, and who it is for.

It is the latter that has driven recent policy developments. Despite references to the greater efficiency of providing social housing only for the duration of acute need, the 'fairness' in question is a dog whistle to the sensibilities of the virtuous, independent, taxpayer. Fair rents, as well as Pay to Stay and the fixed-term tenancies of the Housing and Planning Act 2016 (in England), all sit within the ideology and politics of the small state. In parliamentary debate fixed-term tenancies were thus presented as a means of correcting an inequity heaped on the independent taxpayer, burdened with having to support the dependencies of social tenants:

'The effect … is to ask less well-off taxpayers to subsidise those who, in this case, are not in as much need of public financial support. That, in my view, is not progressive. Indeed, it is the opposite … [we should] consider those who are unable to access a social home, who are subsidising social housing through their taxes but are not benefiting from it.' (Lord O'Shaughnessy, cited in Fitzpatrick and Watts, 2017, p 1025)

In this argument for fixed tenancies it is implied that the subsidy would be recycled, or diverted to those who need it more. But in the context of the dramatic cuts to capital subsidy in the previous five years, this claim is disingenuous. The real intent is to shrink the overall spend on any form of welfare provision. The same intent was explicit in the earlier fair rents debate – which explicitly sought to channel savages back to the Treasury for general use – and in the way that central government clawed back capital receipts from the Right to Buy. In both cases, there was a twofold exit strategy: tenants were to be encouraged to exit social housing, and any fiscal savings were to follow the same exit pathway, to be diverted away from social housing.

However, the principle and practice of a flexible rent system does not have to follow this twofold logic of exit. Higher rents for some – to the extent this is possible in an already residualised system – may in fact strengthen social housing. The strength would come, first, from the use of flexible rents to finance further investment and, second, by broadening the scope of who social housing is 'for', thus reshaping the meaning of what it 'is'. Caution is needed, however. As we saw in Jacobs and colleagues' account of fair rents, greater social mix, with a more affluent social housing population, can be a double-edged sword (Jacobs et al, 2003). A broadening of scope should help insulate social housing from narratives of welfare dependency and underserving dependants. But it also reopens the potential to attack social tenants as underserving because *un*-needy. So a more flexible approach to the financial support available to social tenants is necessary if we wish to head off this resurgent narrative.

Such a system is not, however, unproblematic. The kind of pooled rental system described here may be attractive to many people because it resembles the kind of solidaristic redistribution that is associated with a strong welfare state. Yet it could also be the basis of new distinctions of division and social separation. A flourishing social sector based on this model also holds the threat of exclusion, underpinned by its own success and perceived legitimacy. A self-contained cost-rent system with a means of internal redistribution (through rebates) does not preclude the creation of new in–out groups, perhaps creating a strong corporatist identity that may be attractive, but nevertheless relies on a sense of shared identity that is shaped in part by its uniqueness. Nor would such a system automatically avoid a hierarchy within social housing. This, we should remember, is not an abstract threat. The best of council housing past was also in some respects the worst of it, with households 'graded' by housing officers and often excluded by ethnicity or marital status (Rex and Moore, 1967; Ravetz, 2001; Crowson, 2013).

There are also practical and financial limitations to face. In theory a cost-rent model of social housing can become self-financing over the long term. Once rental income has become sufficient to pay off initial debt finance, future rents could cover ongoing costs and be used to finance new development debt (Gregory et al, 2016). However, taken alone, this form of finance would have little impact on the extent of unmet needs we face today. Even if there were enough social landlords in a position to sustain their current operations, without external sources of finance there would be very limited opportunity for further expansion. Capital subsidy from central government can and should play a role. So should more hybrid forms of finance, such as the sale of homes on the open market to cross-subsidise development of social housing.

My argument here is not intended as a commentary on the design and execution of hybrid housing finance. Aside from the simple observation that we should not rely on one form of financial model to address unmet housing, my assertion is that we should not allow any one tenure to become exclusively associated with one financial model. The capital subsidy necessary for social housing comes with the risk of entrenching further a hard distinction between state and market provision, recreating the kind of social distinctions addressed in this book. The risk lies in a model of capital subsidy that is seen to insulate social housing from the market, and from other finance models. If this were to happen, we would see new meanings attached to 'social housing' as a good.

But even if newer meanings are positive, my argument is that the distinctions themselves – market/state; social/owned – are misleading and ultimately corrosive. As I have suggested, the cost-rent model, based on rent pooling and with a system of rebates, carries a similar risk.

Flexible housing support and progressive universalism

There is a third difference between the flexible rent principles suggested here and the formulation of Pay to Stay. This difference lies in the principle and practice of means testing. This takes us back to the wider issue of targeted welfare goods, in particular the (metaphorical) social distance potentially created by such goods.

Any form of flexible rent requires some form of means testing, as does a system of rebates within social housing. The key point of differentiation lies in the identification of a specific good that is *only* accessible via means testing, compared with goods that may be accessed via means-tested mechanisms, but are not strongly and/or exclusively identified with such mechanisms.

To some extent, this is what the housing benefit system might have achieved prior to the progressively stringent constraints that were imposed from 2008 onwards. But the exclusion of owner-occupiers reinforced tenure distinctions, hardening associations between social tenants and reliance on income support. Viewed anew, we might imagine a kind of universal housing allowance that all individuals carry with them, a kind of pooling and rebate system writ large. The amount of allowance would of course be means tested, but there need be no automatic association with any one tenure.

One way of doing this might be to incorporate the housing costs of all households into the general tax system, creating a form of universal housing tax credit. In this, all households would need to declare their housing costs, either through their employer (streamlining housing cost information with PAYE), or through existing administrative structures. Some households would make a net contribution, while others would receive credit, or a rebate. Surplus from net contributions could be recycled into cross-tenure capital subsidy for new development, and used exclusively for this purpose, creating something like a national housing account.

This is the roughest of outlines – a crude sketch for debate. It is not a new idea, and it shares some of the core principles of the tax credits system introduced by New Labour. The normative basis of a fully developed tax credit system lies in its universal coverage, ultimately dispensing with the need for a separate system dedicated to traditional cash transfers for out-of-work benefits. However, the system developed by New Labour was not a truly universal system, as it did not seek to include either Jobseeker's Allowance or Incapacity Benefit. It has now been supplanted by Universal Credit, which is 'universal' in so far as it brings together a series of means-tested benefits that were previously administered separately (creating the notorious 'benefit interactions'), but is far from universal in terms of the population it covers.

And, taken alone, even the most generous housing allowance would be vulnerable to economic or political change. As we have seen over the past decade, the value of an allowance can change rapidly and dramatically – at the flip of a political switch – by the simplest change in the way that inflation is measured, or by freezing uprating in line with inflation. So we should not forget the primary importance of capital subsidy and the systemic constraints of an integrated mixed economy of housing, with housing allowances systemically linked to new supply. This mix will doubtless create complex interactions, some of which will have unwanted outcomes. Yet complexity can also create systemic resilience. Capital subsidy may be slowly clawed back and assets may be privatised and sold off, but the process will be slow and complex, and difficult to pursue for short-term or ideological purposes.

Conclusion: housing and wellbeing – happiness or human flourishing?

Throughout this book I have foregrounded the contingency of the meanings we attach to social housing. My focus has been on the dominant narrative of social housing that has taken hold over the past 40 years. This narrative portrays social housing, at best, as a tenure of last resort. More often the assumption, if not the explicit assertion, is that social housing also creates a state of welfare dependency. In the face of the evidence I have presented, neither assertion is sustainable. The argument that social housing somehow causes dependency is largely incoherent, and the evidence of the relationship between housing tenure and life chances has been misinterpreted and misused to further undermine the value of social housing (see Chapter 3).

Moreover, the data presented in this book find no difference in either the mental health or 'happiness' of social tenants compared with that of either owner-occupiers or private renters. This conclusion is supported by a number of other studies that have explored the relationship between housing tenure and wellbeing, from across a range of countries (Baker et al, 2013; Popham et al, 2015; Bentley et al, 2016; Acolin, 2020).

Taken at face value, this may be an unremarkable conclusion: why would we expect one type of housing tenure to make you either happy or sad? Yet in the context of the today's housing debate – framed by a persistent and ideologically driven devaluation of social housing – it is an important conclusion.

Nevertheless, it can only take us so far. Even within the subjective wellbeing approach I have used there is room for significant variation. Some of the studies that find no happiness effect still demonstrate a significant relationship between housing tenure and satisfaction with life (Foye et al, 2018; Acolin, 2020; Angel and Gregory, 2021). We also see this kind of divergence in the primary data presented in Chapter 5. Moreover, when we relax some of the controls in the stricter (fixed effects) model in Chapter 6, we find that there *is* a significant relationship between wellbeing and housing tenure: mortgaged owners fare worse across all three wellbeing outcomes.

This might may be taken to imply that the lower levels of wellbeing among mortgaged owners is 'just' compositional. Perhaps there are hidden factors that drive lower levels of wellbeing among mortgaged owners. Some that stand out as potential explanations are greater employment insecurity and later entrance into ownership over the past 20 to 30 years. Untangling these issues is beyond the scope of the book, and possibly beyond the scope of reliable statistical data.

Even so, the 'just' still encompasses a great many people, some of whom may have been better off if they had been able to pursue different options. For this to be possible we need a larger and stronger social housing sector and a functional private rental system, ideally along the lines advocated in this chapter. Greater real choice, based on quality and affordability – and allowing a sense of long-term security – is the foundation of a housing system that would not push people into ownership as soon as they can raise the finance.

Yet choice is not just about supply and affordability. Chapter 1 highlighted the national survey question: 'Would you feel comfortable living next door to a social tenant?' Choice in this context is more complex and subtle. If we are to really expand choice we need to build a social sector that does not invite the question of social 'comfort'. This does not mean that we should tiptoe around the sensibilities of a population that may consider themselves 'better' than social tenants. The point, rather, is to close down the kind of social distance addressed in Chapter 7, and to radically expand the range of people who would be covered by a 'social' system of housing.

I have also discussed the ways in which ownership is embedded in our culture, even to the extent that it can be seen as a developmental good. The strong form of this argument is that ownership is so embedded in our cultural assumptions that it is a vital component of our ontological security. In this sense it is an expression of agency, of our will actualised. The weaker form of the argument is simply that ownership has become so embedded as a norm that it is a marker of social inclusion. Much like Adam Smith's shirtless man, without a home we cannot face society with dignity. Ownership is simply part of what it means to belong in the UK today.

Faced with this argument, we might conclude that the better strategy is to expand homeownership, not to scale it back or to encourage alternative choices. This kind of argument has sometimes been presented in the familiar language of property-owning democracy. The twist, of course, is this property-owning democracy is an egalitarian one, seeking to reclaim it from the ideological grasp of Thatcherism (for a discussion, see Gregory, 2016).

If we were to follow this programme, the aim would be to radically expand ownership, thus closing down social distance by making us all owners. The risk, however, is that there will always be a residual group of non-owners, more stigmatised than ever, and reliant on assistance that has more in common with poor-law era charity than a social democratic welfare state.

Given what we know about the wellbeing of mortgaged owners today, we might also reconsider a strategy of expansion. Even if this expansion were not to the detriment of social housing, any negative relationship between ownership and wellbeing is intrinsically undesirable.

Happy clams and human flourishing

The data used in this book represent just one aspect of individual wellbeing. It should be treated as an indicator and a guide to further research, not the end destination. If we were to extend the kind of approach I employed in Chapter 6, the recommendation would be that we need a deeper exploration of the role of neighbourhoods as determinants of happiness and life satisfaction. In this task researchers could apply a similar analysis to other datasets, some of which have yet to be applied to the housing–wellbeing issue in any great depth. The debate would also benefit from greater consideration of the relationship explored in Chapter 5, digging deeper into the ways in which the 'home' is experienced by people in all tenures.

Of particular value would be a deeper exploration of housing tenure in the Whitehall studies. These longitudinal studies have tracked a broad cohort of civil servants, covering the full range of roles (from clerks for department heads) over five decades (see Marmot and Brunner, 2005). It is from these studies that we have learnt that there is a direct effect of social status (professional seniority) and physical health. Lower-grade roles are associated with greater stress, which, in turn, leads to higher levels of cortisol and a greater risk of cardiovascular disease. Under what circumstances might we see, in the Whitehall studies, a similar status effect driven by housing tenure? Although we do not see an effect on mental health in the BHPS and Understanding Society data used in Chapter 6, it is still possible that an explicitly epidemiological dataset may yield further insights. These could perhaps demonstrate the existence of direct tenure–status effect on health, over and above 'housing factors' such as quality, cost, and location.

Such a finding would, of course, have important policy implications. If tenure really did effect health, some of the negative social relations explored in this book would suggest the need for radical intervention on public health grounds.

Conversely, the absence of any such evidence would not close the case. At most it would be a temporary stopping point for one strand of investigation, with closure (if any) only for those who believe that self-reported 'happiness' fully captures the meaning and value we attach to wellbeing. This does not, I believe, diminish the importance of subjective wellbeing metrics as a guide for public policy. On the contrary, it adds balance to other metrics of impact such as life chances. The latter, although valuable, can lead us towards a rather instrumentalist view of housing outcomes, especially when we are looking at employment-related life chances. It also, no matter how unintentionally, invites tacit moral judgement, whereas 'happiness', crucially, does not – at least not in the first instance.

But here we come full circle back to ideals of 'objective' wellbeing. If happiness metrics do not bring moral judgment in the first instance, it is only ever just around the corner. We can consider, by way of illustration, the finding that social tenants are no more or less likely to be happy than owners. But *should* they be? It would be surprising if readers of this book were to say 'no'. It would not be illogical though. Nor, once we soften the baldness of the question, is it a niche position. Maybe there is a worried concern that social tenants have misunderstood what it is to flourish in life. Something like this is hidden in the conceptual confusion of 'ontological security'. Less generous, and more likely, is the assertion that social tenants should not be happy living the life of the welfare dependant. If they are, something needs to be done, perhaps another dose of welfare reform.

Critics of the 'happiness agenda' would do well to bear these scenarios in mind when they seek to dismiss it as neoliberal Trojan Horse. If a social tenant were to tell us she is happy and satisfied with life, why not instead defend her right to be taken at face value? We could easily construct hypothetical scenarios in which our tenant was in fact wrong, duped by an oppressive system. But the context of social housing in the UK today does not lend itself to this argument. If social housing is good for subjective wellbeing, it should be championed as such.

Definition of variables

Dependent variables

GHQ

Range from 0 to 36, higher score implies higher level of depression

Variable name *scghq1_dv* in BHPS/Understanding Society, subjective wellbeing (GHQ) 1: Likert

Satisfaction with life

Range from 1 (not satisfied at all) to 7 (completely satisfied)

Variable name *lfsato* in BHPS and *sclfsato* in US: satisfaction with life overall

General happiness

Range from 1 (not satisfied at all) to 4 (completely satisfied)

Variable name *scghql* in BHPS/US: GHQ: general happiness

d_happy

Dummy equals 1 if feels happy more than usual, 0 otherwise

Independent variables

Age

Age: 25–49

Reference group: 16–24

Age: 50–64

Age: 65–79

Age: 80

Gender

Male

Ethnicity

Asian or Asian British

Reference group: White

Black or Black British

Other

Marital status

Marital: single

Reference group: married

Marital: cohabiting

Marital: other than single/married/cohabiting

Household size

Hhsize

Number of dependent children

n_depchild: 1

Reference group: no dependent children

n_depchild: 2

(continued)

	n_depchild: 3
	n_depchild: 4+
Education	Edu: GCSE
Reference group: no qualification	Edu: A-level
	Edu: degree or higher
	Edu: other qualification
Two binary health variables	Health: excellent, very good or good
	Health: long-standing illness or impairment
Employment	Employment: self-employed
Reference group: employed	Employment: unemployed
	Employment: retired
	Employment: job_other
Current financial situation	finsit_now: living comfortably
Reference group: just about getting by	finsit_now: doing alright
	finsit_now: quite difficult
	finsit_now: very difficult
Future financial situation	finsit_future: better than now
Reference group: about the same	finsit_future: worse than now
lg_ind_income	Individual income (in logarithm)
lg_rent_gross	Rent including Housing Benefit (in logarithm)
Benefit	Benef: housing benefit
Reference group: no benefits	Benef: other benefit
Tenure	Tenure: owned outright
Reference group: social tenants	Tenure: owned with mortgage
	Tenure: social tenants
	Tenure: other rented (privately or from employer)
Number of rooms	Number of rooms including bedrooms, living room, kitchen etc.
Urban resident	Dummy equals 1 if urban resident
Factor analysis score of **attitudes towards neighbourhood** (larger score implies more positive attitude)	Calculated based on variables scopngbh* (in Understanding Society) and opngbh* (in BHPS)
Likes neighbourhood	Dummy equals 1 if respondent likes current neighbourhood

Appendix A

prb_payhousing	Dummy equals 1 if having problems paying for house
prb_space	Dummy equals 1 if short of space
prb_heating	Dummy equals 1 if not enough heating
prb_damp	Dummy equals 1 if damp walls

Waves and number of observations

Variable	Observa-tions	Mean	Standard deviation	Minimum	Maximum	Waves from
GHQ	247,689	11.143	5.487	0	36	All
Satisfaction with life	214,511	5.193	1.423	1	7	All
General happiness	249,620	2.962	0.567	1	4	All
d_happy	249,620	0.119	0.324	0	1	All
Age group						
16–24	282,602	0.139	0.346	0	1	All
25–49	282,602	0.428	0.495	0	1	All
50–64	282,602	0.231	0.421	0	1	All
65–79	282,602	0.157	0.364	0	1	All
80+	282,602	0.045	0.207	0	1	All
Male	281,553	0.458	0.498	0	1	All
Ethnicity						
White	268,613	0.876	0.329	0	1	All
Asian or Asian British	268,613	0.069	0.254	0	1	All
Black or Black British	268,613	0.034	0.182	0	1	All
Other	268,613	0.020	0.142	0	1	All
Marital status						
Marital: single	282,694	0.225	0.417	0	1	All
Marital: cohabiting	282,694	0.108	0.311	0	1	All
Marital: other than single/ married/ cohabiting	282,694	0.142	0.349	0	1	All
Hhsize	282,970	2.896	1.418	1	7	All
Number of dependent children						
0	257,749	0.642	0.479	0	1	All
1	257,749	0.154	0.360	0	1	All
2	257,749	0.140	0.347	0	1	All

Variable	Observa-tions	Mean	Standard deviation	Minimum	Maximum	Waves from
3	257,749	0.047	0.212	0	1	All
4+ child	257,749	0.017	0.129	0	1	All
Education						
No qualifications	278,304	0.176	0.381	0	1	All
GCSE	278,304	0.220	0.415	0	1	All
A-level	278,304	0.207	0.406	0	1	All
Degree or higher	278,304	0.298	0.457	0	1	ALL
Other	278,304	0.098	0.297	0	1	All
Health						
Health: excellent, very good or good	280,011	0.753	0.431	0	1	All
Health: long-standing illness or impairment	280,300	0.444	0.497	0	1	All
Employment						
Employed	282,494	0.481	0.500	0	1	All
Self_employed	282,494	0.074	0.262	0	1	All
Unemployed	282,494	0.045	0.208	0	1	All
Retired	282,494	0.220	0.414	0	1	All
Job_other	282,494	0.180	0.384	0	1	All
Current financial situation						
Living comfortably	268,595	0.297	0.457	0	1	All
Doing alright	268,595	0.365	0.481	0	1	All
Just about getting by	268,595	0.245	0.430	0	1	All
Quite difficult	268,595	0.065	0.246	0	1	All
Very difficult	268,595	0.029	0.168	0	1	All
Future financial situation						
Better than now	261,092	0.259	0.438	0	1	All
Worse than now	261,092	0.132	0.339	0	1	All
About the same	261,092	0.609	0.488	0	1	All
lg (individual income)	277,096	6.580	1.837	0	8.908618	All
Individual income	277,096	1468.083	1433.027	0	28149.67	All
lg (rent)	275,894	1.339	2.408	0	7.048387	All

(continued)

Variable	Observations	Mean	Standard deviation	Minimum	Maximum	Waves from
Rent	275,892	104.151	533.674	0	127590.7	All
Benefits						
No benefit						All
Housing Benefit	281,173	0.051	0.220	0	1	All
Other benefit	281,173	0.319	0.466	0	1	All
Housing tenure						
Owned outright	280,104	0.305	0.460	0	1	All
Owned with mortgage	280,104	0.410	0.492	0	1	All
Social renters	280,104	0.172	0.378	0	1	All
Other rented (privately or from employer)	280,104	0.113	0.316	0	1	All
Dwelling and neighbourhood						
Number of rooms	280,444	4.834	1.645	2	10	All
prb_space	90,290	0.224	0.417	0	1	BHPS only
prb_heating	90,271	0.065	0.246	0	1	BHPS only
prb_damp	89,253	0.088	0.284	0	1	BHPS only
prb_payhousing	160,285	0.043	0.203	0	1	BHPS only
likes neighbourhood	106,697	0.931	0.254	0	1	BHPS only
Neighbourhood factor	60,198	0.593	0.404	2.49E-05	2.474179	BHPS 8, 13, 18 + Understanding Society 1, 9
Urban resident	171,965	0.768058	0.422074	0	1	Understanding Society 1, 4, 8, 9
Government office region						
North East	282,300	0.035	0.183	0	1	All
North West	282,300	0.095	0.293	0	1	All
Yorkshire and the Humber	282,300	0.077	0.266	0	1	All
East Midlands	282,300	0.067	0.250	0	1	All
West Midlands	282,300	0.076	0.264	0	1	All
East of England	282,300	0.076	0.265	0	1	All

Variable	Observations	Mean	Standard deviation	Minimum	Maximum	Waves from
London	282,300	0.107	0.310	0	1	All
South East	282,300	0.110	0.312	0	1	All
South West	282,300	0.072	0.259	0	1	All
Wales	282,300	0.093	0.290	0	1	All
Scotland	282,300	0.109	0.312	0	1	All
Northern Ireland	282,300	0.084	0.277	0	1	All
Channel Islands	282,300	0.000	0.005	0	1	All
vote2	149,003	0.306	0.461	0	1	All but Understanding Society 8
vote6	218,755	0.432	0.495	0	1	All but Understanding Society 8
jblkche	96,839	0.279	0.449	0	1	BHPS 8, 11, 13, 15, 16, 18+ Understanding Society 4, 8
jblkchd	95,963	0.158	0.365	0	1	BHPS 8, 11, 13, 15, 16, 18+ Understanding Society 4, 8

Satisfaction with life – full fixed and random effects model

JA1:L96	(1)	(2)	(3)	(4)	(5)	(6)	(7)	(8)	(9)	(10)
Variables	fe Life satisfaction	fe Life satisfaction	fe Life satisfaction	fe Life satisfaction	fe Life satisfaction	re Life satisfaction	re Life satisfaction	re Life satisfaction	re Life satisfaction	re Life satisfaction
Age: 25–49	-0.060**	-0.059**	-0.071	-0.087**	-0.020	-0.201***	-0.200***	-0.207***	-0.207***	-0.177***
	(0.024)	(0.024)	(0.063)	(0.036)	(0.029)	(0.008)	(0.015)	(0.027)	(0.019)	(0.021)
Age: 50–64	-0.032	-0.033	-0.033	-0.090**	0.060	-0.165***	-0.168***	-0.152***	-0.200***	-0.069***
	(0.031)	(0.031)	(0.080)	(0.044)	(0.042)	(0.017)	(0.017)	(0.031)	(0.022)	(0.027)
Age: 65–79	0.054	0.052	0.040	0.010	0.098*	0.024	0.019	0.025	-0.030	0.148***
	(0.040)	(0.040)	(0.095)	(0.055)	(0.054)	(0.022)	(0.023)	(0.039)	(0.029)	(0.035)
Age: 80	0.011	0.015	-0.014	0.019	0.004	0.013	0.016	0.035	-0.021	0.113**
	(0.055)	(0.055)	(0.123)	(0.079)	(0.073)	(0.031)	(0.031)	(0.051)	(0.041)	(0.048)
Male	-	-	-	-	-	-0.031***	-0.031***	-0.004	-0.027***	-0.043***
						(0.008)	(0.008)	(0.012)	(0.009)	(0.014)
Asian or Asian British	-	-	-	-	-	-0.065***	-0.065***	-0.084***	-0.068***	-0.199**
						(0.018)	(0.018)	(0.029)	(0.019)	(0.098)
Black or Black British	-	-	-	-	-	0.028	0.036	0.018	0.047*	-0.139**
						(0.026)	(0.026)	(0.043)	(0.028)	(0.068)

JA1:L96 Variables	(1) fe Life satisfaction	(2) fe Life satisfaction	(3) fe Life satisfaction	(4) fe Life satisfaction	(5) fe Life satisfaction	(6) re Life satisfaction	(7) re Life satisfaction	(8) re Life satisfaction	(9) re Life satisfaction	(10) re Life satisfaction
Other	-	-	-	-	-	-0.094***	-0.092***	-0.021	-0.096***	-0.101
						(0.029)	(0.029)	(0.050)	(0.031)	(0.069)
Marital: single	-0.157***	-0.160***	-0.140*	-0.152***	-0.158***	-0.211***	-0.209***	-0.183***	-0.218***	-0.186***
	(0.029)	(0.029)	(0.077)	(0.041)	(0.039)	(0.014)	(0.014)	(0.024)	(0.018)	(0.021)
Marital: cohabiting	0.005	0.007	0.079	0.013	0.007	-0.040***	-0.036***	-0.019	-0.052***	0.007
	(0.020)	(0.020)	(0.054)	(0.028)	(0.028)	(0.011)	(0.011)	(0.020)	(0.014)	(0.018)
Marital: other than single/ married/cohabiting	-0.200***	-0.198***	-0.294***	-0.118***	-0.278***	-0.256***	-0.251***	-0.243***	-0.221***	-0.317***
	(0.030)	(0.030)	(0.061)	(0.045)	(0.040)	(0.015)	(0.015)	(0.024)	(0.020)	(0.024)
Hhsize	-0.013*	-0.015**	-0.047**	-0.008	-0.029***	-0.001	-0.005	-0.012	0.000	-0.018**
	(0.007)	(0.007)	(0.019)	(0.010)	(0.010)	(0.004)	(0.004)	(0.008)	(0.006)	(0.007)
n_depchild: 1	0.001	0.005	0.078**	-0.013	0.045**	-0.003	0.001	-0.007	0.004	0.036**
	(0.015)	(0.015)	(0.039)	(0.022)	(0.020)	(0.010)	(0.010)	(0.019)	(0.014)	(0.016)
n_depchild: 2	-0.019	-0.015	0.100**	-0.041	0.041	-0.000	0.005	0.049**	0.012	0.034
	(0.019)	(0.019)	(0.046)	(0.028)	(0.026)	(0.013)	(0.013)	(0.022)	(0.017)	(0.021)
n_depchild: 3	0.017	0.020	0.228***	-0.005	0.068*	0.025	0.031	0.129***	0.032	0.076**
	(0.030)	(0.030)	(0.076)	(0.044)	(0.040)	(0.020)	(0.020)	(0.034)	(0.026)	(0.032)

(continued)

JA1:L96	(1)	(2)	(3)	(4)	(5)	(6)	(7)	(8)	(9)	(10)
Variables	fe Life satisfaction	fe Life satisfaction	fe Life satisfaction	fe Life satisfaction	fe Life satisfaction	re Life satisfaction	re Life satisfaction	re Life satisfaction	re Life satisfaction	re Life satisfaction
n_depchild: 4+	-0.025	-0.022	0.025	-0.045	0.044	-0.001	0.008	0.009	0.033	0.051
	(0.053)	(0.053)	(0.154)	(0.071)	(0.078)	(0.034)	(0.034)	(0.063)	(0.041)	(0.060)
Edu: GCSE	0.113*	0.112*	-0.105	0.100	0.114	-0.037**	-0.044***	-0.078***	-0.040**	-0.039*
	(0.058)	(0.058)	(0.144)	(0.084)	(0.071)	(0.015)	(0.015)	(0.023)	(0.019)	(0.023)
Edu: A-level	0.068	0.066	-0.082	0.033	0.100	-0.026*	-0.036**	-0.078***	-0.029	-0.054**
	(0.059)	(0.059)	(0.142)	(0.085)	(0.073)	(0.015)	(0.015)	(0.023)	(0.019)	(0.024)
Edu: degree or higher	-0.026	-0.030	-0.215	-0.053	0.011	-0.023	-0.037**	-0.094***	-0.020	-0.097***
	(0.064)	(0.064)	(0.149)	(0.090)	(0.083)	(0.015)	(0.015)	(0.022)	(0.019)	(0.024)
Edu: other qualification	0.115*	0.114*	0.186	0.101	0.108	-0.007	-0.013	-0.046*	-0.004	-0.004
	(0.060)	(0.060)	(0.123)	(0.096)	(0.069)	(0.018)	(0.018)	(0.026)	(0.022)	(0.028)
Health: excellent, very good or good	0.354***	0.353***	0.354***	0.429***	0.272***	0.587***	0.585***	0.599***	0.683***	0.432***
	(0.012)	(0.012)	(0.030)	(0.018)	(0.014)	(0.009)	(0.009)	(0.016)	(0.013)	(0.013)
Health: long-standing illness or impairment	-0.089***	-0.089***	-0.065**	-0.094***	-0.079***	-0.174***	-0.173***	-0.147***	-0.187***	-0.132***
	(0.010)	(0.010)	(0.025)	(0.014)	(0.013)	(0.007)	(0.007)	(0.013)	(0.010)	(0.011)
Employment: self-employed	0.038*	0.037*	0.052	0.050*	0.019	0.016	0.012	-0.002	0.004	0.032
	(0.020)	(0.020)	(0.048)	(0.028)	(0.028)	(0.013)	(0.013)	(0.021)	(0.016)	(0.020)

JA1:L96	(1)	(2)	(3)	(4)	(5)	(6)	(7)	(8)	(9)	(10)
Variables	fe Life satisfaction	fe Life satisfaction	fe Life satisfaction	fe Life satisfaction	fe Life satisfaction	re Life satisfaction	re Life satisfaction	re Life satisfaction	re Life satisfaction	re Life satisfaction
Employment: unemployed	-0.152***	-0.154***	-0.173*	-0.121***	-0.205***	-0.219***	-0.219***	-0.169***	-0.204***	-0.212***
	(0.027)	(0.027)	(0.088)	(0.034)	(0.045)	(0.020)	(0.020)	(0.038)	(0.024)	(0.038)
Employment: retired	0.131***	0.127***	0.070	0.144***	0.088***	0.198***	0.191***	0.159***	0.236***	0.121***
	(0.021)	(0.021)	(0.043)	(0.029)	(0.030)	(0.015)	(0.015)	(0.024)	(0.020)	(0.024)
Employment: job_other	-0.014	-0.014	-0.047	0.016	-0.057**	-0.059***	-0.061***	-0.081***	-0.043***	-0.081***
	(0.017)	(0.017)	(0.044)	(0.023)	(0.025)	(0.012)	(0.012)	(0.021)	(0.015)	(0.020)
finsit_now: living comfortably	0.327***	0.327***	0.349***	0.341***	0.301***	0.518***	0.513***	0.509***	0.550***	0.432***
	(0.013)	(0.013)	(0.034)	(0.018)	(0.017)	(0.009)	(0.009)	(0.017)	(0.012)	(0.014)
finsit_now: doing alright	0.208***	0.208***	0.216***	0.223***	0.184***	0.305***	0.304***	0.296***	0.329***	0.248***
	(0.010)	(0.010)	(0.029)	(0.014)	(0.014)	(0.008)	(0.008)	(0.015)	(0.011)	(0.013)
finsit_now: quite difficult	-0.311***	-0.311***	-0.242***	-0.341***	-0.220***	-0.410***	-0.410***	-0.351***	-0.433***	-0.299***
	(0.019)	(0.019)	(0.060)	(0.024)	(0.029)	(0.015)	(0.015)	(0.030)	(0.018)	(0.027)
finsit_now: very difficult	-0.635***	-0.638***	-0.648***	-0.663***	-0.524***	-0.805***	-0.805***	-0.825***	-0.827***	-0.643***
	(0.033)	(0.033)	(0.111)	(0.041)	(0.057)	(0.026)	(0.026)	(0.051)	(0.030)	(0.050)
finsit_future: better than now	0.038***	0.039***	0.006	0.049***	0.025**	0.049***	0.050***	0.041***	0.055***	0.037***
	(0.009)	(0.009)	(0.026)	(0.013)	(0.012)	(0.007)	(0.007)	(0.014)	(0.010)	(0.011)

(continued)

181

JA1:L96	(1)	(2)	(3)	(4)	(5)	(6)	(7)	(8)	(9)	(10)
Variables	fe Life satisfaction	fe Life satisfaction	fe Life satisfaction	fe Life satisfaction	fe Life satisfaction	re Life satisfaction	re Life satisfaction	re Life satisfaction	re Life satisfaction	re Life satisfaction
finsit_future: worse than now	-0.077***	-0.078***	-0.034	-0.099***	-0.032**	-0.134***	-0.135***	-0.115***	-0.161***	-0.070***
	(0.011)	(0.011)	(0.028)	(0.015)	(0.016)	(0.009)	(0.009)	(0.017)	(0.012)	(0.015)
lg_ind_income	-0.013***	-0.012***	-0.033***	-0.014***	-0.007	-0.023***	-0.023***	-0.030***	-0.022***	-0.020***
	(0.003)	(0.003)	(0.010)	(0.004)	(0.005)	(0.002)	(0.002)	(0.004)	(0.003)	(0.004)
lg_rent_gross	-0.007*	-0.017**	-0.028	-0.052*	-0.009	-0.011***	-0.010**	-0.014**	0.010	-0.044***
	(0.004)	(0.007)	(0.021)	(0.030)	(0.013)	(0.002)	(0.004)	(0.007)	(0.019)	(0.009)
benef_housing	0.017	0.017	-0.080	0.017		-0.119***	-0.112***	-0.162***	-0.099***	
	(0.036)	(0.036)	(0.143)	(0.037)		(0.022)	(0.022)	(0.042)	(0.024)	
benef_other	0.003	0.003	0.006	0.007	0.009	-0.017**	-0.017**	-0.018	-0.014	0.015
	(0.011)	(0.011)	(0.027)	(0.016)	(0.015)	(0.008)	(0.008)	(0.013)	(0.012)	(0.012)
Tenure: owned outright		-0.005	-0.110	-0.204	-0.040		0.051**	0.000	0.131	-0.022
		(0.041)	(0.107)	(0.191)	(0.053)		(0.024)	(0.040)	(0.115)	(0.036)
Tenure: owned with mortgage		-0.050	-0.111	-0.242	-0.090*		0.030	-0.019	0.129	-0.074**
		(0.040)	(0.104)	(0.189)	(0.050)		(0.024)	(0.040)	(0.115)	(0.034)
Tenure: other rented (privately or from employer)		0.025	0.082	0.057	-0.008		0.067***	0.070**	0.043**	0.040
		(0.031)	(0.095)	(0.042)	(0.045)		(0.016)	(0.029)	(0.021)	(0.030)

JA1:L96	(1)	(2)	(3)	(4)	(5)	(6)	(7)	(8)	(9)	(10)
Variables	fe Life satisfaction	fe Life satisfaction	fe Life satisfaction	fe Life satisfaction	fe Life satisfaction	re Life satisfaction	re Life satisfaction	re Life satisfaction	re Life satisfaction	re Life satisfaction
Number of rooms		0.008*	0.001	0.013*	-0.001		0.009***	0.001	0.008**	0.001
		(0.005)	(0.011)	(0.007)	(0.006)		(0.003)	(0.004)	(0.003)	(0.004)
Neighbourhood factor			0.051*					0.135***		
			(0.027)					(0.015)		
Urban resident				-0.053					-0.031***	
				(0.036)					(0.011)	
prb_payhousing					-0.127***					-0.144***
					(0.030)					(0.026)
prb_space					-0.025*					-0.071***
					(0.015)					(0.013)
prb_heating					-0.031					-0.056**
					(0.031)					(0.028)
prb_damp					-0.013					-0.044**
					(0.024)					(0.021)
Likes neighbourhood					0.112***					0.261***
					(0.028)					(0.024)

(continued)

JA1:L96	(1)	(2)	(3)	(4)	(5)	(6)	(7)	(8)	(9)	(10)
Variables	fe Life satisfaction	fe Life satisfaction	fe Life satisfaction	fe Life satisfaction	fe Life satisfaction	re Life satisfaction	re Life satisfaction	re Life satisfaction	re Life satisfaction	re Life satisfaction
Constant	4.820***	4.783***	5.100***	5.054***	4.920***	4.893***	4.833***	5.091***	4.660***	5.038***
	(0.126)	(0.131)	(0.373)	(0.259)	(0.194)	(0.040)	(0.046)	(0.077)	(0.122)	(0.099)
Year dummies controlled										
Region dummies controlled										
Observations	174,506	174,064	48,097	117,627	55,028	174,506	174,064	48,097	117,627	55,028
Number of pidp	74,310	74,209	37,470	56,051	17,927	74,310	74,209	37,470	56,051	17,927
Robust standard errors in parentheses										

*** p<0.01, ** p<0.05, * p<0.1

GHQ-12 – full fixed and random effects model

Variables	(1) fe GHQ	(2) fe GHQ	(3) fe GHQ	(4) fe GHQ	(5) fe GHQ	(6) re GHQ	(7) re GHQ	(8) re GHQ	(9) re GHQ	(10) re GHQ
Age: 25–49	0.384***	0.376***	0.815***	0.454***	0.164	0.500***	0.497***	0.545***	0.368***	0.592***
	(0.087)	(0.088)	(0.303)	(0.135)	(0.131)	(0.055)	(0.055)	(0.110)	(0.075)	(0.090)
Age: 50–64	0.180	0.188*	0.756**	0.308*	0.061	0.159**	0.174***	0.332***	0.033	0.408***
	(0.113)	(0.114)	(0.363)	(0.164)	(0.182)	(0.064)	(0.065)	(0.123)	(0.085)	(0.113)
Age: 65–79	-0.012	0.003	0.807*	0.004	-0.007	-0.364***	-0.324***	-0.240	-0.569***	0.088
	(0.136)	(0.137)	(0.416)	(0.192)	(0.222)	(0.078)	(0.080)	(0.147)	(0.103)	(0.139)
Age: 80	0.337*	0.357**	1.191**	0.146	0.448	0.042	0.093	0.131	-0.369***	0.702***
	(0.178)	(0.179)	(0.492)	(0.251)	(0.280)	(0.106)	(0.107)	(0.185)	(0.140)	(0.180)
Male	–	–	–	–	–	-1.021***	-1.023***	-1.057***	-0.964***	-1.141***
						(0.029)	(0.029)	(0.047)	(0.035)	(0.056)
Asian or Asian British	–	–	–	–	–	-0.348***	-0.327***	-0.479***	-0.366***	0.131
						(0.069)	(0.070)	(0.108)	(0.072)	(0.437)
Black or Black British	–	–	–	–	–	-1.250***	-1.252***	-1.371***	-1.458***	0.226
						(0.096)	(0.097)	(0.162)	(0.105)	(0.272)

(continued)

Variables	(1) fe GHQ	(2) fe GHQ	(3) fe GHQ	(4) fe GHQ	(5) fe GHQ	(6) re GHQ	(7) re GHQ	(8) re GHQ	(9) re GHQ	(10) re GHQ
Other	-	-	-	-	-	-0.001	-0.006	-0.101	-0.082	-0.080
						(0.111)	(0.112)	(0.198)	(0.123)	(0.271)
Marital: single	-0.133	-0.134	-0.518	-0.045	-0.273*	-0.014	-0.008	-0.035	0.157**	-0.348***
	(0.104)	(0.105)	(0.339)	(0.156)	(0.162)	(0.052)	(0.052)	(0.095)	(0.069)	(0.086)
Marital: cohabiting	-0.131*	-0.118	-0.685***	-0.081	-0.128	0.081*	0.099**	0.069	0.251***	-0.182**
	(0.074)	(0.074)	(0.246)	(0.104)	(0.119)	(0.043)	(0.043)	(0.081)	(0.054)	(0.078)
Marital: other than single/married/cohabiting	0.563***	0.564***	0.444*	0.105	0.890***	0.487***	0.487***	0.440***	0.322***	0.471***
	(0.107)	(0.108)	(0.269)	(0.174)	(0.156)	(0.058)	(0.058)	(0.093)	(0.081)	(0.092)
Hhsize	0.013	0.005	0.084	-0.041	0.050	-0.011	-0.028*	-0.014	-0.074***	0.004
	(0.025)	(0.026)	(0.077)	(0.037)	(0.041)	(0.016)	(0.016)	(0.029)	(0.021)	(0.029)
n_depchild: 1	0.038	0.027	-0.056	0.007	0.045	-0.081**	-0.095**	-0.020	-0.088	-0.064
	(0.055)	(0.055)	(0.164)	(0.081)	(0.087)	(0.040)	(0.040)	(0.076)	(0.054)	(0.069)
n_depchild: 2	0.106	0.094	-0.168	0.143	0.090	-0.111**	-0.126***	-0.096	-0.104	-0.053
	(0.070)	(0.071)	(0.199)	(0.102)	(0.112)	(0.048)	(0.049)	(0.090)	(0.064)	(0.088)
n_depchild: 3	-0.102	-0.112	-0.497	-0.053	-0.229	-0.281***	-0.295***	-0.380***	-0.257***	-0.278**
	(0.109)	(0.109)	(0.320)	(0.160)	(0.169)	(0.074)	(0.074)	(0.133)	(0.096)	(0.132)

Variables	(1) fe GHQ	(2) fe GHQ	(3) fe GHQ	(4) fe GHQ	(5) fe GHQ	(6) re GHQ	(7) re GHQ	(8) re GHQ	(9) re GHQ	(10) re GHQ
n_depchild: 4+	0.176	0.174	-0.158	0.166	-0.074	-0.142	-0.137	-0.238	-0.139	-0.175
	(0.186)	(0.186)	(0.557)	(0.251)	(0.295)	(0.126)	(0.127)	(0.233)	(0.159)	(0.218)
Edu: GCSE	0.127	0.158	-0.361	0.090	0.020	-0.025	-0.032	0.040	0.168**	-0.288***
	(0.195)	(0.194)	(0.603)	(0.283)	(0.296)	(0.053)	(0.053)	(0.081)	(0.070)	(0.087)
Edu: A-level	0.146	0.190	-0.120	0.115	0.334	0.094*	0.089*	0.165**	0.309***	-0.128
	(0.195)	(0.194)	(0.606)	(0.289)	(0.288)	(0.054)	(0.054)	(0.084)	(0.070)	(0.090)
Edu: degree or higher	0.582***	0.631***	0.016	0.679**	0.718**	0.184***	0.170***	0.153*	0.394***	-0.070
	(0.216)	(0.216)	(0.646)	(0.313)	(0.336)	(0.052)	(0.053)	(0.081)	(0.068)	(0.092)
Edu: other qualification	0.094	0.112	-0.763	-0.110	0.397	-0.159**	-0.156**	-0.136	-0.001	-0.283***
	(0.188)	(0.189)	(0.498)	(0.313)	(0.259)	(0.063)	(0.063)	(0.093)	(0.081)	(0.105)
Health: excellent, very good or good	-1.866***	-1.863***	-1.896***	-2.058***	-1.658***	-2.597***	-2.596***	-2.796***	-2.930***	-2.229***
	(0.044)	(0.044)	(0.133)	(0.071)	(0.061)	(0.036)	(0.036)	(0.067)	(0.052)	(0.052)
Health: long-standing illness or impairment	0.553***	0.555***	0.639***	0.580***	0.549***	0.973***	0.975***	1.047***	1.071***	0.770***
	(0.036)	(0.036)	(0.106)	(0.048)	(0.057)	(0.027)	(0.027)	(0.050)	(0.036)	(0.044)
Employment: self-employed	-0.149**	-0.148**	-0.052	-0.259***	-0.014	-0.118***	-0.121***	0.070	-0.197***	0.031
	(0.072)	(0.073)	(0.215)	(0.096)	(0.122)	(0.045)	(0.046)	(0.080)	(0.055)	(0.085)

(continued)

Variables	(1) fe GHQ	(2) fe GHQ	(3) fe GHQ	(4) fe GHQ	(5) fe GHQ	(6) re GHQ	(7) re GHQ	(8) re GHQ	(9) re GHQ	(10) re GHQ
Employment: unemployed	1.077***	1.076***	0.176	1.066***	1.168***	1.104***	1.107***	0.806***	1.100***	1.144***
	(0.101)	(0.102)	(0.367)	(0.132)	(0.179)	(0.077)	(0.077)	(0.147)	(0.094)	(0.150)
Employment: retired	-0.427***	-0.398***	-0.407**	-0.390***	-0.379***	-0.336***	-0.301***	-0.242***	-0.356***	-0.216**
	(0.069)	(0.069)	(0.159)	(0.092)	(0.119)	(0.050)	(0.051)	(0.085)	(0.064)	(0.095)
Employment: job_other	0.473***	0.483***	0.339*	0.531***	0.510***	0.811***	0.821***	0.836***	0.917***	0.681***
	(0.064)	(0.064)	(0.194)	(0.088)	(0.104)	(0.046)	(0.046)	(0.086)	(0.060)	(0.081)
finsit_now: Living comfortably	-1.210***	-1.207***	-1.171***	-1.228***	-1.150***	-1.601***	-1.603***	-1.691***	-1.671***	-1.470***
	(0.044)	(0.044)	(0.143)	(0.061)	(0.068)	(0.033)	(0.033)	(0.064)	(0.043)	(0.057)
finsit_now: doing alright	-0.826***	-0.826***	-0.955***	-0.817***	-0.795***	-1.013***	-1.014***	-1.087***	-1.042***	-0.929***
	(0.037)	(0.037)	(0.125)	(0.052)	(0.058)	(0.030)	(0.030)	(0.060)	(0.039)	(0.051)
finsit_now: quite difficult	1.445***	1.450***	1.303***	1.301***	1.594***	1.736***	1.740***	1.517***	1.648***	1.810***
	(0.074)	(0.074)	(0.264)	(0.096)	(0.129)	(0.061)	(0.061)	(0.123)	(0.074)	(0.117)
finsit_now: very difficult	3.362***	3.360***	3.482***	3.288***	3.159***	3.689***	3.692***	3.334***	3.603***	3.543***
	(0.137)	(0.137)	(0.511)	(0.174)	(0.239)	(0.111)	(0.111)	(0.229)	(0.134)	(0.214)
finsit_future: better than now	-0.236***	-0.234***	-0.134	-0.211***	-0.248***	-0.297***	-0.297***	-0.340***	-0.261***	-0.330***
	(0.034)	(0.034)	(0.116)	(0.047)	(0.053)	(0.028)	(0.028)	(0.056)	(0.035)	(0.046)
finsit_future: worse than now	0.498***	0.496***	0.376***	0.559***	0.353***	0.756***	0.755***	0.736***	0.867***	0.491***
	(0.041)	(0.041)	(0.119)	(0.054)	(0.068)	(0.036)	(0.036)	(0.067)	(0.045)	(0.062)

Appendix D

Variables	(1) fe GHQ	(2) fe GHQ	(3) fe GHQ	(4) fe GHQ	(5) fe GHQ	(6) re GHQ	(7) re GHQ	(8) re GHQ	(9) re GHQ	(10) re GHQ
lg_ind_income	0.022*	0.022*	0.076*	0.027*	0.012	0.066***	0.066***	0.101***	0.068***	0.080***
	(0.012)	(0.012)	(0.041)	(0.015)	(0.021)	(0.009)	(0.009)	(0.017)	(0.011)	(0.017)
lg_rent_gross	0.012	0.044*	0.030	0.091	0.012	0.006	0.046***	0.018	0.048	0.103***
	(0.016)	(0.026)	(0.082)	(0.113)	(0.052)	(0.007)	(0.016)	(0.029)	(0.073)	(0.037)
benef_housing	0.298**	0.302**	0.084	0.274**		0.430***	0.418***	0.400**	0.436***	
	(0.134)	(0.134)	(0.514)	(0.137)		(0.086)	(0.086)	(0.161)	(0.091)	
benef_other	0.077**	0.076**	0.029	0.031	0.070	-0.017	-0.016	-0.044	0.070*	0.042
	(0.039)	(0.039)	(0.112)	(0.055)	(0.065)	(0.028)	(0.028)	(0.052)	(0.042)	(0.052)
Tenure: owned outright		-0.019	-0.234	0.092	0.095		0.045	0.079	0.175	0.187
		(0.151)	(0.437)	(0.715)	(0.205)		(0.093)	(0.162)	(0.437)	(0.140)
Tenure: owned with mortgage		0.188	-0.123	0.273	0.280		0.213**	0.216	0.316	0.324**
		(0.144)	(0.425)	(0.712)	(0.194)		(0.090)	(0.161)	(0.437)	(0.133)
Tenure: other rented (privately or from employer)		-0.035	-0.245	-0.176	0.029		-0.064	-0.027	-0.028	0.061
		(0.113)	(0.384)	(0.166)	(0.186)		(0.061)	(0.110)	(0.081)	(0.121)
Number of rooms		0.019	0.086*	-0.000	0.038		0.031***	0.065***	0.039***	0.049***
		(0.018)	(0.049)	(0.028)	(0.025)		(0.010)	(0.016)	(0.012)	(0.017)

(continued)

Variables	(1) fe GHQ	(2) fe GHQ	(3) fe GHQ	(4) fe GHQ	(5) fe GHQ	(6) re GHQ	(7) re GHQ	(8) re GHQ	(9) re GHQ	(10) re GHQ
Neighbourhood factor			-0.253**					-0.311***		
			(0.111)					(0.055)		
Urban resident				0.020					0.126***	
				(0.140)					(0.043)	
prb_payhousing					0.686***					0.743***
					(0.119)					(0.105)
prb_space					-0.008					0.137**
					(0.063)					(0.054)
prb_heating					-0.068					0.011
					(0.132)					(0.115)
prb_damp					0.030					0.128
					(0.097)					(0.084)
Likes neighbourhood					-0.685***					-1.044***
					(0.118)					(0.099)
Constant	12.822***	12.713***	11.550***	13.016***	12.611***	13.504***	13.232***	12.463***	13.228***	13.018***
	(0.528)	(0.552)	(1.701)	(1.085)	(0.845)	(0.149)	(0.172)	(0.295)	(0.467)	(0.431)

Variables	(1) fe GHQ	(2) fe GHQ	(3) fe GHQ	(4) fe GHQ	(5) fe GHQ	(6) re GHQ	(7) re GHQ	(8) re GHQ	(9) re GHQ	(10) re GHQ
Year dummies controlled										
Region dummies controlled										
Observations	195,513	194,909	47,881	117,469	68,420	195,513	194,909	47,881	117,469	68,420
Number of pidp	76,413	76,303	37,304	56,065	19,172	76,413	76,303	37,304	56,065	19,172

Robust standard errors in parentheses

*** p<0.01, ** p<0.05, * p<0.1

APPENDIX E

Happiness – full fixed and random effects model

Variables	(1) fe happy	(2) fe happy	(3) fe happy	(4) fe happy	(5) fe happy	(6) re happy	(7) re happy	(8) re happy	(9) re happy	(10) re happy
Age: 25–49	-0.026**	-0.025**	-0.025	-0.040**	0.009	-0.065***	-0.064***	-0.042***	-0.060***	-0.060***
	(0.011)	(0.011)	(0.038)	(0.017)	(0.017)	(0.006)	(0.006)	(0.013)	(0.008)	(0.010)
Age: 50–64	-0.018	-0.019	-0.045	-0.040*	0.010	-0.072***	-0.069***	-0.064***	-0.067***	-0.071***
	(0.014)	(0.014)	(0.045)	(0.021)	(0.023)	(0.007)	(0.007)	(0.014)	(0.009)	(0.013)
Age: 65–79	-0.013	-0.015	-0.070	-0.021	0.009	-0.055***	-0.054***	-0.054***	-0.041***	-0.067***
	(0.017)	(0.017)	(0.051)	(0.024)	(0.028)	(0.009)	(0.009)	(0.017)	(0.011)	(0.016)
Age: 80	-0.017	-0.021	-0.058	-0.024	-0.005	-0.063***	-0.064***	-0.050**	-0.042***	-0.090***
	(0.021)	(0.022)	(0.061)	(0.030)	(0.034)	(0.011)	(0.011)	(0.020)	(0.014)	(0.019)
Male	–	–	–	–	–	0.034***	0.034***	0.049***	0.034***	0.034***
						(0.003)	(0.003)	(0.005)	(0.004)	(0.006)
Asian or Asian British	–	–	–	–	–	0.048***	0.044***	0.055***	0.045***	0.005
						(0.007)	(0.007)	(0.012)	(0.007)	(0.044)
Black or Black British	–	–	–	–	–	0.097***	0.096***	0.113***	0.106***	0.029
						(0.010)	(0.010)	(0.018)	(0.011)	(0.026)

Variables	(1) fe happy	(2) fe happy	(3) fe happy	(4) fe happy	(5) fe happy	(6) re happy	(7) re happy	(8) re happy	(9) re happy	(10) re happy
Other	-	-	-	-	-	0.015	0.016	0.031	0.024*	-0.018
						(0.011)	(0.011)	(0.022)	(0.013)	(0.026)
Marital: single	0.008	0.008	0.070	0.025	0.008	0.004	0.004	0.019*	-0.004	0.025***
	(0.013)	(0.013)	(0.043)	(0.019)	(0.022)	(0.006)	(0.006)	(0.011)	(0.007)	(0.009)
Marital: cohabiting	0.033***	0.029***	0.108***	0.020	0.030*	0.013***	0.009*	0.022**	-0.008	0.039***
	(0.010)	(0.010)	(0.031)	(0.013)	(0.016)	(0.005)	(0.005)	(0.009)	(0.006)	(0.009)
Marital: other than single/married/cohabing	-0.029**	-0.028**	0.043	0.013	-0.049**	-0.022***	-0.022***	-0.012	-0.017**	-0.013
	(0.013)	(0.013)	(0.034)	(0.021)	(0.020)	(0.006)	(0.006)	(0.010)	(0.008)	(0.009)
Hhsize	-0.005	-0.002	-0.008	0.002	-0.007	-0.001	0.003	0.002	0.005**	0.001
	(0.003)	(0.003)	(0.009)	(0.005)	(0.005)	(0.002)	(0.002)	(0.003)	(0.002)	(0.003)
n_depchild: 1	0.005	0.007	0.008	0.008	0.003	0.013***	0.014***	0.005	0.014***	0.016*
	(0.007)	(0.007)	(0.020)	(0.010)	(0.011)	(0.004)	(0.004)	(0.009)	(0.006)	(0.008)
n_depchild: 2	-0.024***	-0.022**	-0.006	-0.034***	-0.013	-0.003	-0.003	-0.007	-0.006	0.000
	(0.009)	(0.009)	(0.024)	(0.013)	(0.015)	(0.005)	(0.005)	(0.010)	(0.007)	(0.010)
n_depchild: 3	0.007	0.008	0.032	0.001	0.026	0.020**	0.020**	0.011	0.018*	0.029*
	(0.013)	(0.013)	(0.039)	(0.019)	(0.021)	(0.008)	(0.008)	(0.015)	(0.010)	(0.016)
n_depchild: 4+	-0.040*	-0.039	-0.062	-0.017	-0.027	0.014	0.011	-0.006	0.027	0.001
	(0.024)	(0.024)	(0.064)	(0.031)	(0.039)	(0.014)	(0.014)	(0.025)	(0.017)	(0.026)

(continued)

Variables	(1) fe happy	(2) fe happy	(3) fe happy	(4) fe happy	(5) fe happy	(6) re happy	(7) re happy	(8) re happy	(9) re happy	(10) re happy
Edu: GCSE	-0.004 (0.024)	-0.009 (0.024)	-0.090 (0.072)	0.003 (0.035)	0.001 (0.038)	-0.020*** (0.005)	-0.018*** (0.005)	-0.021** (0.008)	-0.031*** (0.007)	-0.003 (0.008)
Edu: A-level	0.028 (0.024)	0.023 (0.024)	-0.025 (0.071)	0.047 (0.036)	0.001 (0.038)	-0.018*** (0.005)	-0.016*** (0.005)	-0.017** (0.009)	-0.029*** (0.007)	-0.001 (0.009)
Edu: degree or higher	-0.004 (0.027)	-0.011 (0.027)	-0.077 (0.077)	0.022 (0.038)	-0.063 (0.044)	-0.021*** (0.005)	-0.018*** (0.005)	-0.012 (0.008)	-0.029*** (0.007)	-0.010 (0.009)
Edu: other qualification	-0.013 (0.022)	-0.018 (0.022)	-0.027 (0.064)	-0.026 (0.037)	-0.019 (0.031)	-0.008 (0.006)	-0.007 (0.006)	-0.008 (0.009)	-0.016** (0.008)	-0.000 (0.010)
Health: excellent, very good or good	0.135*** (0.005)	0.135*** (0.005)	0.130*** (0.016)	0.144*** (0.008)	0.123*** (0.007)	0.177*** (0.004)	0.178*** (0.004)	0.164*** (0.007)	0.194*** (0.005)	0.155*** (0.006)
Health: long-standing illness or impairment	-0.047*** (0.004)	-0.048*** (0.004)	-0.050*** (0.013)	-0.047*** (0.006)	-0.056*** (0.007)	-0.062*** (0.003)	-0.062*** (0.003)	-0.055*** (0.006)	-0.065*** (0.004)	-0.055*** (0.005)
Employment: self-employed	0.015 (0.009)	0.015* (0.009)	0.030 (0.026)	0.033*** (0.012)	-0.002 (0.015)	0.018*** (0.005)	0.020*** (0.005)	0.013 (0.009)	0.029*** (0.006)	0.001 (0.009)
Employment: unemployed	-0.071*** (0.012)	-0.070*** (0.012)	-0.024 (0.044)	-0.061*** (0.016)	-0.092*** (0.022)	-0.080*** (0.009)	-0.079*** (0.009)	-0.067*** (0.016)	-0.077*** (0.010)	-0.082*** (0.017)
Employment: retired	0.049*** (0.008)	0.045*** (0.008)	0.053*** (0.021)	0.028** (0.011)	0.062*** (0.015)	0.027*** (0.005)	0.026*** (0.005)	0.022** (0.010)	0.023*** (0.007)	0.033*** (0.011)

Variables	(1) fe happy	(2) fe happy	(3) fe happy	(4) fe happy	(5) fe happy	(6) re happy	(7) re happy	(8) re happy	(9) re happy	(10) re happy
Employment: job_other	-0.015*	-0.017**	-0.016	-0.017	-0.022*	-0.038***	-0.038***	-0.031***	-0.044***	-0.026***
	(0.008)	(0.008)	(0.023)	(0.011)	(0.013)	(0.005)	(0.005)	(0.009)	(0.007)	(0.009)
finsit_now: living comfortably	0.107***	0.107***	0.090***	0.101***	0.111***	0.114***	0.116***	0.109***	0.115***	0.113***
	(0.005)	(0.005)	(0.017)	(0.008)	(0.009)	(0.004)	(0.004)	(0.007)	(0.005)	(0.007)
finsit_now: doing alright	0.073***	0.073***	0.082***	0.068***	0.073***	0.074***	0.075***	0.074***	0.075***	0.070***
	(0.005)	(0.005)	(0.015)	(0.006)	(0.007)	(0.003)	(0.003)	(0.007)	(0.004)	(0.006)
finsit_now: quite difficult	-0.122***	-0.123***	-0.125***	-0.109***	-0.145***	-0.137***	-0.137***	-0.096***	-0.127***	-0.156***
	(0.009)	(0.009)	(0.032)	(0.011)	(0.016)	(0.007)	(0.007)	(0.013)	(0.008)	(0.014)
finsit_now: very difficult	-0.300***	-0.299***	-0.289***	-0.289***	-0.299***	-0.311***	-0.310***	-0.273***	-0.298***	-0.323***
	(0.016)	(0.016)	(0.055)	(0.020)	(0.028)	(0.012)	(0.012)	(0.024)	(0.015)	(0.024)
finsit_future: better than now	0.038***	0.038***	0.026*	0.036***	0.038***	0.050***	0.050***	0.048***	0.047***	0.050***
	(0.004)	(0.004)	(0.014)	(0.006)	(0.007)	(0.003)	(0.003)	(0.007)	(0.004)	(0.006)
finsit_future: worse than now	-0.029***	-0.028***	-0.024	-0.034***	-0.018**	-0.048***	-0.047***	-0.039***	-0.054***	-0.032***
	(0.005)	(0.005)	(0.015)	(0.007)	(0.009)	(0.004)	(0.004)	(0.007)	(0.005)	(0.008)
lg_ind_income	0.001	0.001	-0.010**	-0.000	0.003	-0.005***	-0.005***	-0.007***	-0.005***	-0.005***
	(0.002)	(0.002)	(0.005)	(0.002)	(0.003)	(0.001)	(0.001)	(0.002)	(0.001)	(0.002)

(continued)

Variables	(1) fe happy	(2) fe happy	(3) fe happy	(4) fe happy	(5) fe happy	(6) re happy	(7) re happy	(8) re happy	(9) re happy	(10) re happy
lg_rent_gross	0.002	-0.005	-0.009	-0.029**	0.001	0.003***	-0.005***	-0.006*	-0.013*	-0.007*
	(0.002)	(0.003)	(0.010)	(0.013)	(0.006)	(0.001)	(0.002)	(0.003)	(0.008)	(0.004)
benef_housing	-0.019	-0.019	0.021	-0.021		-0.028***	-0.025***	-0.032*	-0.029***	
	(0.016)	(0.016)	(0.057)	(0.016)		(0.009)	(0.009)	(0.017)	(0.010)	
benef_other	-0.012**	-0.011**	-0.015	-0.009	-0.004	-0.002	-0.003	-0.003	-0.009*	0.003
	(0.005)	(0.005)	(0.014)	(0.007)	(0.008)	(0.003)	(0.003)	(0.006)	(0.005)	(0.006)
Tenure: owned outright		0.000	0.063	-0.134*	-0.004		-0.025***	-0.032*	-0.084*	-0.034**
		(0.019)	(0.055)	(0.082)	(0.026)		(0.010)	(0.018)	(0.048)	(0.015)
Tenure: owned with mortgage		-0.027	0.034	-0.154*	-0.027		-0.034***	-0.039**	-0.089*	-0.045***
		(0.018)	(0.055)	(0.081)	(0.024)		(0.010)	(0.018)	(0.048)	(0.014)
Tenure: other rented (privately or from employer)		0.019	0.092**	0.037*	0.022		0.016**	0.024*	0.019**	0.011
		(0.014)	(0.046)	(0.020)	(0.023)		(0.006)	(0.012)	(0.009)	(0.014)
Number of rooms		-0.006**	-0.011*	-0.007**	-0.005		-0.006***	-0.006***	-0.007***	-0.005***
		(0.002)	(0.006)	(0.003)	(0.003)		(0.001)	(0.002)	(0.001)	(0.002)
Neighbourhood factor			0.014					0.037***		
			(0.014)					(0.006)		

Variables	(1) fe happy	(2) fe happy	(3) fe happy	(4) fe happy	(5) fe happy	(6) re happy	(7) re happy	(8) re happy	(9) re happy	(10) re happy
Urban resident				0.009					-0.010**	
				(0.018)					(0.004)	
prb_payhousing					-0.056***					-0.048***
					(0.015)					(0.013)
prb_space					0.005					-0.003
					(0.008)					(0.006)
prb_heating					0.001					-0.006
					(0.017)					(0.014)
prb_damp					-0.003					-0.013
					(0.012)					(0.010)
Likes neighbourhood					0.061***					0.095***
					(0.015)					(0.011)
Constant	2.721***	2.747***	2.839***	2.913***	2.729***	2.827***	2.874***	2.907***	2.934***	2.875***
	(0.064)	(0.067)	(0.186)	(0.128)	(0.100)	(0.016)	(0.018)	(0.033)	(0.051)	(0.048)

(continued)

Variables	(1) fe happy	(2) fe happy	(3) fe happy	(4) fe happy	(5) fe happy	(6) re happy	(7) re happy	(8) re happy	(9) re happy	(10) re happy
Year dummies controlled										
Region dummies controlled										
Observations	196,908	196,295	48,247	118,151	69,048	196,908	196,295	48,247	118,151	69,048
Number of pidp	76,726	76,619	37,557	56,335	19,218	76,726	76,619	37,557	56,335	19,218

Robust standard errors in parentheses

*** p<0.01, ** p<0.05, * p<0.1

Notes

Chapter 1

[1] Grenfell Tower was a high-rise housing block in West London that was destroyed by a fire in June 2017. Although built solely for social housing, at the time of the fire it was home to owners and private renters as well as social tenants, The fire was accelerated by the use of inferior building materials and led to the loss of 72 lives.

[2] These five social ills were identified by a committee, led by William Beveridge, formed in the early stages of World War Two. Driven by a sense of wartime solidarity, the task was to outline the structure of a new welfare state, to improve the lives of all citizens once the war had been won. The full report can be accessed here: https://www.nationalarchives. gov.uk/education/resources/attlees-britain/five-giants/

[3] Eneurin (Nye) Bevan was appointed Secretary of State in 1945 Labour Government, which was committed to tackling Beveridge's 'five giants', Bevan also held responsibility for housing (tackling squalor) and famously called for the creation of mass housing which would create a "living tapestry", "where the doctor, the grocer, the butcher and the farm labourer all lived in the same street" (https://api.parliament.uk/historic-hansard/comm ons/1949/mar/16/housing-bill).

Chapter 2

[1] For the best recent discussion of neoliberalism see Davies, 2016.

[2] See Doyal and Gough, 1991 for a more contemporary account of human need.

[3] Rawls later revised his account to embrace an egalitarian version of property owning democracy (Rawls, 2001). This adds a new perspective but does not alter the terms of debate I discuss in this and the following section. For discussion see Gregory, 2016 and O'Neill and Williamson, 2012.

Chapter 3

[1] Octavia Hill was a central figure in the development creation of 'model dwellings companies', sometimes referred to as 'philanthropy at five percent', in the second half of the 19th Century. Famous names still providing social housing include the Peabody Trust, founded in 1862, and the Guinness Trust, founded in 1890. While not an investor herself, Hill was managing 3000 such homes in the 1870s, and developed a management style that the imposed strict conditions on tenants but, at the same time, a high level of support from managers. Today Hill is sometimes used as a byword for control and paternalism.

[2] Compare Weber. This bears some resemblance to Marshall's celebrated account of the development of individual rights, from legal to political to social rights (Marshall, 1950, pp 14–28).

[3] 'The term salutogenesis is associated with a variety of meanings that Aaron Antonovsky introduced in his 1979 book *Health, Stress and Coping* and expounded in many subsequent works. In its most particular meaning, salutogenesis is almost equivalent to the sense of coherence. In its more general meaning, salutogenesis refers to a scholarly orientation focusing attention on the study of the origins of health, contra the origins of disease. Salutogenesis – model, sense of coherence and orientation – is in harmony with developments across the social sciences that seek better understanding of positive aspects of human experience' (Mittelmark et al, 2017).

Chapter 4

[1] Peter Rachman was a private landlord based in Notting Hill, London, in the 1950s and 1960s. He acquired a number of houses in poor repair, sub-dividing them into flats and letting them to Afro-Caribbean immigrants, whose housing options were otherwise restricted, in both the social and private rental sectors. Rachman's properties were often in very poor condition and he is regarded as a 'slum landlord'.

Chapter 5

[1] See also Padgett's research on homelessness and mental health in New York City (Padgett, 2007).

[2] The full report can be found here: https://www.birmingham.ac.uk/documents/college-social-sciences/social-policy/chasm/2021/wellbeing-and-tenure-final-report.pdf

[3] The full report can be found here: https://www.vividhomes.co.uk/media/516/homes-and-wellbeing-full-report.pdf

Chapter 6

[1] I use Likert; Foye et al (2018) use caseness.

[2] Sometimes this ordering implicitly follows a narrative structure revealing an often quite dramatic tenure–wellbeing relationship before using a more robust model to put the rabbit back into the magician's hat. In this narrative fixed effects are a kind of gold standard and, indeed, the results I present could be interpreted in this way, by the extent and richness of tenure variation that disappears in the fixed effect model. However, this is not the whole story. There are a number of experts who dispute this and argue for the superiority of a random effects approach using longitudinal data (Cameron and Trivedi, 2009; Nikolaev, 2016). There is also a body of work in the broader methodological literature that seeks to move beyond an either/or debate, and which argues that the apparent distortions of a random effects model can be exaggerated and, moreover, that the price of the fixed effects model can be very high if we are interested in the relationship between our dependent variables (wellbeing) and not just tenure alone, but tenure in its country specific cultural and institutional context (Bell et al, 2019).

[3] 'pidp' refers to the cross-wave person identifier used in BHPS/US to track identifiable individuals over time.

Chapter 7

[1] In 1967 Rex and Moore published the results of a study of racial discrimination in the housing market of Sparkbrook in Birmingham (Rex and Moore, 1967). At the time of publication private landlords had a legal right to exclude tenants on the basis of race or ethnicity.

[2] A very similar account has since been developed, independently, by Sayer (2020).

[3] www.estatewatch.london/research

[4] The local authority responded with the counter-claim that all residents were offered a new home in the same borough (Southwark Council, n.d.).

References

Acolin, A. (2020) Owning vs. renting: The benefits of residential stability? *Housing Studies*, 1–24.

Adler, A. and Seligman, M.E. (2016) Using wellbeing for public policy: Theory, measurement, and recommendations. *International Journal of Wellbeing*, *6*(1), pp 1–35.

Affordable Housing Commission (2020) Making housing affordable again: Rebalancing the nation's housing system. The final report of the Affordable Housing Commission. Affordable Housing Commission, [online] 23 March, Available from: www.affordablehousingcommission. org/news/2020/3/23/making-housing-affordable-again-rebalancing-the-nations-housing-system-the-final-report-of-the-affordable-housing-commission

Alesina, A. and Ferrara, E.L. (2000) Participation in heterogeneous communities. *Quarterly Journal of Economics*, *115*(3), pp 847–904.

Alkire, S. (2005) *Valuing freedoms: Sen's capability approach and poverty reduction.* New York: Oxford University Press.

Angel, S. (2021) Housing regimes and residualization of the subsidized rental sector in Europe 2005–2016. *Housing Studies*, pp 1–21.

Angel, S. and Gregory, J. (2021) Does housing tenure matter? Owner-occupation and wellbeing in Britain and Austria. *Housing Studies*, 1-21. DOI: 10.1080/02673037.2021.1912714.

Araya, R., Dunstan, F., Playle, R., Thomas, H., Palmer, S. and Lewis, G. (2006) Perceptions of social capital and the built environment and mental health. *Social Science and Medicine*, *62*(12), pp 3072–3083.

Archer, T., Green, S. and Wilson, I. (2018) *Effective housing for people on low incomes in the Welsh valleys.* York: Joseph Rowntree Foundation.

Baba, C., Kearns, A., McIntosh, E., Tannahill, C. and Lewsey, J. (2017) Is empowerment a route to improving mental health and wellbeing in an urban regeneration (UR) context? *Urban Studies*, *54*(7), pp 1619–1637.

Bacchi, C. (2009) *Analysing policy.* Sydney: Pearson Higher Education AU.

Badland, H., Foster, S., Bentley, R., Higgs, C., Roberts, R., Pettit, C. and Giles-Corti, B. (2017) Examining associations between area-level spatial measures of housing with selected health and wellbeing behaviours and outcomes in an urban context. *Health & Place*, *43*, pp 17–24.

Baker, E., Bentley, R. and Mason, K. (2013) The mental health effects of housing tenure: Causal or compositional? *Urban Studies*, *50*(2), pp 426–442.

Bamfield, L. (2007) *Born unequal: Why we need a progressive pre-birth agenda.* London: Fabian Society.

Banting, K.G. and Kymlicka, W. (2006) *Multiculturalism and the welfare state: Recognition and redistribution in contemporary democracies.* New York: Oxford University Press.

Barker, N. (2017) Revealed: The scale of ex-RTB home conversions to private rent. Inside Housing, [online] 7 December, Available from: https://www.insidehousing.co.uk/insight/insight/revealed-the-scale-of-ex-rtb-home-conversions-to-private-rent-53525

Barlow, J. and Duncan, S. (1988) The use and abuse of housing tenure. *Housing Studies, 3*(4), pp 219–231.

Bassett, K.A. and Short, J.R. (1980) Patterns of building society and local authority mortgage lending in the 1970s. *Environment and Planning A, 12*(3), pp 279–300.

Batty, E. and Flint, J. (2013) Talking 'bout' poor folks (thinking 'bout my folks): Perspectives on comparative poverty in working class households. *International Journal of Housing Policy, 13*(1), pp 1–19.

Bauer, T.K., Fertig, M. and Vorell, M. (2011) Neighborhood effects and individual unemployment, Available from: https://papers.ssrn.com/sol3/papers.cfm?abstract_id=1965950

BBC News (2008) 'Work or lose home' says minister. BBC News, [online] 5 February, Available from www.news.bbc.co.uk/1/hi/7227667.stm

BBC News (2018) The sacrifices you make to get on the housing ladder. BBC News, [online] 3 October, Available from: www.bbc.co.uk/news/av/business-45733911

Bentley, R.J., Pevalin, D., Baker, E., Mason, K., Reeves, A. and Beer, A. (2016) Housing affordability, tenure and mental health in Australia and the United Kingdom: A comparative panel analysis. *Housing Studies, 31*(2), pp 208–222.

Beresford, P., Green, D., Lister, R. and Woodard, K. (1999) *Poverty first hand: Poor people speak for themselves.* London: CPAG.

Berger, P.L. and Luckmann, T. (1991 [1966]) *The social construction of reality: A treatise in the sociology of knowledge.* London: Penguin.

Birch, J. (2020) We need to talk about tax reform. Jules Birch, [blog] 12 November, Available from: https://julesbirch.com/2020/11/12/we-need-to-talk-about-tax-reform

Blume, L. and Durlauf, S.N. (2001) The interactions-based approach to socioeconomic behavior. *Social Dynamics, 15.*

Bond, L., Kearns, A., Mason, P., Tannahill, C., Egan, M. and Whitely, E. (2012) Exploring the relationships between housing, neighbourhoods and mental wellbeing for residents of deprived areas. *BMC Public Health, 12*(1), p 48.

Bourdieu, P. (1977) *Outline of a theory of practice.* Cambridge: Cambridge University Press.

Bright, S. (1998) Of estates and interests: A tale of ownership and property rights. In S. Bright and J. Dewar (eds) *Land law: Themes and perspectives*. Oxford: Oxford University Press: pp 529–546.

Bright, S. and Hopkins, N. (2011) Home, meaning and identity: Learning from the English model of shared ownership. *Housing, Theory and Society*, *28*(4), pp 377–397.

Buck, N. (2001) Identifying neighbourhood effects on social exclusion. *Urban Studies*, *38*(12), pp 2251–2275.

Burchardt, T. (2004) Capabilities and disability: The capabilities framework and the social model of disability. *Disability & Society*, *19*(7), pp 735–751.

Burchardt, T. and Vizard, P. (2011) 'Operationalizing' the capability approach as a basis for equality and human rights monitoring in twenty-first-century Britain. *Journal of Human Development and Capabilities*, *12*(1), pp 91–119.

Burrows, R. (2003) How the other half lives: An exploratory analysis of the relationship between poverty and home-ownership in Britain. *Urban Studies*, *40*(7), pp 1223–1242.

Carter, H. (2007) Housing madness. *The Guardian*, [online] 3 October, Available from: www.theguardian.com/commentisfree/2007/oct/03/housingmadness

Chapman, J. (2015) 'We'll create a job for everyone that wants one': Cameron pledges to create highest employment rate in developed world, *Daily Mail*, [online] 31 March, Available from: www.dailymail.co.uk/news/article-3018675/David-Cameron-pledges-create-highest-employment-rate-developed-world-exclusive-interview-Mail.html

Chartered Institute of Housing (2021) *UK housing review 2021*. Coventry: Chartered Institute of Housing.

Cheung, F. and Lucas, R.E. (2016) Income inequality is associated with stronger social comparison effects: The effect of relative income on life satisfaction. *Journal of Personality and Social Psychology*, *110*(2), p 332–341.

Clair, A. (2021) The effect of local housing allowance reductions on overcrowding in the private rented sector in England. *International Journal of Housing Policy*, pp 1–19.

Clair, A., Reeves, A., Loopstra, R., McKee, M., Dorling, D. and Stuckler, D. (2016) The impact of the housing crisis on self-reported health in Europe: Multilevel longitudinal modelling of 27 EU countries. *European Journal of Public Health*, *26*(5), pp 788–793.

Clapham, D. (1997) The social construction of housing management research. *Urban Studies*, *34*(5–6), pp 761–774.

Clapham, D. Foye, C. and Christian, J. (2018) The concept of subjective well-being in housing research. *Housing, Theory and Society*, *35*, pp 261–280.

Clark, A.E. (2015) SWB as a measure of individual well-being. In M.D. Adler and M. Fleurbaey (eds) *The Oxford handbook of well-being and public policy*. Oxford: Oxford University Press.

Clark, A.E. and Oswald, A.J. (1996) Satisfaction and comparison income. *Journal of Public Economics*, *61*(3), pp 359–381.

Clark, A.E., Frijters, P. and Shields, M.A. (2008) Relative income, happiness, and utility: An explanation for the Easterlin paradox and other puzzles. *Journal of Economic Literature*, *46*(1), pp 95–144.

Clark, J. and Kearns, A. (2012) Housing improvements, perceived housing quality and psychosocial benefits from the home. *Housing Studies*, *27*(7), pp 915–939.

Clark, A.E., Fleche, S., Layard, R., Powdthavee, N. and Ward, G. (2018) *The origins of happiness: The science of well-being over the life course*. Princeton: Princeton University Press.

Conservative Party (2019) 5 key points you must know about our new housing policy, Conservatives, [online] 30 September, Available from: www.conservatives.com/news/2019/5-key-points-you-must-know-about-our-new-housing-policy

Corbyn, J. (2015) Tackling the housing crisis. Jeremy Corbyn: Housing policy, [online], Available from: https://d3n8a8pro7vhmx.cloudfront.net/jeremyforlabour/pages/106/attachments/original/1438782182/housing.pdf?1438782182

Cowan, D., Carr, H. and Wallace, A. (2018) Ownership, narrative, things. In D. Cowan, H. Carr and A. Wallace (eds) *Ownership, narrative, things*. London: Palgrave Macmillan, pp 1–41.

Curchin, K. (2017) Using behavioural insights to argue for a stronger social safety net: Beyond libertarian paternalism. *Journal of Social Policy*, *46*(2), 231-249.

Crane, J. (1991) The epidemic theory of ghettos and neighborhood effects on dropping out and teenage childbearing. *American Journal of Sociology*, *96*(5), pp 1226–1259.

Crisis (2019) *Cover the cost: How gaps in Local Housing Allowance are impacting homelessness*. London: Crisis, Available from: www.crisis.org.uk/media/240377/cover_the_cost_2019.pdf

Crawford, J. and McKee, K. (2018) Hysteresis: Understanding the housing aspirations gap. *Sociology*, *52*(1), pp 182–197.

Crockett, R. (1995) *Thinking the unthinkable*. London: Fontana.

Crook, A.T. and Whitehead, C. (2019) Capturing development value, principles and practice: Why is it so difficult? *The Town Planning Review*, *90*(4), pp 359–381.

Crowson, N.J. (2013) Revisiting the 1977 Housing (Homeless Persons) Act: Westminster, Whitehall, and the homelessness lobby. *Twentieth Century British History*, *24*(3), pp 424–447.

CSJ (Centre for Social Justice) (2008) *Housing poverty: From social breakdown to social mobility*. London: CSJ.

Cullingworth, J.B. (1969) *Council housing: Purposes, procedures and priorities. Ninth report of the Housing Management Sub-Committee of the Central Housing Advisory Committee*. London: HMSO.

Curchin, K. (2017) Using behavioural insights to argue for a stronger social safety net: Beyond libertarian paternalism. *Journal of Social Policy*, *46*(2), pp 231–249.

Curry, R. (2019) Why are so many housing associations turning their backs on fixed-term tenancies? *Inside Housing*, [online] 2 May, Available from: www.insidehousing.co.uk/insight/insight/why-are-so-many-housing-associations-turning-their-backs-on-fixed-term-tenancies-61200

Daly, G., Mooney, G., Poole, L. and Davis, H. (2005) Housing stock transfer in Birmingham and Glasgow: The contrasting experiences of two UK cities. *European Journal of Housing Policy*, *5*(3), pp 327–341.

Davies, W. (2016) *The limits of neoliberalism: Authority, sovereignty and the logic of competition*. London: Sage.

DBIS (Department for Business, Innovation and Skills) (2010) The Spending Review 2010. DBIS, [online] 20 October, Available from: www.gov.uk/government/news/the-spending-review-2010

Defend Council Housing (DCH) (2006) *The case for council housing in 21st century Britain*. London: Defend Council Housing.

Dean, H. (2009) Critiquing capabilities: The distractions of a beguiling concept. *Critical Social Policy*, *29*(2), pp 261–278.

Dietz, R.D. and Haurin, D.R. (2003) The social and private micro-level consequences of homeownership. *Journal of Urban Economics*, *54*(3), pp 401–450.

Diener, E., Lucas, R.E. and Oishi, S. (2002) Subjective well-being: The science of happiness and life satisfaction. In C.R. Snyder and S.J. Lopez (eds) *Handbook of positive psychology*. Oxford: Oxford University Press, pp 63–73.

Department for Work and Pensions (DWP) (2009) *Supporting people into work: The next stage of Housing Benefit reform. Public consultation*. London: DWP, Available from: https://assets.publishing.service.gov.uk/government/uploads/system/uploads/attachment_data/file/422155/Supporting_people_into_work-Housing_Benefit_consultation.pdf

DWP (2013) Households below average income (HBAI) statistics. DWP, [online] 14 June, Available from: www.gov.uk/government/collections/households-below-average-income-hbai--2

DWP (2021) Family Resources Survey: Financial year 2019 to 2020, 4. Tenure: Households by tenure, FYE2010 to FYE 2020, United Kingdom. DWP, [online] 25 March, Available from: www.gov.uk/government/statistics/family-resources-survey-financial-year-2019-to-2020/family-resources-survey-financial-year-2019-to-2020#tenure-1

Diener, E., Oishi, S. and Tay, L. (2018) Advances in subjective well-being research. *Nature Human Behaviour*, *2*(4), pp 253–260.

DiPasquale, D. and Glaeser, E.L. (1999) Incentives and social capital: Are homeowners better citizens? *Journal of Urban Economics*, *45*(2), 354–384.

DLHC and MHCLG (Department for Levelling Up, Housing and Communities) and MHCLG (Ministry of Housing, Communities & Local Government) (2021a) English Housing Survey data on attitudes and satisfaction, Table FA5401: satisfaction with accommodation, 2019–20. DLHC and MHCLG, [online] 8 July, Available from: www.gov.uk/government/statistical-data-sets/attitudes-and-satisfaction

DLHC and MHCLG (2021b) English Housing Survey data on social and private renters. DLHC and MHCLG, [online] 8 July, Available from: www.gov.uk/government/statistical-data-sets/social-and-private-renters

DLHC and MHCLG (2022) Live tables on dwelling stock (including vacants), Chart 103: by tenure, Great Britain, historical series (chart). DHLC and MHCLG, [online] 27 January, Available from: www.gov.uk/government/statistical-data-sets/live-tables-on-dwelling-stock-including-vacants

Dolan, A. and Bentley, P. (2013) Vile product of welfare UK: Man who bred 17 babies by five women to milk benefits system is guilty of killing six of them. *Daily Mail*, [online] 24 May, Available from: www.dailymail.co.uk/news/article-2303120/Mick-Philpott-vile-product-Welfare-UK-Derby-man-bred-17-babies-milk-benefits-GUILTY-killing-six.html

Dolan, P. and Metcalfe, R. (2012) Measuring subjective wellbeing: Recommendations on measures for use by national governments. *Journal of Social Policy*, *41*(2), pp 409–427.

Dolan, P., Kavetsos, G. and Tsuchiya, A. (2013) Sick but satisfied: The impact of life and health satisfaction on choice between health scenarios. *Journal of Health Economics*, *32*(4), pp 708–714.

Donnison, D.V. (1967) *The government of housing*. London: Penguin.

Donnison, D.V. and Ungerson, C. (1982) *Housing policy*. London: Penguin.

Doyal, L. and Gough, I. (1991) *A theory of human need*. Basingstoke: Macmillan.

Dujardin, C. and Goffette-Nagot, F. (2005) Neighborhood effects, public housing and unemployment in France. Amsterdam: SSRN, Elsevier.

Dujardin, C. and Goffette-Nagot, F. (2010) Neighborhood effects on unemployment?: A test à la Altonji. *Regional Science and Urban Economics*, *40*(6), pp 380–396.

Dunleavy, P. (1981) *The politics of mass housing in Britain, 1945–1975: A study of corporate power and professional influence in the welfare state*. Oxford: Oxford University Press.

Dupuis, A. and Thorns, D.C. (1998) Home, home ownership and the search for ontological security. *The Sociological Review*, *46*(1), pp 24–47.

Edinburgh Evening News (2018) Edinburgh housing crisis as rent prices soar. *Edinburgh Evening News*, [online] 28 November, Available from: www.edinburghnews.scotsman.com/news/politics/edinburgh-housing-crisis-rent-prices-soar-200640

Ellen, I.G. and Turner, M.A., (1997) Does neighborhood matter? Assessing recent evidence. *Housing Policy Debate*, 8(4), pp 833–866.

Esping-Andersen, G. (1990) *The three worlds of welfare capitalism.* Princeton: Princeton University Press.

Evans, G.W. (2003) The built environment and mental health. *Journal of Urban Health*, 80(4), pp 536–555.

Feinstein, L. (2003) Inequality in the early cognitive development of British children in the 1970 cohort. *Economica*, 70(277), pp 73–97.

Feinstein, L., Lupton, R., Hammond, C., Mujtaba, T., Salter, E. and Sorhaindo, A. (2008) *The public value of social housing: A longitudinal analysis of the relationship between housing and life chances.* London: Smith Institute.

Field, F. (2010) *The Foundation Years: Preventing poor children becoming poor adults. The report of the Independent Review on Poverty and Life Chances.* London: The Stationery Office.

Financial Times (2021) Foreign ownership of homes in England and Wales triples. *Financial Times*, [online] 12 November, Available from: www.ft.com/content/e36cec28-7acd-4154-b57d-923b5d1610da

Fitzpatrick, S. and Pawson, H. (2014) Ending security of tenure for social renters: Transitioning to 'ambulance service' social housing? *Housing Studies*, 29(5), pp 597–615.

Fitzpatrick, S. and Watts, B. (2017) Competing visions: Security of tenure and the welfarisation of English social housing. *Housing Studies*, 32(8), pp 1021–1038.

Flint, J. (2003) Housing and ethopolitics: Constructing identities of active consumption and responsible community. *Economy and Society*, 32(4), pp 611–629.

Flint, J. and Nixon, J. (2006) Governing neighbours: Anti-social behaviour orders and new forms of regulating conduct in the UK. *Urban Studies*, 43(5–6), pp 939–955.

Flint, J. and Powell, R. (2012) The English city riots of 2011: 'Broken Britain' and the retreat into the present. *Sociological Research Online*, 17(3), pp 153–162.

Forrest, R. and Murie, A. (1983) Residualization and council housing: Aspects of the changing social relations of housing tenure. *Journal of Social Policy*, 12(4), pp 453–468.

Forrest, R. and Wu, Y. (2014) People like us? Social status, social inequality and perceptions of public rental housing. *Journal of Social Policy*, 43(1), pp 135–151.

Forrest, R., Murie, A. and Williams, P. (1990) *Home ownership: Differentiation and fragmentation.* London: Routledge.

Foye, C. (2017) The relationship between size of living space and subjective well-being. *Journal of Happiness Studies*, 18(2), pp 427–461.

Foye, C., Clapham, D. and Gabrieli, T. (2018) Home-ownership as a social norm and positional good: Subjective wellbeing evidence from panel data. *Urban Studies*, 55(6), pp 1290–1312.

Francis, M. (2012) 'A crusade to enfranchise the many': Thatcherism and the 'property-owning democracy'. *Twentieth Century British History*, 23(2), pp 275–297.

Frankfurt, H.G. (1971) Freedom of the will and the concept of a person. *The Journal of Philosophy*, 68(1), pp 5–20.

Franklin, B. and Clapham, D. (1997) The social construction of housing management. *Housing Studies*, 12(1), pp 7–26.

Fraser, N. and Gordon, L. (1994) A genealogy of dependency: Tracing a keyword of the US welfare state. *Signs: Journal of Women in Culture and Society*, 19(2), pp 309–336.

Freeden, M. (2003) The coming of the welfare state. In T. Ball and R. Bellamy (eds) *The Cambridge history of twentieth-century political thought*. Cambridge: Cambridge University Press, pp 7–44.

Freud, Lord D. (2007) *Reducing dependency, increasing opportunity: Options for the future of welfare to work*. Leeds: Corporate Document Services.

Freud, Lord D. (2011) Speech: Housing and welfare reform. UK Government, [online] 22 June, Available from: www.gov.uk/government/speeches/housing-and-welfare-reform

Freud, Lord D. (2014) Speech: Transforming welfare. UK Government, [online] 27 January, Available from: www.gov.uk/government/speeches/transforming-welfare

Freud, Lord D. (2016) Speech: Reforms to support social sector tenants. UK Government, [online] 30 June, Available from: www.gov.uk/government/speeches/reforms-to-support-social-sector-tenants

Frost, L. and Hoggett, P. (2008) Human agency and social suffering. *Critical Social Policy*, 28(4), pp 438–460.

Foucault, M. (1991) *The Foucault effect: Studies in governmentality*. Chicago: University of Chicago Press.

Fujiwara, D. (2013) *The social impact of housing providers*. London: HACT.

Gadamer, H.G. (2013 [1960]) *Truth and method*. London: A&C Black.

Galster, G., Andersson, R., Musterd, S. and Kauppinen, T.M. (2008) Does neighborhood income mix affect earnings of adults? New evidence from Sweden. *Journal of Urban Economics*, 63(3), pp 858–870.

Gamble, A. (1994) *The free economy and the strong state: The politics of Thatcherism*. Basingstoke: Palgrave.

Giddens, A. (1990) *The consequences of modernity*. Cambridge: Polity Press.

Giddens, A. (1991) *Modernity and self-identity: Self and society in the late modern age*. Cambridge: Polity Press.

Gilligan, A. (2010) Rush-hour silence in a welfare ghetto. *The Telegraph*, [online] 10 October, Available from: www.telegraph.co.uk/news/politics/8053265/Rush-hour-silence-in-a-welfare-ghetto-Sink-estate-by-passed-by-the-rush-hour.html

Ginsburg, N. (2005) The privatization of council housing. *Critical Social Policy*, *25*(1), pp 115–135.

Glass, N. (1999) Sure Start: The development of an early intervention programme for young children in the United Kingdom. *Children & Society*, *13*(4), pp 257–264.

Golding, P. and Middleton, S. (1982) *Images of welfare: Press and public attitudes to poverty*. Oxford: Martin Robertson & Co.

Goodchild, B. and Cole, I. (2001) Social balance and mixed neighbourhoods in Britain since 1979: A review of discourse and practice in social housing. *Environment and Planning D: Society and Space*, *19*(1), pp 103–121.

Green, A.E. and White, R.J. (2007) *Attachment to place, social networks, mobility and prospects of young people*. York: Joseph Rowntree Foundation.

Gregory, J. (2014) The search for an 'asset-effect': What do we want from asset-based welfare? *Critical Social Policy*, *34*(4), pp 475–494.

Gregory, J. (2015) Engineering compassion: The institutional structure of virtue. *Journal of Social Policy*, *44*(2), 339–356.

Gregory, J., Mullins, D., Murie, A. and Redman, P. (2016) Social housing and the good society. *Housing and Communities Research Group*, Available from: https://www.birmingham.ac.uk/Documents/college-social-sciences/social-policy/SPSW/Housing/2017/WMT-final-NOV-12th-Clean-Version.pdf

Gregory, J. (2016) How not to be an egalitarian: The politics of homeownership and property-owning democracy. *International Journal of Housing Policy*, *16*(3), pp 337–356.

Gregory, J., Lymer, A., Espenlaub, S., Khurshed, A., Mohamed, A. and Giunti, G. (2018) *Homes and wellbeing: Breaking down housing stereotypes*. Portsmouth: VIVID in association with Universities of Birmingham and Manchester, Available from: www.vividhomes.co.uk/media/516/homes-and-wellbeing-full-report.pdf

Guite, H.F., Clark, C. and Ackrill, G. (2006) The impact of the physical and urban environment on mental well-being. *Public Health*, *120*(12), pp 1117–1126.

Gurney, C.M. (1999) Pride and prejudice: Discourses of normalisation in public and private accounts of home ownership. *Housing Studies*, *14*(2), pp 163–183.

Halpern, D. (2005) *Social capital*. Cambridge: Polity Press.

Hamptons (2021) Has the door closed on Buy-to-let? Hamptons, [online], Available from: https://mr1.homeflow.co.uk/files/site_asset/image/4541/0317/buy-to-let-reports.pdf#

Hancock, L. and Mooney, G. (2013) 'Welfare ghettos' and the 'broken society': Territorial stigmatization in the contemporary UK. *Housing, Theory and Society, 30*(1), pp 46–64.

Harloe, M. (2008) *The people's home?: Social rented housing in Europe and America.* Chichester: John Wiley & Sons.

Harris, J., Cowan, D. and Marsh, A. (2020) *Improving compliance with private rented sector legislation: Local authority regulation and enforcement.* Glasgow: UK Collaborative Centre for Housing Evidence.

Hastings, A. (2000) Discourse analysis: What does it offer housing studies? *Housing, Theory and Society, 17*(3), pp 131–139.

Hastings, A. (2004) Stigma and social housing estates: Beyond pathological explanations. *Journal of Housing and the Built Environment, 19*(3), pp 233–254.

Hastings, A. and Dean, J. (2003) Challenging images: Tackling stigma through estate regeneration. *Policy & Politics, 31*(2), pp 171–184.

Hayton, R. (2012) Fixing broken Britain. In T. Heppell and D. Seawright (eds) *Cameron and the Conservatives: The transition to coalition government.* Basingstoke: Palgrave Macmillan, pp 136–148.

Hewstone, M. (2015) Consequences of diversity for social cohesion and prejudice: The missing dimension of intergroup contact. *Journal of Social Issues, 71*(2), pp 417–438.

Honneth, A. (1996) *The struggle for recognition: The moral grammar of social conflicts.* Cambridge: MIT Press.

Hick, R. (2012) The capability approach: Insights for a new poverty focus. *Journal of Social Policy, 41*(2), pp 291–308.

Hicks, S., Tinkler, L. and Allin, P. (2013) Measuring subjective well-being and its potential role in policy: Perspectives from the UK office for national statistics. *Social Indicators Research, 114*(1), pp 73–86.

Hills J. (2007) *Ends and means: The future roles of social housing in England.* CASE Report 34. London: London School of Economics.

Hills, J. (2013) *Wealth in the UK: Distribution, accumulation, policy.* Oxford: Oxford University Press.

Hiscock, R., Kearns, A., MacIntyre, S. and Ellaway, A. (2001) Ontological security and psycho-social benefits from the home: Qualitative evidence on issues of tenure. *Housing, Theory and Society, 18*(1–2), pp 50–66.

Hiscock, R., Macintyre, S., Kearns, A. and Ellaway, A. (2003) Residents and residence: factors predicting the health disadvantage of social renters compared to owner-occupiers. *Journal of Social Issues, 59*(3), 527–546.

HMT (Her Majesty's Treasury) (2015) *Fixing the foundations: Creating a more prosperous nation.* Cm 9098. London: HMT.

Hodkinson, S. and Robbins, G. (2013) The return of class war conservatism? Housing under the UK coalition government. *Critical Social Policy, 33*(1), pp 57–77.

Hoggett, P. (2001) Agency, rationality and social policy. *Journal of Social Policy*, *30*(1), pp 37–56.

Holding, E., Blank, L., Crowder, M., Ferrari, E. and Goyder, E. (2020) Exploring the relationship between housing concerns, mental health and wellbeing: A qualitative study of social housing tenants. *Journal of Public Health*, *42*(3), pp e231–e238.

Horton, T. and Gregory, J. (2009) *The solidarity society*. London: The Fabian Society.

Inside Housing (2017) Inside Housing, [online], Available from: https://www.insidehousing.co.uk/insight/insight/revealed-the-scale-of-ex-rtb-home-conversions-to-private-rent-53525

Howker, E. (2010) Spectator exclusive: Britain's welfare ghettos. *The Spectator*, [online] 9 October, Available from: www.spectator.co.uk/article/spectator-exclusive-britain-s-welfare-ghettos

Jackson, B. (2005) Revisionism reconsidered: 'Property-owning democracy' and egalitarian strategy in post-war Britain. *Twentieth Century British History*, *16*(4), pp 416–440.

Jacobs, K., Kemeny, J. and Manzi, T. (2003) Power, discursive space and institutional practices in the construction of housing problems. *Housing Studies*, *18*(4), pp 429–446.

Jensen, T. (2014) Welfare commonsense, poverty porn and doxosophy. *Sociological Research Online*, *19*(3), pp 1–7.

Jenson, T. and Tyler, I. (2015) Benefits broods: The cultural and political crafting of anti-welfare commonsense. *Critical Social Policy*, *35*(4), pp 470–491.

Jones, C. and Murie, A. (2008) *The right to buy: Analysis and evaluation of a housing policy*. Vol. 18. Chichester: John Wiley & Sons.

Jones, C., Morgan, J. and Stephens, M. (2018) *An assessment of historic attempts to capture land value uplift in the UK*. Inverness: Scottish Land Commission.

Judge, L. (2019) Social renting: A working hypothesis. Resolution Foundation, [online] 10 April, Available from: www.resolutionfoundation.org/comment/social-renting-a-working-hypothesis

Kahneman, D., Krueger, A.B., Schkade, D.A., Schwarz, N. and Stone, A.A. (2004) A survey method for characterizing daily life experience: The day reconstruction method. *Science*, *306*(5702), pp 1776–1780.

Kearns, A., Hiscock, R., Ellaway, A. and Macintyre, S. (2000) 'Beyond four walls': The psycho-social benefits of home – Evidence from west central Scotland. *Housing Studies*, *15*(3), pp 387–410.

Kearns, A., Whitley, E., Bond, L. and Tannahill, C., (2012) The residential psychosocial environment and mental wellbeing in deprived areas. *International Journal of Housing Policy*, *12*(4), pp 413–438.

Kemeny, J. (1992) *Housing and social theory*. London: Routledge.

Kemp, P.A. (2000) Images of council housing. In R. Jowell, J. Curtice, A. Park and K. Thomson (eds) *British Social Attitudes. The 17th report: Focusing on diversity*. London: Sage, pp 137–154.

Kemp, P. (2002) *Private renting in transition*. Coventry: Chartered Institute of Housing.

Kemp, P.A. and Kofner, S. (2010) Contrasting varieties of private renting: England and Germany. *International Journal of Housing Policy*, *10*(4), pp 379–398.

King, P. (2009) Using theory or making theory: Can there be theories of housing? *Housing, Theory and Society*, *26*(1), pp 41–52.

Kleinhans, R. and Elsinga, M. (2010) 'Buy your home and feel in control': Does home ownership achieve the empowerment of former tenants of social housing? *International Journal of Housing Policy*, 10(1), pp 41–61.

Kofner, S. (2017) Social housing in Germany: An inevitably shrinking sector? *Critical Housing Analysis*, 4(1), pp 61–71.

Laing, R. (2010 [1965]) *The divided self: An existential study in sanity and madness*. London: Penguin.

Langhamer, C. (2005) The meanings of home in postwar Britain. *Journal of Contemporary History*, *40*(2), pp 341–362.

Lansley, S. and Mack, J. (2015) *Breadline Britain: The rise of mass poverty*. London: Oneworld Publications.

Larsen, C.A. (2008) The institutional logic of welfare attitudes: How welfare regimes influence public support. *Comparative Political Studies*, *41*(2), pp 145–168.

Laurence, J. (2011) The effect of ethnic diversity and community disadvantage on social cohesion: A multi-level analysis of social capital and interethnic relations in UK communities. *European Sociological Review*, *27*(1), pp 70–89.

Lawrence, J. (2019) *Me, me, me? Individualism and the search for community in post-war England*. Oxford: Oxford University Press.

Leather, P. and Nevin, B. (2013) The housing market renewal programme: Origins, outcomes and the effectiveness of public policy interventions in a volatile market. *Urban Studies*, *50*(5), pp 856–875.

Leather, P., Nevin, B., Cole, I. and Eadson, W. (2012) *The Housing Market Renewal Programme in England: Development, impact and legacy*. Shrewsbury and Sheffield: Nevin Leather Associates and Centre for Regional, Economic and Social Research, Sheffield Hallam University.

Lees, L. and White, H. (2020) The social cleansing of London council estates: Everyday experiences of 'accumulative dispossession'. *Housing Studies*, *35*(10), pp 1701–1722.

Lees, L. (2008) Gentrification and social mixing: Towards an inclusive urban renaissance? *Urban Studies*, *45*(12), pp 2449–2470.

Letki, N. (2008) Does diversity erode social cohesion? Social capital and race in British neighbourhoods. *Political Studies, 56*(1), pp 99–126.

Leunig, T. and Swaffield, J. (2007) *Cities limited*. London: Policy Exchange.

Lindblad, M.R. and Quercia, R.G. (2015) Why is homeownership associated with nonfinancial benefits? A path analysis of competing mechanisms. *Housing Policy Debate, 25*(2), 263–288.

Lind, H. (2017) The Swedish housing market from a low income perspective. *Critical Housing Analysis, 4*(1), pp 150–160.

Lister, R. (2003) *Poverty*. Cambridge: Polity Press.

Lister, R. (2015) 'To count for nothing': Poverty beyond the statistics. *Journal of the British Academy, 3*, pp 139–165.

Liu, Y., Dijst, M. and Geertman, S. (2017) The subjective well-being of older adults in Shanghai: The role of residential environment and individual resources. *Urban Studies, 54*(7), pp 1692–1714.

Locke, J. (1962 [1689]) *Second treatise on government*. Cambridge: Cambridge University Press.

Lowe, S. (2011) *The housing debate*. Bristol: Policy Press.

Ludwig, J., Duncan, G.J., Gennetian, L.A., Katz, L.F., Kessler, R.C., Kling, J.R. and Sanbonmatsu, L. (2013) Long-term neighborhood effects on low-income families: Evidence from moving to opportunity. *American Economic Review Papers and Proceedings, 103*(3), pp 226–231.

Lund, B. (2016) *Housing politics in the United Kingdom: Power, planning and protest*. Bristol: Policy Press.

Lupton, R., Tunstall, R., Sigle-Rushton, W., Obolenskaya, P., Sabates, R., Meschi, E., Kneale, D. and Salter, E. (2009) *Growing up in social housing in Britain: A profile of four generations from 1946 to the present day*. York: Joseph Rowntree Foundation.

Luttmer, E.F. (2005) Neighbors as negatives: Relative earnings and well-being. *The Quarterly Journal of Economics, 120*(3), pp 963–1002.

Macdonald, R., Shildrick, T. and Furlong, A. (2014) In search of 'intergenerational cultures of worklessness': Hunting the Yeti and shooting zombies. *Critical Social Policy, 34*(2), pp 199–220.

MacIntyre, A.C. (1985) *After virtue* (2nd edn). London: Duckworth.

Macmillan, L. (2014) Intergenerational worklessness in the UK and the role of local labour markets. *Oxford Economic Papers, 66*(3), pp 871–889.

Malpass, P. (2005) *Housing and the welfare state: The development of housing policy in Britain*. Basingstoke: Palgrave Macmillan.

Malpass, P. (2008) Housing and the new welfare state: Wobbly pillar or cornerstone? *Housing Studies, 23*(1), pp 1–19.

Malpass, P. and Mullins, D. (2002) Local authority housing stock transfer in the UK: From local initiative to national policy. *Housing Studies, 17*(4), pp 673–686.

Marmot, M. (2005) *Status syndrome: How your social standing directly affects your health*. London: A&C Black.

Marmot, M. and Brunner, E. (2005) Cohort profile: The Whitehall II study. *International Journal of Epidemiology*, *34*(2), 251–256.

Marsh, A. and Gibb, K. (2019) *The private rented sector in the UK An overview of the policy and regulatory landscape*. Glasgow: UK Collaborative Centre for Housing Evidence.

Marshall, T.H. (1950) *Citizenship and social class and other essays*. Cambridge: Cambridge University Press.

Marston, G. (2002) Critical discourse analysis and policy-orientated housing research. *Housing, Theory and Society*, *19*(2), pp 82–91.

Maslow, A.H. (1943) A theory of human motivation. *Psychological Review*, *50*(4), p 370.

Maslow, A.H. (1981 [1954]) *Motivation and personality*. New Delhi: Prabhat Prakashan.

McCabe, B.J. (2013) Are homeowners better citizens? Homeownership and community participation in the United States. *Social Forces*, *91*(3), 929–954.

McCabe, B.J. (2016) *No place like home: Wealth, community, and the politics of homeownership*. Oxford: Oxford University Press.

McCormack, J. (2009) 'Better the devil you know': Submerged consciousness and tenant participation in housing stock transfers. *Urban Studies*, *46*(2), pp 391–411.

McKee, K. (2009) Post-Foucauldian governmentality: What does it offer critical social policy analysis? *Critical Social Policy*, *29*(3), pp 465–486.

Mead, G.H. (1934) *Mind, self and society*. Vol. 111. Chicago: University of Chicago Press.

Merrett, S. (1979) *State housing in Britain*. London: Routledge.

Miller, D. (1990) *Market, state, and community: Theoretical foundations of market socialism*. Oxford: Oxford University Press.

Miller, D. (1999) *Principles of social justice*. Cambridge: Harvard University Press.

Ministry of Housing, Communities & Local Government (MHCLG) (2012) Councils given the freedom to stop people playing the social housing system. MHCLG, [online] 5 January, Available from: www.gov.uk/government/news/councils-given-the-freedom-to-stop-people-playing-the-social-housing-system

MHCLG (2016) English housing survey 2014: housing and well-being report. MHCLG, [online] 21 July, Available from: https://www.gov.uk/government/statistics/english-housing-survey-2014-housing-and-well-being-report

MHCLG (2018) *A new deal for social housing*. Cm9671. London: MHCLG.

MHCLG (2019) *Public attitudes to social housing: Findings from the British Social Attitudes Survey 2018*. London: MHCLG.

MHCLG (2020a) English Housing Survey Headline Report, 2019-20. MHCLG, [online] 17 December, Available from: https://assets.publishing. service.gov.uk/government/uploads/system/uploads/attachment_data/ file/945013/2019-20_EHS_Headline_Report.pdf

MHCLG (2020b) *The charter for social housing residents: Social housing White Paper.* London: MHCLG.

Mittelmark, M.B., Sagy, S., Eriksson, M., Bauer, G.F., Pelikan, J.M., Lindström, B. and Arild Espnes, G. (2017) *The handbook of salutogenesis.* Cham: Springer Nature.

Montada, L. and Schneider, A. (1989) Justice and emotional reactions to the disadvantaged. *Social Justice Research, 3,* pp 313–344.

Montgomerie, J. and Büdenbender, M. (2015) Round the houses: Homeownership and failures of asset-based welfare in the United Kingdom. *New Political Economy, 20*(3), pp 386–405.

Mooney, G. and Poole, L. (2005) Marginalised voices: Resisting the privatisation of council housing in Glasgow. *Local Economy, 20*(1), pp 27–39.

Moore, J. (2018) Millions of millennials will never own homes so it's time to make renting work better. *Independent,* [online] 17 April, Available from: www.independent.co.uk/news/business/comment/generation-rent-millennials-home-ownership-house-prices-resolution-foundation-a8308396.html

Morphet, J. and Clifford, B. (2020) *Reviving local authority housing delivery: Challenging austerity through municipal entrepreneurialism.* Bristol: Policy Press.

Morton, A. (2010) Making housing affordable. London: Policy Exchange.

Mullins, D. and Jones, T. (2015) From 'contractors to the state' to 'protectors of public value'? Relations between non-profit housing hybrids and the state in England. *Voluntary Sector Review, 6*(3), pp 261–283.

Mullins, D. and Pawson, H. (2010) Housing associations: Agents of policy or profits in disguise? In D. Billis (ed) *Hybrid organizations and the third sector: Challenges for practice, theory and policy.* Basingstoke: Palgrave Macmillan, pp 197–218.

Mullins, D., Czischke, D. and van Bortel, G. (2012) Exploring the meaning of hybridity and social enterprise in housing organisations. *Housing Studies, 27*(4), pp 405–417.

Murie, A. (1975) *The sale of council houses: A study in social policy.* Birmingham: Centre for Urban and Regional Studies, University of Birmingham.

Murie, A. (1997) The social rented sector, housing and the welfare state in the UK. *Housing Studies, 12*(4), pp 437–461.

Murie, A. (2016) *The Right to Buy: Selling off public and social housing.* Policy Press.

National Audit Office (NAO) (2019) *Help to Buy: Equity loan scheme – progress review*. London: NAO, Available from: www.nao.org.uk/report/help-to-buy-equity-loan-scheme-progress-review

Nettleton, S. and Burrows, R. (1998) Mortgage debt, insecure home ownership and health: An exploratory analysis. *Sociology of Health & Illness*, *20*(5), pp 731–753.

Nissan, D. and Le Grand, J. (2000) *A capital idea: Start-up grants for young people*. London: Fabian Society.

Nozick, R. (1974) *Anarchy, state, and utopia* (vol. 5038). New York: Basic Books.

Nussbaum, M.C. (1992) Human functioning and social justice: In defense of Aristotelian essentialism. *Political Theory*, *20*(2), pp 202–246.

Nussbaum, M.C. (2006) *Frontiers of justice: Disability, nationality, species membership*. Cambridge: Belknap Press.

O'Neill, M. and Williamson, T. (eds) (2012) *Property-owning democracy: Rawls and beyond*. Chichester: John Wiley & Sons.

ONS (Office for National Statistics) (2016) Housing affordability in England and Wales: 2016. ONS, [online], Available from: www.ons.gov.uk/peoplepopulationandcommunity/housing/bulletins/housingaffordability inenglandandwales/1997to2016

ONS (2020) One in eight British households has no garden. ONS, [online] 14 May, Available from: www.ons.gov.uk/economy/environmentalaccounts/articles/oneineightbritishhouseholdshasnogarden/2020-05-14

Opotow, S. (1990) Moral exclusion and injustice: An introduction. *Journal of Social Issues*, *46*(1), pp 1– 20.

Padgett, D.K. (2007) There's no place like (a) home: Ontological security among persons with serious mental illness in the United States. *Social Science & Medicine*, *64*(9), 1925–1936.

Pahl, R.E. (1984) *Divisions of labour*. Oxford: Basil Blackwell.

Pantazis, C. (2016) Policies and discourses of poverty during a time of recession and austerity. *Critical Social Policy*, *36*(1), pp 3–20.

Pattison, B. and Cole, I. (2020) Opening a new route into home ownership? The extension of the Right to Buy to housing associations in England. *International Journal of Housing Policy*, *20*(2), pp 203–228.

Pawson, H. and Mullins, D. (2010) *After council housing: Britain's new social landlords*. Basingstoke: Palgrave Macmillan.

Pawson, H. and Smith, R. (2009) Second generation stock transfers in Britain: Impacts on social housing governance and organisational culture. *European Journal of Housing Policy*, *9*(4), pp 411–433.

Peasgood, T.M. (2008) *Measuring well-being for public policy*. Doctoral thesis, University of London.

Peck, J. and Tickell, A. (2007) Conceptualizing neoliberalism, thinking Thatcherism. In H. Leitner, J. Peck and E.S. Sheppard (eds) *Contesting neoliberalism: Urban frontiers*. New York: The Guilford Press, pp 26–50.

Percival, J. (2001) Self-esteem and social motivation in age-segregated settings. *Housing Studies*, 16(6), pp 827–840.

Permentier, M., Bolt, G. and van Ham, M. (2011) Determinants of neighbourhood satisfaction and perception of neighbourhood reputation. *Urban Studies*, 48(5), pp 977–996.

Pettigrew, T.F. (1998) Intergroup contact theory. *Annual Review of Psychology*, 49, pp 65–85.

Pevalin, D.J., Taylor, M.P. and Todd, J. (2008) The dynamics of unhealthy housing in the UK: A panel data analysis. *Housing Studies*, 23(5), pp 679–695.

Philpot, R. (ed) (2011) *The purple book*. London: Biteback Publishing.

Pierson, P. (1993) When effect becomes cause: Policy feedback and political change. *World Politics*, 45(4), pp 595–628.

Popham, F., Williamson, L. and Whitley, E. (2015) Is changing status through housing tenure associated with changes in mental health? Results from the British Household Panel Survey. *Journal of Epidemiology and Community Health*, 69(1), pp 6–11.

Prabhakar, R. (2008) *The assets agenda: Principles and policy*. Basingstoke: Palgrave Macmillan.

Putnam, R.D. (2000) *Bowling alone: The collapse and revival of American community*. New York: Simon & Schuster.

Rawls, J. (1971) *A theory of justice*. Cambridge: Harvard University Press.

Rawls, J. (2001) *Justice as fairness: A restatement*. Cambridge: Harvard University Press.

Ravetz, A. (2001) *Council housing and culture: The history of a social experiment*. London: Routledge.

Rees-Mogg, J. and Tylecote, R. (eds) (2019) *Raising the roof: How to solve the United Kingdom's housing crisis*. London: Institute of Economic Affairs.

Rex, J. and Moore, R.S. (1969) *Race, community and conflict: A study of Sparkbrook*. Oxford: Oxford University Press.

Ritchey, L.H., Ritchey, P.N. and Dietz, B.E. (2001) Clarifying the measurement of activity. *Activities, Adaptation & Aging*, 26(1), pp 1–21.

Robeyns, I. (2011) The capability approach. In E.N. Zalta (ed) *The Stanford encyclopedia of philosophy* (Summer 2011 Edition), Available from: https://plato.stanford.edu/archives/win2021/entries/capability-approach/

Rohe, W.M. and Basolo, V. (1997) Long-term effects of homeownership on the self-perceptions and social interaction of low-income persons. *Environment and Behavior*, 29(6), pp 793–819.

Rohe, W.M., Van Zandt, S. and McCarthy, G. (2002) Social benefits and costs of homeownership. In N.P. Retsinas and E.S. Belsky (eds) *Low-income homeownership: Examining the unexamined goal*, Washington, DC: Brookings Institution Press, pp 381–406.

Rohe, W.M., Quercia, R.G. and Van Zandt, S. (2007) The social-psychological effects of affordable homeownership. In W.M. Rohe and H.L. Watson (eds) *Chasing the American dream: New perspectives on affordable homeownership*. New York: Cornell University Press, pp 304–325.

Ronald, R. (2008) *The ideology of home ownership: Homeowner societies and the role of housing*. Basingstoke: Palgrave Macmillan.

Rossi, P.H. and Weber, E. (1996) The social benefits of homeownership: Empirical evidence from national surveys. *Housing Policy Debate*, 7(1), pp 1–35.

Rothstein, B. (1998) *Just institutions matter: The moral and political logic of the universal welfare state*. Cambridge: Cambridge University Press.

Ruonavaara, H. (1993) Types and forms of housing tenure: Towards solving the comparison/translation problem. *Scandinavian Housing and Planning Research*, 10(1), pp 3–20.

Sanbonmatsu, L., Ludwig, J., Katz, L.F., Gennetian, L.A., Duncan, G.J., Kessler, R.C., Adam, E., McDade, T. and Lindau, S.T. (2011) *Moving to Opportunity for Fair Housing demonstration program: Final impacts evaluation*. Washington, DC: US Department of Housing and Urban Development, Office of Policy Development and Research.

Saugeres, L. (1999) Social construction of housing management discourse: Objectivity, rationality and everyday practice. *Housing, Theory and Society*, 16(3), pp 93–105.

Saunders, P. (1990) *A nation of home owners*. London: Routledge.

Savills (2018) UK housing wealth tops £7 trillion mark for first time ever. Savills, [online] 19 January, Available from: www.savills.co.uk/insight-and-opinion/savills-news/226807/uk-housing-wealth-tops-%C2%A37-trillion-mark-for-first-time-ever

Sayer, A. (2020) Critiquing – and rescuing – 'character'. *Sociology*, 54(3), pp 460–481.

Schwartz, H.M. and Seabrooke, L. (2009) Varieties of residential capitalism in the international political economy: Old welfare states and the new politics of housing. In H. Schwartz and L. Seabrooke (eds) *The politics of housing booms and busts*. Basingstoke: Palgrave Macmillan, pp 1–27.

Scottish Housing News (2018) 13% of Scots believe social housing provides best choice for high quality home. *Scottish Housing News*, [online] 17 September, Available from: www.scottishhousingnews.com/articles/13-of-scots-believe-social-housing-provides-best-choice-for-high-quality-home

Searle, B. (2008) *Well-being: In search of a good life?* Bristol: Policy Press.

Sen, A. (1980) Equality of what? In S.M. McMurrin (ed) *The Tanner lectures on human values: Volume 1*. Cambridge: Cambridge University Press.

Sen, A. (1992) *Inequality reexamined*. Oxford: Oxford University Press.

Sen, A. (1993) Capability and well-being. *The Quality of Life*, 30, pp 1–445.

Sen, A. (1999) *Development as freedom*. New York: A. Knopf.

Shelter Scotland (2017) *Impact report 2016/17*. Edinburgh: Shelter Scotland. Available from: https://scotland.shelter.org.uk/professional_resources/policy_library/shelter_scotland_impact_report_201617

Shelter Scotland (2018) Housing and homelessness statistics. Shelter Scotland, [online], Available from: https://scotland.shelter.org.uk/housing_policy/key_statistics/homelessness_facts_and_research

Sherraden, M. (1991) *Assets and the poor: A new American welfare policy*. New York: M.E. Sharpe.

Slater, T., 2014. The myth of 'Broken Britain': welfare reform and the production of ignorance. *Antipode, 46*(4), pp 948–969.

Smith, A. (1776) *An enquiry into the nature and causes of the wealth of nations*. London: W. Strahan and T. Cadell.

Smith, S.J. (2008) Owner-occupation: At home with a hybrid of money and materials. *Environment and Planning A, 40*(3), pp 520–535.

Smith, S.J., Searle, B.A. and Cook, N. (2009) Rethinking the risks of home ownership. *Journal of Social Policy, 38*(1), pp 83–102.

Smyth, S. (2013) The privatization of council housing: Stock transfer and the struggle for accountable housing. *Critical Social Policy, 33*(1), pp 37–56.

Southwark Council (n.d.) Elephant and Castle: Background to the Elephant Park development site. Southwark Council, [online], Available from: www.southwark.gov.uk/regeneration/elephant-and-castle?chapter=4

Stephens, M. (2005) An assessment of the British housing benefit system. *European Journal of Housing Policy, 5*(2), pp 111–129.

Stephens, M. and Leishman, C. (2017) Housing and poverty: A longitudinal analysis. *Housing Studies, 32*(8), pp 1039–1061.

Stephens, M., Dailly, M. and Wilcox, S. (2008) *Developing safety nets for home-owners*. York: Joseph Rowntree Foundation.

Stillman, S. and Liang, Y. (2010) Does homeownership improve personal wellbeing, Available from: https://bia.unibz.it/discovery/fulldisplay/alma991005772672601241/39UBZ_INST:ResearchRepository

Sutcliffe-Braithwaite, F. (2012) Neo-liberalism and morality in the making of Thatcherite social policy. *The Historical Journal, 55*(2), pp 497–520.

Taylor, C. (1992) *Sources of the self: The making of the modern identity*. Cambridge: Harvard University Press.

Taylor, D. (2011) Wellbeing and welfare: A psychosocial analysis of being well and doing well enough. *Journal of Social Policy, 40*(4), pp 777–794.

Tennant, R., Hiller, L., Fishwick, R., Platt, S., Joseph, S., Weich, S., Parkinson, J., Secker, J. and Stewart-Brown, S. (2007) The Warwick-Edinburgh mental well-being scale (WEMWBS): Development and UK validation. *Health and Quality of Life Outcomes, 5*(1), pp 1–13.

The Guardian (2018) More than 1m families waiting for social housing in England. *The Guardian*, [online] 9 June, Available from: www.theguardian.com/society/2018/jun/09/more-than-1m-families-waiting-for-social-housing-in-england

Thomson, H. and Thomas, S. (2015) Developing empirically supported theories of change for housing investment and health. *Social Science & Medicine, 124*, pp 205–214.

Torgersen, U. (1987) Housing: The wobbly pillar under the welfare state. *Scandinavian Housing and Planning Research*, 4(S1), pp 116–126.

Tunstall, R. and Fenton, A. (2006) *In the mix: A review of mixed income, mixed tenure and mixed communities – What do we know?* York, London: Joseph Rowntree Foundation, Housing Corporation, English Partnerships.

Tunstall, R., Bevan, M., Bradshaw, J., Croucher, K., Duffy, S., Hunter, C., Jones, A., Rugg, J., Wallace, A. and Wilcox, S. (2013) *The links between housing and poverty: An evidence review*. York: Joseph Rowntree Foundation.

van Ham, M. and Manley, D. (2009) The effect of neighbourhood housing tenure mix on labour market outcomes: A longitudinal investigation of neighbourhood effects. *Journal of Economic Geography, 10*(2), pp 257–282.

van Oorschot, W. (2000) Who should get what, and why? On deservingness criteria and the conditionality of solidarity among the public. *Policy & Politics, 28*(1), pp 33–48.

van Praag, B.M., Frijters, P. and Ferrer-i-Carbonell, A. (2003) The anatomy of subjective well-being. *Journal of Economic Behavior & Organization, 51*(1), pp 29–49.

Waddell, G. and Burton, A.K. (2006) *Is work good for your health and well-being?*. London: The Stationery Office.

Wallace, A. (2010) *Public attitudes to housing*. York: Joseph Rowntree Foundation.

Wallace, A., Rhodes, D. and Roth, F. (2018a) *Home-owners and poverty in Northern Ireland*. York: Joseph Rowntree Foundation.

Wallace, A., Rhodes, D. and Roth, F. (2018b) *Home-owners and poverty*. York: Joseph Rowntree Foundation.

Walzer, M. (1983) *Spheres of justice: A defense of pluralism and justice*. New York: Basic Books.

Walzer, M. (2006) *Frontiers of justice*. Cambridge: Harvard University Press.

Watt, P. (2008) 'Underclass' and 'ordinary people' discourses: Representing/re-presenting council tenants in a housing campaign. *Critical Discourse Studies, 5*(4), pp 345–357.

Watt, P. (2021) *Estate regeneration and its discontents: Public housing, place and inequality in London*. Bristol: Policy Press.

Watts, B., Fitzpatrick, S. and Johnsen, S. (2018) Controlling homeless people? Power, interventionism and legitimacy. *Journal of Social Policy, 47*(2), pp 235–252.

Welshman, J. (2007) *Underclass: A history of the excluded, 1880–2000.* London: A&C Black.

White, S. (2012) Property-owning democracy and republican citizenship. In M. O'Neill and T. Williamson (eds) *Property-owning democracy: Rawls and beyond.* Chichester: John Wiley & Sons, pp 129–147.

Williams, O. (2013) Britain's benefits ghettos: Report reveals growing number of estates where half those of working age are dependent on handouts. *Daily Mail*, [online] 22 May, Available from: www.dailymail.co.uk/news/article-2327033/Britains-benefits-ghettos-Report-reveals-growing-number-estates-half-working-age-dependent-handouts.html

Wilson, W.J. (2012 [1987]) *The truly disadvantaged: The inner city, the underclass, and public policy.* Chicago: University of Chicago Press.

Wilson, W. and Barton, C. (2021a) *Overcrowded housing (England).* London: House of Commons Library, Available from: https://researchbriefings.files.parliament.uk/documents/SN01013/SN01013.pdf

Wilson, W. and Barton, C. (2021b) *Leasehold and commonhold reform.* London: House of Commons Library, Available from: https://researchbriefings.files.parliament.uk/documents/CBP-8047/CBP-8047.pdf

Winnicott, D.W. (2018) *The maturational processes and the facilitating environment: Studies in the theory of emotional development.* Oxford: Routledge.

Wintour, P. (2008) Labour: If you want a council house, find a job. *The Guardian*, [online] 5 February, Available from: www.theguardian.com/politics/2008/feb/05/uk.topstories3

Young, M. and Wilmott, P. (2013) *Family and kinship in East London.* Oxford: Routledge.

Zavisca, J.R. and Gerber, T.P. (2016) The socioeconomic, demographic, and political effects of housing in comparative perspective. *Annual Review of Sociology*, *42*, pp 347–367.

Zielewski, E.H., Ratcliffe, C.E., McKernan, S.M., Johnson, L. and Sherraden, M.W. (2009) Evaluation design for the next phase of the assets for independence program: Final literature review, Available from: https://papers.ssrn.com/sol3/papers.cfm?abstract_id=2206606

Zumbro, T. (2014) The relationship between homeownership and life satisfaction in Germany. *Housing Studies*, *29*(3), pp 319–338.

Index

References to endnotes show both the page number and the note number (231n3)